Border and Boundaries

Contesting Identities between Nations

Border and Boundaries

Contesting Identities between Nations

Col. T.N. Marwah (Retd.)

Gaurav Book Centre Pvt Ltd

Delhi

Publisher
GAURAV BOOK CENTRE PVT LTD
4832/24,Prahlad Lane,S-207 Ansari
Road, Daryaganj, Delhi-110002
Ph.: 43570976, 23278261
Email: gauravbookcentre@gmail.com

Edition: 2016

ISBN: 978-93-83316-49-6

Laser Typesetting
JEE-VEE Graphics, Delhi

Price: 1295/-

Printed
Vikas Computers, Delhi

Preface

The terms "border" and " boundary" are physical in origin. The original imagery is not quite abandonedand is even intentionally played outwhen the terms are used in reference to culture. Cultural border and boundary often connote the border and boundary of a nation, a state or a tribal community, which are clearly identifiable markers.

Changing borders and boundaries are not a new phenomenon. Most tend to think of maps as inviolate and certain, but the dimensions of the international system have changed dramatically over time and are frequently ill defined.

Borders are geographic boundaries of political entities or legal jurisdictions, such as governments, sovereign states, federated states, and other subnational entities. Some borders—such as a state's internal administrative border, or inter-state borders within the Schengen Area—are open and completely unguarded. Other borders are partially or fully controlled, and may be crossed legally only at designated border checkpoints and border zones may be controlled. Some, mostly contentious, borders may even foster the setting up of buffer zones.

In the end, all borders, boundaries and borderlands have to be studies from the a local perspective, because all are situated in particular contexts and locations, are part of a discursive landscape. Borders come to life at the level of the narrative, anecdote and communication, through everyday experiences of individuals. The meanings of borders are constantly changing, the more borders are crossed, the more they are reproduced along other dimensions, ranging from the cultural to the symbolic.

The book may be found useful for those who have interest in the subject and the region.

—Editor

Contents

1

Introduction

DEFINING THE BORDER

Customs officers define the border as any place at, or within, the 12-mile limit where the state exercises statutory authority. But this definition is not as clear-cut as it might have been some years ago. The new administrative arrangements for Advanced Passenger Information and Advanced Passenger Processing (API/APP), part of the new "layered systems" approach to enhancing border security, seem to be pushing the borders out beyond this. Indeed, it appears that no country in the Pacific region has a single border. In all countries of the region there are different borders for different purposes.

The New Zealand border that defines its sovereign territory includes the Cook Islands, Niue and the Tokelaus. But its border for customs and biosecurity purposes excludes these islands. One border demarcates the twelve mile maritime limit and a quite different border defines the country's 200 mile Exclusive Economic Zone. The United Nations Convention on the Law of the Sea defined two other zones within which states have limited rights. The contiguous zone – from the edge of the territorial sea to 24 nautical miles from the coastal baselines – is not sovereign territory but states have limited authority here to enable them to better manage certain sovereign rights within their territory.

And in cases where the continental shelf extends beyond the EEZ, states can exercise sovereign rights to explore and exploit the natural resources of the seabed and subsoil. Pre-importation rulings and advance passenger processing can be arranged from anywhere in the world. FIC foreign exchange controls are effectively implemented in New York, London and Frankfurt. Tax rules which differentiate between the tax treatments accorded to income earned in different countries add a further dimension of complexity. National border controls may be challenged at any point in the country that can be accessed directly from abroad e.g. at any inland airport accessed by international flights, at an Automated Teller Machine or at a computer linked by wireless to the internet. The vision of the border as a unique physical barrier no longer represents its reality.

The internet, in particular, poses a serious challenge to traditional border structures. Many of the goods and services available via the internet - such as auction and gambling services, computer programmes and downloaded music - can be imported without ever passing through an official border. In this environment, for example, it will be very difficult to maintain separate national censorship regimes. Either censorship regimes will have to be internationalized or countries may have to accept in effect that they must mutually recognize each other's censorship standards. Developments in cyberspace may also make it increasingly difficult to ensure compliance with international commitments relating to trade in intellectual property.

Commonly, there are also internal borders, especially for biosecurity purposes. In Samoa, for example, the bio-security authorities have established an internal "sanitary cordon" between Upolu and Savaii to prevent the spread of coconut beetle and, recently in New Zealand, there was a bio-security barrier to the movement of bees between the North and South Islands to prevent the spread of the veroa mite. Internal borders are sometimes created for security purposes; Papua New Guinea has created internal security borders from time to time to prevent entry to Bougainville or to areas adjacent to the land border with Indonesia.

Borders can also be categorized in terms of their relative "hardness". Some borders are permeable because movement is negotiable e.g. movement of people with visas, while others are intended to be very hard and non-negotiable e.g. biosecurity borders. Some borders do not appear to be seriously enforced and others may be enforced more strongly on one side of the border than on the other. Cultural factors and history may have a strong influence on attitudes to national borders and the extent to which they are enforced.

Arguably, the link between national borders and nationality – the permanent population - is now becoming more tenuous when a large proportion of the population of some FICs (such as Samoa and Tonga) already resides outside their national borders.

All this underlines both the particularity and the complexity of border management issues and the need for great care in generalizing from particular examples. It is important to bear in mind some of the conditions facing border management agencies in the region. By definition all the FICs are islands, with sea borders and most have lengthy coastlines. Many are extensive archipelagos, with populations that are sparse and unevenly spread. Most have large exclusive economic zones. They are distant from other countries and from each other. None are rich in human or physical resources for border supervision and control, and the cost of a great deal of the hardware required to do the job properly is relatively high.

It is also worth remembering that there are always two sides to a border. Managing a national border is necessarily a collaborative process that cannot be conducted effectively or efficiently by one national administration alone: it requires at least bilateral collaboration on a wide range of issues – and regional collaboration may be an even more sensible approach in many areas.

EFFECTIVE AND EFFICIENT BORDER MANAGEMENT

Effective and efficient border management is also needed to facilitate trade in goods and services and travel by people for legitimate purposes, such as for business, family reunions or tourism. Finally, many states still depend heavily upon the revenue from taxes imposed at the border and want to ensure that this tax base is not impaired or eroded.

Within any one country some of these objectives may conflict with each other. For example, there is a tension between the immediate importance of maintaining revenues from tariffs and the argument that lower tariffs and the removal of quantitive restrictions will increase economic growth in the longer term. Other objectives may be inconsistent with other national policies. For example, migration criteria might limit the availability of skilled or unskilled labour needed for key domestic industries.

Between countries, objectives may also conflict. There are periodic disagreements between individual FICs over trade issues (Vanuatu's ban on the importation of ships biscuits from Fiji being the most recent) and arguments about the need for such stringent bio-security measures on, for example the export of salmon from Papua New Guinea to Australia or on the trade in kava into Australia (under threat, apparently, because of the effects this might have on indigenous communities). There are also disagreements between New Zealand and some FICs relating to the treatment of fruit to ensure that fruit fly is not imported into New Zealand. For some countries in the region, migration and labour market policies are designed to attract inflows of skilled labour; for other countries, labour market policy is all about stemming the outflow of skilled labour. To some extent, these differences reflect different national perceptions of risk. Risk depends upon what a country has to lose. Countries with highly developed and valuable agricultural sectors, for example, have much more to lose from any serious breach of their bio-security regime than countries with agricultural sectors that contribute relatively little to national welfare. And some objectives may not be as firmly adhered to as others. Sometimes, indeed, there is a difference between the officially stated national objectives and the objectives really supported by officials, traders and individuals. The historical reluctance (until quite recently) to levy customs duties on trade between American and (Western) Samoa; and the tolerance of informal migration between Indonesia and PNG are two examples that come to mind.

In short, border policies and managerial arrangements are shaped by a variety of influences and the relative importance of each of these changes from time to time. Border management objectives do not always seem to evolve in an entirely rational way but that is not entirely surprising: after all, border management objectives reflect the outcome of attempts by national authorities to mediate between politically powerful domestic pressures and almost equally strong external pressures.

The Economic, Social and Political Implications of Border Interventions

Borders intersect the economic and social space of the region, sometimes in apparently haphazard ways that may hinder or block access by people of the region to many of the important assets they need to earn their livelihoods and/or maintain the human networks needed for social and economic support. In some cases, this may leave people seriously discontented and unwilling to acknowledge the border or comply with border controls. The rationality and legitimacy of some national borders have simply never been accepted by people in some FICs. The borders between Papua New Guinea and Indonesia, between Bougainville and Solomon Islands, and between American and (Western) Samoa are all the result of historical agreements between colonial powers over which the indigenous peoples affected had little say. And the new border between Tuvalu and Kiribati created at the time of their independence was an arrangement that not all citizens of the former Gilbert and Ellice Islands agreed with. Disagreements of this nature can make border enforcement much more difficult.

The assets to which people in general and entrepreneurs in particular, need access include capital, labour, foreign exchange, information, goods and services (such as transport and risk management products). To remain internationally competitive, assets should be available at, or close to, international prices. Border interventions can increase the cost of business by driving a wedge between international prices and local prices. They can also increase business risk by creating uncertainty about the ability of entrepreneurs to obtain the assets they need at the time they are needed. Border regulations may also unduly restrict travel for legitimate purposes and disrupt family life.

On the other hand, effective borders can enhance the security of individuals and of property, minimize the entry of undesirable plants and animals that could threaten local ecosystems or livelihoods, maintain the integrity of the tax system and, more arguably, protect local businesses and jobs from 'unfair' competition. In practice, most particular government interventions at the border will create both winners and losers.

Each country explicitly or implicitly attempts to structure its interventions so as to obtain net national benefits from the totality of its border management arrangements. But decision making is heavily influenced by the national political process and the resulting outcome is frequently biased in favour of domestic producers and manufacturers, for example, (who stand to benefit most from particular border interventions and who are usually the most well organized) and against consumers (who are widely dispersed, less well organized and who do not individually appreciate the full extent of the losses imposed upon them collectively by the border interventions that discriminate against them). This kind of bias typically leads to systemic inertia: it creates strong incentives to maintain the status quo.

But to what extent does the totality of all such arrangements in the individual countries of the Pacific region contribute to, or detract from, the economic and social performance of the region as a whole? Or, to put the same point in a different way, do many of these border interventions detract from potential regional output because individual nation states are using partial analysis in the calculation of net national benefits?

This is a key question in thinking about the consequences of government interventions at the border. Would the region be better off without some of these impediments to the free flow of goods, services, people and capital?

Typically, border interventions increase transaction costs, lessen the intensity of competition, reduce the scope for gaining economies of scale and increase uncertainty and business risk. There is also an argument that more open economies gain less easily quantifiable but very real benefits from the propagation of ideas and values across borders – including democratic values and practices.

More cooperative approaches to the detection of criminal or terrorist activities within the region and to joint monitoring of public and animal health may provide benefits to the region over and above those that could be obtained by states operating alone. This may yield some unexpected synergies. For example, it is likely that counter-terrorism measures, to the extent that they lessened the incidence of corrupt practices and strengthened revenue collections, would help to improve governance and fiscal stability in FICs.

There can also be important political implications. Any country's failures in border management may have consequences for its neighbours. In a globalized and (post 9/11) more anxious world, the word neighbour has become less spatially restricted. Countries assess their vulnerability by the vulnerability of the weakest link in the global supply chains that link with their markets. The consequences for any country of being deemed not to comply with the relevant international standards are potentially severe, and include the disruption of its trade. All members of the Pacific Islands Forum, including Australia and New Zealand, have a common interest in not being seen as a region in which conformance with international standards and obligations at the border is lax.

Borders in the New International Environment

The Pacific region faces a range of threats and risks created by its openness to the external environment. Some are familiar and well known e.g. threats to government revenues from "normal" smuggling activities and long established risks to the region's biosecurity from traditional diseases and pathogens. Others are relatively new and, perhaps, unexpected.

The most serious is a growing and serious threat from transnational organized crime groups, whose activities –including the importation and/or production of drugs, illegal gambling, arms smuggling, counterfeiting and corruption - constitute a serious assault on good governance within the region. Illegal migration within the region is a growing concern for many FIC governments and the region remains very exposed to money-laundering activities and financial fraud.

The region also remains vulnerable to potential penetration by terrorist groups (even if the risk is not high). Wildlife trafficking is not an immediate problem but could expand rapidly as an alternative source of illicit income when the region's fisheries and logging resources are depleted.

There are serious risks surrounding the potential for the introduction of new infectious diseases such as the H5N1 strain of avian flu, which could present a serious threat to human health and to the economy, while bio-security agencies must be on constant alert for any signs of a range of animal and plant diseases that could impact adversely upon the productive base and bio-diversity of the region. Bio-security risks have increased markedly in recent years because of the rapid increase in trade and travel volumes and pathways.

Many of these risks and threats are inter-related in subtle and complex ways. For example, while corruption is not a new phenomenon in the region, it has become a much more insidious and dangerous threat when linked to the wider activities of transnational organised criminal groups that are undermining the financial stability of some states even as they attempt to suborn the ruling class in an effort to expand their political influence.

THE CONCEPT OF COLLABORATIVE BORDER MANAGEMENT

Whereas the international community has discussed integrated border management and coordinated border management, this book—to denote more than mere coordination, while avoiding the more threatening connotations of organizational integration— uses the term *collaborative border management*. Collaborative border management is based on the need for agencies and the international community to work together to achieve common aims. The model suggests that border management agencies can increase control while providing a more efficient service, and that they can do so while retaining their own organizational mandates and integrity.

In collaborative border management a virtual border encompasses the entire transport and supply chain, assessing goods and passengers for admissibility and clearance in advance of arriving at the physical border. Border management agencies work together, sharing information. As they gather, collate, and share more data, a complete view of risks and opportunities emerges, encouraging a knowledge sharing culture and a border management strategy built on proactive decisionmaking.

Typically collaborative border management is not achieved through forced organizational change— which invariably creates conflict—but by creating an overarching governance body charged with establishing a border management vision and ensuring that all stakeholders work together to achieve it. This requires strong political will and commitment and appropriate incentives and disincentives. While collaborative border management can be achieved under a single border management agency, the creation of such an agency is not a precondition for success. Well managed, collaborative border management results in reduced documentation, a more appropriate treatment of traders through more thorough and accurate data collection and analysis, and a combination of lower costs and greater control for border management agencies. It can also preserve the independence and specific mandates of customs and other agencies involved in border management. Collaborative border management also benefits the customer, reducing administrative and compliance costs while saving time and making service more predictable. Collaborative border management makes possible a set of defined business outcomes, including:

- Distinctive border management agency operations in areas that make a real difference to trade and industry.
- Objective measures of performance in all key result areas.
- Cost savings through the avoidance of unnecessary duplication of effort.
- A trading environment that is more business friendly and responsive.

THE INDO-BANGLADESH BORDER FENCING PROJECT

The Government of India sanctioned the erection of fencing in two phases. The Indo-Bangladesh Border Works under Phase-

I had been initiated in 1989. Fencing in 854.35 kilometres was erected and 2606.35 kilometres of road was completed as. Under Phase II, the government had approved additional fencing of 2429.5 kilometres and 797 kilometres road at an estimated cost of Rs 287.617 million. This project was budgeted at Rs. 10.5 billion in 1998. It involved the construction of 900 km of border fence, 2800 km of border roads and 24 km of bridges along the India-Bangladesh border in the states of West Bengal, Assam, Meghalaya, Tripura and Mizoram. The Assamese government and media were not satisfied with the fence on the Assamese side. As a local newspaper had put it, 'crossing the fence border remained as easy as slicing butter with a knife '.

In 2001, the Director General of the Border Road Organization calculated that 1 km of border fence cost Rs. 2.2 million and 1 km of border road Rs 4.5 million. A high BSF official admitted that 80 percent of the 4000 km border was unfenced, while the Indian External Affairs Minister claimed in a statement to Parliament that the border would completely be fenced in 2006-07. In 2001, BSF and BDR exchanged gunfire leading to the killing of BSF personnel which obviously had a negative impact on India-Bangladesh relations. Former Prime Minister of Bangladesh Sheikh Hasina resolved the dispute jointly with Indian Prime Minister Vajpayee. Work on erecting barbed wire fences along the Indo-Bangladesh border was again resumed by the NDA government headed by Vajpayee in 2002.

The Indian government tripled its budget for border security in 2003. The work had been in actual progress from early 2004, when tenders were called and closed. Various public sector institutions of India undertook activities to fence different parts of the border, such as Indian Railways Construction Corporation (NBCC), Borders Road Organization (BRO), the Central Public Works Department (CPWD), and the state Public Works Departments in Assam, Tripura, Meghalaya and West Bengal. In May 2004, the Central government of India changed and BJP-led National Democratic Alliance handed over power to the United Progressive Alliance (UPA) led by the Indian National Congress. After the newly formed government assumed power and formed their coalition government in 2004, the construction of fence was put on hold for review in June. According to Karlekar, one of the main reasons was the strong opposition of the Bangladesh government that argued that the fence violated the India-Bangladesh Agreement in 1974 which prohibited the construction of any defence structure within 150 yard of the border and the fence was a defensive structure.

National level talks were held between the Home Secretaries of Bangladesh and India in Dhaka in September 2004 to cover security issues, implementation of the 1974 Land Boundary Agreement, cooperation in combating the problems of drugs and narcotics, border patrolling be security forces, cross border movements, visa regime and extradition treaty and agreements on mutual legal assistance in criminal matters. Construction resumed after a meeting on 14 October 2004 in Delhi where the Cabinet Committee on Security decided to continue fencing the border. The UPA government allocated funds for border fencing, road and maintenance as well as for boats and aircraft for the BSF. India's seriousness about the fence was demonstrated by the fact that they spent Rs 2404.7 million for fencing the Bangladesh border during 2004-5. This was stated in the Indian Lok Sabha by the State Minister for Home Affairs Mr. S. Raghupathy.

According to the Annual Report 2005-2006 of Indian Ministry of Home Affairs, fencing was necessary in order to prevent illegal infiltration and other anti-national activities from across the border. By the year 2004-2005, 1502 kilometres had been fenced. Similarly, work was completed on 2670 kilometres out of 3663 kilometres of roads to be constructed. To date, a total of 2535.80 kilometres fencing has been completed in Phase I and II out of 4096.7 km long Indo-Bangladesh border. For border roads 3250.60 kilometres has been completed in Phase I and II.

In 2007, India decided to replace the entire 861 km. of fence constructed under Phase-I in West Bengal, Assam and Meghalaya, as most of this fence have been damaged by adverse climatic conditions and repeated submergence. The replacement work has already commenced in the States of Assam and West Bengal. 193.70 km. of fencing has been replaced so far.

Illegal Migration and the Census of India 2001

According to the Census 2001 report released in 2005, the number of Bangladeshi migrants during the decade 1991-2001 was about 280,000, which was a decrease of 53% from almost 600,000 migrants between 1981 and 1991. In the 2001 Census, about 5.1 million persons were reported as migrant by last residence from across the international border from India's neighbour countries mainly Pakistan, Afghanistan, Sri Lanka, Nepal, Bhutan and Bangladesh. About 97% of these migrants by last residence were from eight neighbouring countries including Afghanistan. Of these migrants, 3 million were from Bangladesh, 0.9 million from Pakistan, 0.5 million from Nepal and 0.1 million from Sri Lanka. About 65.2% of these migrants from neighbouring countries had migrated to India at least 20 years ago perhaps many of them during the time of partition and later during the Bangladesh liberation war in 1971.

The total number of migrants by last residence from neighbouring countries by duration of residence is 3.08 million from Bangladesh -all residents living in India for more than 20 years. The '20 years or above' category indicates migration at the time of the 1949 partition or the formation of Bangladesh in 1971. Yet the report also revealed the number of migrants who came from Bangladesh during the decade 1991-2001. In case of Bangladesh as the last place of residence, the total number of migrants with duration from 0 to 9 years is 279,878 in 2001 and 591,572 in 1991.

Another notable figure in the report was the flow of migrants from another neighbouring country Nepal-175,195 in 1991 and 261,451 in the 2001 census which is close to the total number of Bangladeshi migrants. The decadal variation during 1991 –2001 has been negative -a reduction of 52.7% for Bangladesh and an increase for Nepal by 49.2%. It can be assumed that most of the migrants coming from Nepal were Hindu. According to the census 2001 in Nepal, 80.6% of the population is Hindu, 10.7% is Buddhist, 4.2% of the population is Muslim and 3.6% of the population follows the indigenous Kirant Mundum religion. Christianity is practiced by less than 0.5% of the population. It is very significant that the Shiv Sena-BJP government never complained about the migrants from Nepal, though statistics indicate the number of migrants was larger. They kept quiet on illegal Nepalese migrants as far as the literature and media are concerned. It can be interpreted that they did not take Hindu illegal migrants from Nepal as an economic or security threat to India. Another interesting feature of their campaign on detection and deportation of illegal Bangladeshi migrants is that, BJP appeared to be sympathetic towards Hindu migrants from Bangladesh. So this was not about jobs or security ;it is really an anti-Muslim campaign.

THE IDENTITY OF INDIA

The identity of India refers to the kind of country it is, and wishes to be. The essence of Indian security policy lies in its quest for strategic autonomy. To understand this, it must be realised that India is largely friendless in the world today. India has friendly relations with many states but friendship with none. India's relationship with the US is constrained by many factors, including the latter's security links with Pakistan.

An important factor that places limits on US-India security relations is that the former does not regard India as a member of the 'democratic core' of states, as it is not a part of any security pact led by the US. India, therefore, cannot rely on the US for security back-up as it successfully depended for two decades upon the Soviet Union. Also, India is just too big to be accommodated in any security pact as a junior partner. Faced by varied threats and adversaries, India has no option but to rely on its own capabilities. These capabilities, while significant in certain contexts, are by no means sufficient and are prone to debilitating weakness in critical areas.

Geography, history and resources have been key elements in strategic thinking throughout the millennia and remain important sources of strategic culture. Maintaining democracy and promoting development—and treating both as equally important and necessary—is the biggest security challenge facing India. Over 60 years of genuine liberal democracy in a pluralist, multicultural, socio-economically deprived, continent-sized setting is surely an achievement of world historical importance that deserves to be recognised.

In 1947, India inherited many disadvantages—the accumulated subtractions of many centuries — but one great advantage, that of resurgent nationalism. There are five important features of the Indian identity. These are:

- India is a republic, i.e. a democracy with an elected head.
- It is a secular country. The state is not committed to a particular religion.
- India is committed to social justice and equality for its citizens. The Directive Principles of the Constitution are an egalitarian vision of Indian society.
- India is a plural society. It cherishes its diversity and allows its different communities full freedom to express themselves.
- India is not just a nation-state but a distinct civilisation with its own perspective on the world. India sees the world through its own eyes, avoids being tied to a particular country or bloc, and brings to the international community its own distinct voice. India's traditional neutrality is a political expression of this.

India has not inherited any strategic thought, as it has always been a land divided geographically and otherwise. History shows that there had been little opportunity or reason for conceptualising any such thought, as it was never considered a *sine qua non* of statecraft. Against this backdrop, to understand better the security challenges that confront India, there is a need to analyse who we are, what moves us, what we stand for, where we are planning to go, why we want to go there and how we propose to get there. "Deeply embedded habits of thoughts related to Indian geography, history, culture.... exert a powerful influence....they will, in the foreseeable future, help to shape its strategic thinking and its strategy."

A strategic culture serves to explain how a country's culture influences its strategic behaviour. Equally important is how the political and military elite of a country view an adversary or potential adversary. A nation-state's view of itself—its national character, its intended regional and global roles, and its perceptions of its eventual destiny—are important facets. National culture, thus, plays a significant role in influencing security policy. Interests, power, and violence are staples of international relations. States cannot avoid the responsibility of pursuing their national interest. Nor can they be indifferent to the cultivation of power—their own and that of other states.

States must look after themselves in a world in which violence is a regrettable last resort. India's view is that international laws and institutions, military restraint, negotiations and compromise, cooperation, free intercourse between societies, and regard for the well-being of people everywhere and not just one's own citizens can overcome the rigours of the international system.

India is an ancient civilisation and Hinduism is the oldest of the world's religions. It is a country where the burden of history hangs heavy over the national psyche. Its way of looking at the world and at itself is unique, shaped by its geography, history and religious influence.

Its civilisational heritage makes it place morality above reality, yet it has the ability to absorb or permanently subdue other influences. It is a country where ethnic identity can transcend national identity, yet nationalism is placed at a high pedestal in the minds of the people. It, therefore, shapes national behaviour and defines values in discernible and measurable ways. India's historical experience has generated various ideas on issues of national strategy and policy.

India's approach to the world is naturally a function of its values, history and geography, and of how it defines its interests. India has several strategic issues that are yet to be resolved in its quest for its rightful place in the comity of nations. Pakistan and India share the world's most dangerous nuclear border. The rise of China looms large against the backdrop of a long-standing border conflict. India's geographical location—at the natural junction of busy international shipping lanes that crisscross the Indian Ocean—has a major impact upon the formulation of her maritime strategy in support of the pursuit of her national interests.

There are many shibboleths about India's strategic culture, perhaps because it has not been clearly articulated. The country is both a continental and maritime nation. Its location at the base of continental Asia and the top of the Indian Ocean gives it a vantage point in relation to both West, Central, continental and Southeast Asia, and the littoral states of the Indian Ocean, from East Africa to Indonesia. India's projection into this vast and critically important waterway gives it a major stake in its security and stability.

Continental Aspects

While geography is the study of the physical environment, its centrality is to discover in what ways and to what extent this environment affected history. Geographical analysis can offer more towards the understanding of international politics than just an appreciation of the facts of location. Borders define nationhood and sovereignty. India never had borders till Independence. Essentially, its boundaries over the centuries can best be termed as 'frontiers' i.e. a demarcation between territories with independent sovereignties. A frontier constitutes "an area of separation" between two regions of "more or less homogeneous, and usually denser, population." It is of such frontiers that Lord Curzon spoke when, in his classic essay bearing that name, he described them as "the razor's edge" on which hang the modern issues of war and peace and of life or death to nations. Warfare has always occurred for the defence of frontiers.

In the making of frontiers, international law has a significant role to play. The recognition of the existence, sanctity and permanence of frontiers is one of the foundations on which the law of nations has been built. Frontiers once negotiated and demarcated cannot be altered unilaterally. They are inviolate and unalterable save through negotiation, for any use of *force majeure* in such cases would be a denial of international law itself. Vital as the element of power politics is, human geography plays an equally important part. What makes for frontiers, and frontier problems, are such factors as race, population, language, geography and access to the sea. Religion also plays an important role in varying degrees, e.g. the birth of Pakistan and Israel. Also, self determination has been a powerful weapon in creating new frontiers by disrupting ancient ones.

There is a further distinction between a boundary and a frontier. Geographical and historical boundaries, represent the edges of frontiers. A boundary does not merely demarcate geographical regions or divide human societies but represents the optimum limits of growth of a particular society. In an address to the Royal Society of Arts in 1935, Sir Henry McMahon maintained that a frontier meant a wide tract of border land which, because of its ruggedness or other difficulties, served as a buffer between two states. A boundary, on the other hand, was a clearly defined line expressed either as a verbal distinction (delimited) or as a series of physical marks on the ground (demarcated); the former thus roughly signified a region, while the latter was a positive and precise statement of the limits of sovereignty.

The Great Wall of China connoted the domain that it was thought proper to include in the *tien h'sia*, marking it from the outer darkness of the barbarians. So too did the Roman Empire's frontiers along the Danube, which separated it from the uncivilised tribes beyond its pale. Much the same holds true of the northern mountain ranges in Indian history. The issue here was not only one of keeping the barbarians out, but also of setting limits to the imperial rule.

The long and sprawling land frontier between India and China is now the subject of a bitterly raging conflict between the two countries. The Himalayas were always considered as a natural barrier 'forbidding' or 'preventing' passage. A mountain system – and the extent to which it is a barrier is inversely proportional to the ease with which it can be crossed – tends to mark a separation between economic and strategic regions. While mountains were a barrier to older societies, they do not pose insurmountable problems to an industrialised society that is equipped with airplanes or the frightening armoury of thermo-nuclear weapons; here it is not nature that has changed, but man.

Today, the sea, the desert, the mountain and the river no longer guarantee natural security as they once did. Even artificial contrivances as a neutral territory, state or zone, or a buffer state, e.g. Afghanistan and Tibet during the British period, do not inspire in the guarantors, much less among those so guaranteed, any measure of confidence. Frontiers today have evolved from being mere geographical barriers into human bulwarks against political ideologies and systems of government, each of them claiming ultimate perfection and allowing at best a modicum of peaceful, if highly competitive, coexistence.

The frontier, in both geo-political, as well as the human geography contexts, has played a significant role in India's long and sprawling and frontier to the northeast which, for most of its length, is co-terminous with Tibet. For further understanding of its intricacies, it is imperative to analyse its historical geography under its obvious sub-divisions of northwest and northeast segments.

From the very inception of its recorded history and the fight of Chandragupta Maurya against the Greeks, India's northwest frontier has been a subject of considerable concern to her rulers. It was to protect the Khyber and other passes from the northwest against these onslaughts from 'barbaric hordes' that every powerful Indian Empire evolved a 'frontier' policy. Thus, the policy of Chandragupta Maurya against the post-Alexander Greeks, of Anangpal vis-à-vis the Ghaznavids, of Balban against the Mongols, or of Akbar or Aurangzeb when faced with threats from Central Asia was essentially the same. Ranjit Singh's acumen in the handling of the frontier in the post-Nadir Shah /Ahmad Shah Abdali period, earned him a well-merited tribute from his British successors. The latter, whose span has been the most recent in Indian history, deserves close examination, if only to understand the present situation in that region.

For India, the Himalayas comprised a frontier of both ingress and egress. With Tibet in the north, the intercourse was largely one of religious doctrines and their practice, the mountain barrier being far too formidable to mount any large-scale invasion. But on the western side, the Khyber did provide a route for any hostile power to challenge the northern Indian polity, unless the latter was in a position to defend itself. As to the southern frontier, the peninsular barrier did not constitute any major obstacle; though both Ashoka (273-237 BC) and the Mughals (1565-1820) did hold sway over lands south of the Vindhyas.

It is difficult to sum up the British epoch in a nutshell, but it may suffice to suggest that during the colonial period, the theory and practice of the frontier, as also the foreign and defence policy of a united India, rested on the evolution of a buffer state. Both Afghanistan and Tibet fulfilled this role.

BOUNDARY DELIMITATION

Boundary delimitation (or simply delimitation) is the drawing of boundaries, particularly of electoral precincts, states, counties or other municipalities. In the context of elections, it can be called redistribution and is used to prevent unbalance of population across districts. Unbalanced or discriminatory delimitation is called "gerrymandering." Though there are no internationally agreed processes that guarantee fair delimitation, several organizations, such as the Commonwealth Secretariat, the European Union and the International Foundation for Electoral Systems have proposed guidelines for effective delimitation.

In international law, the related national delimitation is the process of legally establishing the outer limits ("borders") of a state within which full territorial or functional sovereignty is exercised. Occasionally this is used when referring to the maritime boundaries as well, in this case called maritime delimitation.

DEMOCRATIC DELIMITATION

Methods

Countries delimit electoral districts in different ways. Sometimes these are drawn based on traditional boundaries, sometimes based on the physical characteristics of the region and, often, the lines are drawn based on the social, political and cultural contexts of the area. This may need to be done in any form of electoral system even though it is primarily done for plurality or majority electoral system. These processes of boundary delimitation can have a variety of legal justifications. Often, because of the powerful effects this process can have on constituencies, the legal framework for delimitation is specified in the constitution of a country. The Institute for Democracy and Electoral Assistance (IDEA) recommends the following pieces of information be included in this legal framework:

- The frequency of such determination;
- The criteria for such determination;
- The degree of public participation in the process;
- The respective roles of the legislature, judiciary and executive in the process;and
- The ultimate authority for the final determination of the electoral units.

Established democracies

Delimitation is regularly used in the United States and Commonwealth countries. This is called redistricting or redistribution respectively. In these countries non-partisan commissions draw new districts based on the distribution of population according to a census.

International Standards

A number of international organizations including the Organization for Security and Co-operation in Europe, the European Commission for Democracy Through Law (the Venice Commission), the Commonwealth Secretariat, and the Electoral Institute of Southern Africa (EISA) have established standards which their members are encouraged to prescribe to. Among these standards the International Foundation for Electoral Systems (IFES) lists the most common as being Impartiality, Equality, Representativeness, Non-Discrimination and Transparency.

Venice Commission

As part of its report, *European Commission for Democracy Through Law: Code of Good Practice in Electoral Matters, Guidelines and Explanatory Reports adopted October 2002*, the Venice Commission proposed the following guidelines:

Equal voting power: seats must be evenly distributed between the constituencies.

i. This must at least apply to elections to lower houses of parliament and regional and local elections:
ii. It entails a clear and balanced distribution of seats among constituencies on the basis of one of the following allocation criteria: population, number of resident nationals (including minors), number of registered voters, and possibly the number of people actually voting. An appropriate combination of these criteria may be envisaged.
iii. The geographical criterion and administrative, or possibly even historical, boundaries may be taken into consideration.
iv. The permissible departure from the norm should not be more than 10%, and should certainly not exceed 15% except in special circumstances (protection of a concentrated minority, sparsely populated administrative entity).
v. In order to guarantee equal voting power, the distribution of seats must be reviewed at least every ten years, preferably outside election periods.
vi. With multimember constituencies, seats should preferably be redistributed without redefining constituency boundaries, which should, where possible, coincide with administrative boundaries.
vii. When constituency boundaries are redefined—which they must be in a single-member system—it must be done:
    - impartially;
    - without detriment to national minorities;
    - taking account of the opinion of a committee, the majority of whose members are independent; this committee should preferably include a geographer, a sociologist, and a balanced representation of the parties and, if necessary, representatives of national minorities.

Commonwealth Secretariat

In the publication *Good Commonwealth Electoral Practices: A Working Document, June 1997,* the Commonwealth Secretariat identifies the following practices as necessary for proper delimitation:

The delimitation of constituency boundaries is a function occasionally performed by an election commission or otherwise by an independent boundaries commission, and in some cases after a population census.

General principles guiding the drawing of constituency boundaries include community of interest, convenience, natural boundaries, existing administrative boundaries and population distribution, including minority groups. There should be no scope for any "gerrymandering", and each vote should, to the extent possible, be afforded equal value or weight, in recognition of the democratic principle that all those of voting age participate equally in the ballot.

It is important that the general public play a part in the whole process and that the political parties also have an opportunity to respond to proposals before they are finalized. Where the size of a particular constituency is markedly out of line with the target "quota" of voters per seat, the reasons should be capable of being readily understood by both the parties and the general public.

IFES

In her study sponsored by the International Foundation for Electoral Systems, Dr. Lisa Handley recommends the following considerations:

1. population density
2. ease of transportation and communication
3. geographic features
4. existing patterns of human settlement
5. financial viability and administrative capacity of electoral area
6. financial and administrative consequences of boundary determination
7. existing boundaries
8. community of interest

Also, she suggests that the process should:

- be managed by an independent and impartial body that is representative of society, comprising persons with the appropriate skills;
- be conducted on the basis of clearly identified criteria such as population, distribution, community of interest, convenience, geographical features and other natural or administrative boundaries;
- be made accessible to the public through a consultation process;
- be devoid of manipulation of electoral boundaries to favour political groups or political interests;
- be conducted by one body;
- include all spheres of government, both national and local.

NATIONAL DELIMITATION

The negotiations surrounding the modification of a states borders is called National delimitation. This event often takes place as part of the negotiations seeking to end a conflict over resource control, popular loyalties, or political interests.

2

Cultural Border and Boundary

The terms "border" and " boundary" are physical in origin. The original imagery is not quite abandonedand is even intentionally played outwhen the terms are used in reference to culture. Cultural border and boundary often connote the border and boundary of a nation, a state or a tribal community, which are clearly identifiable markers. The equation between a culture and a territory has dominated the discourse in anthropology. The assumption is that as long as two distinct societies remain separate from each other, their boundaries exist and cultural distinctiveness is expected. It is further assumed that if two societies, identified with two distinct cultures, come in contact, a cultural border is expected to form between them. If an individual from Culture A is to voluntarily or involuntarily become part of Culture B, she/he is expected to literally leave his/her own society, cross the border and enter a new society. This physical implication of the cultural border is fully entertained by scholars of Mexican immigrants, for whom crossing the border is a literal as well as a figurative experience.

To many scholars a border is not a neutral demarcation line. It is a symbol of power that imposes inclusion and exclusion. The more privileged dominant, hegemoniousside will actively control the border to keep border-crossers out. Erickson accentuated the political nature of a border by differentiating it from a boundary:

A cultural boundary refers to the presence of some kind of cultural difference cultural boundaries are characteristic of all human societies, traditional as well as modern. A border is a social construct that is political in origin. Across a border power is exercised, as in the political border between two nations.

A cultural border connotes a barrier that a more powerful side constructs to guard its own political power, cultural knowledge and privileges.

The cultural border rhetoric is grounded in the essentialist view of culture. This view makes several assumptions regarding culture: (1) a culture is viewed as a bounded system which is separate and distinguishable from others; (2) a culture is expected to be "homogeneous" ; (3) a culture is expected to be shared by members of the society.

The first assumption is evident in the work of many anthropologists. The cultural boundary is viewed as coterminous with a nation, a state, a tribe, a community or an organization that is clearly defined by an identifiable markeroften physical borders. Good enough attributed this notion of culture to Franz Boas, a pioneer German-American anthropologist:

At the end of the nineteenth century, Franz Boas began to use "culture" to refer to the distinctive body of customs, beliefs, and social institutions that seemed to characterize each separate society.

The notion of one-distinct-culture-for-each-separate-society suggests that one culture represents a society and vice versa. This close match makes the conceptual interchange of culture and society acceptable. Henze and Vanett further explore this assumption of culture in the metaphor of "walking in two worlds" in their study of native Alaskan and Native American students.

The second assumption of cultural homogeneity suggests that a homogeneous, patterned prototype of a culture can be abstracted. It implies that a "pure" form of a culture exists. Any variation from the pure form is treated as an exception, peripheral to "the culture." This assumption ignores the dynamic nature of culture, in which people of a society change at different rates for different reasons. The diffusionist view of culture argues against this notion of cultural homogeneity, for all cultures include elements borrowed from other cultures.

The third assumption of the cultural border is that a culture is "shared" by members of a society. The extent of sharedness is debatable, yet sharedness is considered a trademark of culture. This assumption suggests that people within a cultural system share a set of traits unique to their group membership. Sharedness is considered a product of cultural transmission and acquisition which often take place through personal interactions among members of physical proximity. In other words, an Asian is expected to share with other Asians traits unique to Asian culture. When a group is small and specific, the extent of sharedness among members may be higher. However, if a group presents a large, cross-sectional or cross-national cultural identity, such as "female culture," "middle-class culture" and "Muslim culture," the sharedness of that particular culture is blurred by other cultural identities. Ewing examined how the cultural identity of Muslims shifts relative to national borders and the gender line.

This territory-oriented rhetoric of culture, cultural border and boundary faces a great challenge in a multicultural society because intense contacts between various cultural carriers blur the clarity of demarcation lines.

CULTURAL BORDERLAND

"Cultural borderland" is a notion created to accommodate a multicultural society. Foley explores the cultural borderland as a "space" created when two or more cultures and races occupy the same territory. He considers the space psychological and political: [According to Rosaldo and Clifford, the borderland] generally refers to a psychological space at the conjuncture of two cultures. A cultural borderland is also a political space in which ethnic groups actively fuse and blend their culture with the mainstream culture.

The borderland is viewed as a psychological space in which border-crossers struggle with their bicultural or multicultural identities. In this borderland individuals decide how much they want to identify with their cultures of origin or of adoption. Too much of either can be the subject of ridicule. Saenz compared two distinguished Mexican-American writers who try to come to terms with their ethnic identities. He argued that Gloria Anzaldua is "completely mortgaged to a nostalgia" a nostalgia to the Aztec origin of the Mexican culture. Richard Rodriguez, on the other hand, "is completely mortgaged to an ideology that privileges the category of individual". In the eyes of Saenz, Rodriguez has taken too much of his adopted culture. In between lies Saenz's Mexican-American college student who refused to read "gringo" (White) poetry and Saenz himself who insists on his identity as a Chicano writer.

The borderland is also highly political. The borderland is never on centre stage. It is often viewed as a marginal space for cultural hybrids—those who have adopted "foreign," distinctly different, cultural traits—who therefore do not fit the homogeneous prototypes of their original cultures. In Foleys Mesquaki Indian study the borderland is viewed as a threat to the integrity of the Indian culture. It was a space for Indian progressives (who proposed to modernize the Indian community and to collaborate with Whites), White "wannabes" (who tried to adopt the Indian culture) and "mixed-bloods" (biracial individuals of White and Indian parents).

The borderland rhetoric is still embedded in the essentialist view of culture. For example, Foleys notion of cultural borderlands creates an image of three separate zones: the "pure" Indian culture that is being guarded by "traditionalists" (Lets call it Culture A); the "pure" White culture that is distinguished from the Indian (Culture B); and the borderland between them, a space for border-crossers. Chang quesitons this essentialist presumption of culture by wondering, "just where the Indian culture ends and the White culture begins for border crossers".

How Real is Cultural Border

The cultural border and boundary rhetoric focuses on a societal culture. If cultural diversity is viewed at the societal level, cultural borders seem authentic and real. Skin colour, national origin, gender, religious affiliation, identification of disability, and group membership all serve as identifiable markers for subgroups. Since these categories are socially constructed and validated, cultural differences are assumed and expected. But when the cultures of individuals are under scrutiny, it becomes clear that cultural borders do not hold their dividing power. Cultural boundaries within individuals become blurred as components from diverse cultures become incorporated into their individual cultural identity, instead of remaining separate from each other.

Let us take a close look at four multicultural individuals who had a close connection with Korea but who live in the pluralistic U.S. society.

Jean Kohl, a 9-year-old daughter of a German father and a Korean mother, was born and raised in the United States. Her parents, fluent speakers of German and Korean respectively, adopted English as the primary language at home. "I am an American," proclaimed she, but she often ended her proclamation with an addendum that she was also German and Korean. For several summers she travelled to visit her maternal or paternal grandparents in Korea or Germany, during which she was exposed to her parents native cultures and languages. The German, Korean and U. S. heritage blended in her cultural repertoire. For Jean, where does the "American" cultural border end and other cultural borders begin?

Carrie Baumstein, a 20-year-old woman, was born in Korea and adopted by a Messianic Jewish-American couple when she was 2 years old. She has lived in the States ever since. She was not exposed to much Korean culture and language when she was growing up, but was instead surrounded by her parents Jewish tradition. Despite her primary identity with the Jewish culture, she was often reminded by her relatives and neighbors of her Koreanor Asianlinkage. She was in an identity search for Asianness when she was attending a small Christian college on the East Coast. For Carrie, where do the cultural borders lie between the Korean and the American and between the Messianic Jew and the Christian?

Peter Lee, a 15-year-old, was born in the States to immigrant parents from Korea. His parents own and operate a dry cleaning shop in a suburb of Philadelphia. Their English is functional for the business but they prefer speaking Korean on all other occasions.

Peters family attends a Korean church regularly, which usually serves as a cultural community as much as a religious one. Peters Korean is so limited that he usually speaks English, although his parents speak Korean to him. He is definitely an American in his mind and heart, perhaps a Korean-American occasionally. But his preference of Korean-American peers to others is a curious phenomenon. Where lies the cultural border that divides the Korean and the "American" for Peter?

Elaine Sook-Ja Cho, 50 years old, immigrated to the States 30 years ago to marry a Korean bachelor 10 years her senior. Her husband came to the States as a student and found employment upon completion of his study. Elaine was a housewife for 20 years before undertaking a small grocery business. She speaks "Konglish" (a mixture of Korean sentence structure and English words) but she seems to be at ease speaking English. She is Korean in her heart but "Americanized" in her own words and by her life style. For Sook-Ja how far does the Korean cultural border stretch to meet the "American" culture?

I wonder how I would map the cultural topology (again a physical metaphor) of Jean Kohl, Carrie Baumstein, Peter Lee and Elaine Sook-Ja Cho. How would I draw up the boundary of the Korean culture for each case? Would they cross cultural borders from the Korean to the German and so on daily? How cognizant would they be of crossing? Would it be possible for one to become culturally more Korean in the morning, German for lunch, "American" in the afternoon, and back to Korean in the evening?

The early illustration of an individual leaving his/her society, crossing the border and entering a new society may shed light on the problem with the cultural border rhetoric. Once you acquire cultural traits, whether in a certain territorial context or not, leaving the territory does not make an individual "lose" the culture. Sook-Ja is not any less Korean culturally now because she left her homeland 30 years ago. Carries minimal identity as a Korean is not surprising despite her origin. Peter and Jean who were born and raised in the States have acquired Korean cultural traits from their parents. In other words, the physical proximity or distance to Korea does not serve as an accurate gauge for their Koreanness in culture. It is also hardly imaginable that Jeans notion of the Korean culture is similar to that of Sook-Ja, although both claim to be Korean. What would Peter share about the Korean culture with others and to what extent? How would I compare these peoples Korean culture with that of Koreans who have never left the country? The essentialist image of culturein particular, the Korean cultureseems to lose the clarity of its boundary as I probe into each individuals personal version of culture.

Conclusion

Everyone is cultural and multicultural : "cultural" in that culture is not a property of an exotic people but "standards" that all human beings adopt for their daily operations; "multicultural" in the sense of being competent in multiple macro or microcultural systems.

In a pluralistic society in which people from diverse cultures come in constant contact, the cultural metamorphosis takes place noticeably in individual cultures. Thus the Boas-Benedict legacy of the "plural, separate, distinct, historically homogeneous" culture offers little help in understanding the multicultural society and its residents. Rosaldo also critiqued the fallacy of cultural homogeneity, especially in the pluralistic setting:

uman cultures are neither necessarily coherent nor always homogeneous. More often than we usually care to think, our everyday lives are crisscrossed by border zones, pockets and eruptions of all kinds.

It also becomes clear that a culture is not bounded by a territory as earlier anthropologists believed. Rather, people are the carriers, movers, consumers, and inventors of a culture. When they move from one place to the other, they carry their culturestheir personal outlookswith them. Good enough coined a term, "propriospect," to refer to the "private, subjective view of the world and of its content," which includes the various standards for perceiving, evaluating, believing, and doing that an individual attributes to other persons as a result of his or her experience of their actions and admonitions. Wolcott elaborated on the meaning of the term "propriospect" to illustrate how individuals develop personal versions of a culture through personal contacts with others with different sets of standards. Through these contacts they acquire some of the new standards. As a result, they become increasingly multicultural.

This concept of culture sheds light on cultural differences. Since everyone has a unique cultural make-up, cultural differences are not really divisive and separable. Individual cultural differences are really different combinations of standards. Once different standards are embraced by individuals, the differences are incorporated into their individual cultures. In other words, the cultural differences are reframed into multiculturalism. It seems logical to me that we understand our individual multiculturalism as a pathway to understand our societal multiculturalism. The constructive view of individual cultures would be too useful and insightful to ignore.

OF BOUNDARIES AND BORDERS

Amongst the hundreds of thousand of visitors to the 1988 Calgary Olympics were a few hundred travellers returning home after absences of up to 300 years. As early as 1668, they had left to tell the "Old" World of another; to act as witness to the expanding dominion of those explorers with whom they travelled. They also offered evidence of the complexity and history of this seeming "New" World. In 1988, as the Olympics' flagship exhibit, these "cultural objects" were invited back to the Glenbow Museum to speak of the moment of that diversity and richness. Their presence, their hosts declared, attested to "the richness, diversity and complexity of Canada's Native cultures", which had enabled the survival of their creators' descendants.

But within their narratives were painful silences; powerful absences. They were not asked to speak of the disruption and extinction, the change or the loss, that was evident on their return. Their invitation specified public homecoming stories of a culture that flourished centuries ago, but demanded silence on their subsequent travels and the circumstances that had led to their leaving. The selective muteness of these works however engendered other voices, other stories. This exhibit, *The Spirit Sings*, was the object of a vocal boycott by the Lubicon Lake Cree of Northern Alberta and the catalyst for a national review of the relationship between Canada's museum and Native communities.

The Lubicon boycott was initiated to draw public attention to two critical points. The first was the exhibit's focus on the period of contact and its lack of contemporary Native voice and presence. While the extraordinary beauty and power of the works was never contested, the Lubicon argued that the museum needed to promote, rather than deny, the relationship between the historical pieces and the realities of contemporary Native life. One of those realities was the target of the second criticism. The exhibit was sponsored by Shell Canada, an oil company which had been drilling since the 1950s in what the Lubicon believe to be their traditional lands; lands that are the subject of an ongoing land claim dispute. How was it, asked Bruce Trigger who resigned from the McCord Museum when it refused to join the boycott, that a "show glorifying the creativity of Native peoples at the time of European discovery should be sponsored by an oil company that was...engaged in destroying the traditional economy and way of life of the Lubicon Lake Cree"?.

The exhibit's organizers answered, with a resounding echo from many in the Canadian museum community, that these were inappropriate questions to ask for they drew the players into the political realm where museums could not, and would not, speak. They were not, it was stated, political entities. I would like to argue here that, despite this overwhelming denial, museums are by their very nature political institutions. At the symposium called to address "the outstanding issues between museums and First Nations", Native and non-Native voices, both curatorial and public, challenged the fundamental premises of an institution rooted in colonial practice. The museum's mandate—to collect, preserve, interpret, and educate—is inherently an assumption of power: of the power to define and limit the meanings of those objects, and those cultures, it provides homes to. Museum's arm's-length policies, designed according to many to protect them from hostage taking by special interest groups, more effectively distances them from those whose histories they have become responsible for. The

Lubicon boycott made clear that the arm's length space which stands between the museum discourse and the many sites of what might be called contemporary practice, is that in which the Other is constructed: a space that allows the museum image to ultimately depoliticize and delegitimate those created outside it. The symposium and the disciplinary debates that have been engendered by these questions, make painfully obvious that exhibits are constructs, representations which reflect not only particular and situated interpretations of history, but more importantly create a particular vision of contemporary Canada which has the potential to defuse much of what may seem to threaten it.

CREATING THE MUSEUM'S OTHER

Bourdieu has argued that "[w]hat is at stake in the struggles about the meaning of the social world is power over the classificatory schemes and systems which are the basis of the representations of the groups and therefore of their mobilization and demobilization". The museum's claim to apolitical (rather than *a political* status) is based in the argument that once transferred into the "preserve" of the museum environment, this struggle over meaning ceases.

Removed from circulation and daily contexts of use and exchange, the objects' meanings are fixed and known. Knowledge, it is insisted, is neutral, free of influence, and free to all. And this knowledge becomes centralized in the seemingly stable object, effectively and necessarily erasing the more volatile represented subject.

Perhaps it would be more accurate to say that the original subject is replaced by the *exhibitor* as subject. An oft repeated observation made about museums is that they speak more clearly of themselves, of the exhibitor, than they do of the culture that is exhibited. These objects, which in the museum environment come to speak of a "subjected" population, speak through a known, specific, and entirely different subject: an articulative or speaking subject. Kopytoff writes that this assumption or appropriation of subjectivity is an assumption of power: the power to singularize an object, to make its meaning secure and unquestionable. What is significant about the adoption of foreign objects, Kopytoff continues, is not the fact that they are adopted, but the way they are culturally redefined and put to use. The rhetoric employed to validate colonial collecting argued the necessity of protecting and conserving a culture facing inevitable extinction of assimilation. Certainly this was the case in the collection of Native art and artefact. As Doxtator has noted: "The ethnographic museum gallery was born in the nineteenth century when, at the heart of `Indianness,' was the belief that Indian cultures were technologically and intellectually inferior and incapable of surviving in competition with Euro-Canadian society". This rhetoric of salvage, the ability to determine what deserves to be kept, remembered, and treasured is the product of an ideology of conquest.

In the collection of another culture, the museum constructs a history which situates that Other in the theoretical and institutional framework of the collector's world. Breckenridge has argued that the collection in which a piece falls contains and bounds the represented culture. An order is imposed inherent not necessarily to the objects or the displayed culture, but to the interests and goals the exhibition will serve. In making an object one's own, through its acquisition into a collection, the object is removed from a potentially threatening environment and provided a safe, and seemingly comprehensible, meaning. In a review of *The Spirit Sings*, the editor of the *Edmonton Journal* voiced this near obsession on the parts of Canadian exhibitors and publics: "It has long been clear that we actually prefer our native culture in museums. We certainly do not prefer it running the Department of Indian Affairs. Nor do we prefer it announcing the news on national television or determining its own political destiny". Continued mastery over the boundaries within which the received object and recovered history is situated guarantees control over the message that is ultimately created and passed on to the audience. While the museum then is making its exhibits more accessible, it is always careful to shape and supply the very terms on which those exhibits can be encountered.

At the Canadian Museum of Civilization's History Hall, visitors are offered a "true exploration of Canada's history" and the *History*

Hall Guide promises that its authenticity "has been established through painstakingly thorough historical research." There is no suggestion, no suspicion, that such research is powerfully limited by its methodology and sources. The language of the museum's texts and brochures is an objective one, inhabited by references to a single definitive interpretation: a *known* history. The museum's director writes: "In a sense, a national museum elevates culture by *recognizing it...*". Public exhibition then, is not simply an exchange of knowledge, but a recognition, a legitimation of objects and cultures which had, it is implied, descended into obscurity. The "come discover" invitation used so repeatedly in museums only extends the illusion that began with Columbus' "discovery" of America. Truths are discovered and illuminated. The Museum's *Souvenir Booklet* tells us that the Grand Hall "*reveals* the culture, lifestyle and monumental art of Canada's Pacific Coast", again as if earlier concealed or lost to all. And it is a *singular* culture, a singular lifestyle and art, conflating a complex and diverse history and people into a surprising homogeneity, which I will argue below has important political ramifications.

The museum then presents the illusion of an objective, authorless and truthful experience. The Canadian Museum of Civilization envisions these truths to be the glue our multicultural mosaic has lost. In fact, this is its announced mandate. In a statement that quite eerily suggests the "subjected" nature of Canada's First People, the museum's director suggests: "The more visitors can intimately experiment with the cultures on display the more likely they will make a true contact with these cultures". This true contact is dependent upon the metaphor of "experimentation," with its overtones of powerless subjects and human manipulation. We can, it is argued, participate and seemingly control the nation's collective memory, for this is how the Museum identifies its collections. But what does this collective memory, as structured in more traditional Canadian museums, recall of Native Canadians and how does that memory inform contemporary realities? I would like to suggest that, in fact, Native Canadian history has been situated outside this collective memory. Despite its ubiquitous presence in Canadian history and anthropology museums, it has remained distanced both from the exhibitor's world and from the complexities of contemporary Native life.

Marginalization in the museum setting is accomplished by the erection of barriers which demarcate the distance between the exhibited and the exhibitor: the creation of the Other. The Colonial Other is that which is not self-defining: he or she exists in opposition to those who have the power to construct and enforce boundaries of race, gender, and ethnicity. The Other is marked by *difference*—in location, time, colour, custom, history or gender. This distance, which lies behind what Fabian has called "the West and the Rest", is most recognizable by its emptiness and lack. It is not a difference that is defined by characteristics of its own identity or subjectivity (in other words, by its femaleness, blackness or Indianness), but by *absence*; by its not being male, white or First World. Fixed as the subaltern in seemingly inescapable binaries (tradition /progress, past /present, spirituality/rationality, myth /science, craft /art), the Other is at one and the same time inferior (for they are marked by lack) and threatening. His or her presence outside those boundaries is a continued reminder of possible vulnerability. What is emphasized in this construction of distance is the space not between the centre (so often impossible to identify and locate, and so impossible to penetrate) and a population with its own history, but the space between ourselves and "not us." This barrier, erected between exhibited and exhibitor, defines cultural boundaries and determines who exists within and who "without."

MAPPING COLONIAL HISTORY

In the remainder of this chapter, I would like to consider two alternative methods of looking at history museums and their exhibits, both which are situated within what Kaplan has termed the language of the atlas. The ongoing debate around how museums can best serve diverse communities echoes with geographical descriptors—boundaries, distances, inside and out—which point to the very powerful relationship between identity and place (be it spatial or temporal). In considering the shifting character of this relationship in the museum, I have adopted the working metaphor of "mapping." We will consider the way in which we might use this metaphor to critically analyse how the spatial configurations and boundaries of these museums continue to perpetuate colonial structures of power. This will allow me to set out in a very abbreviated form some of the criticisms that have recently been levelled at museums. While I strongly sympathize with the critiques of this methodology—that it can be seen as a passive and purely deconstructive move—I remain convinced that it is an important and necessary starting point. I would like, however, in the paper's second section, to move beyond this and suggest that the linear and boundary-enforcing colonial model that best describes current museums be replaced with a reconfigured "border" location or "borderland." This interpretation of place and time attempts to defuse any given centre of power and asks that we look more closely at intersections; at the interfaces between peoples and the places from which they speak and act. I believe the latter model more clearly expresses a goal identified in *The Task Force Report on Museums and First Peoples* to forge "new partnerships" that work from within a "commonality of interest".

Museums, like maps, exist in order to orient their users: to indicate where one has been, where they can go, and how that travel may best be accomplished. In the map, the unknown loses its threat of confusion. These museological maps define and negotiate spatial and temporal distances, constructing boundaries between the place where one is and is not. Their "major centres" and "capitals" of history and culture privilege certain places, indicating in the process their relationship to others on or off the map. As Fabian has argued in his discussion of the anthropological construction of time: "The history of our discipline reveals that such use of Time almost invariably is made for the purpose of distancing those who are observed from the Time of the observer". It is an argument, I believe, equally revealing of museum's construction of space. As visitors to the museum, as readers of its map, we travel *through* histories that are fixed in space and time for our perusal.

Again, in a discussion of anthropology, Appadurai has noted: "These outsiders, these observers, are regarded as quintessentially mobile; they are the movers, the seers, the knowers. The natives are immobilized by their belonging to a place". In this sense then, the user of the map is not forever tied to a single location like the Other she or he visits. That Other, Appadurai has argued, remains "somehow incarcerated, or confined, in those places" ; not simply in space, but in thought and belief as well. The visitor's is a linear journey, the progress of which is marked by these captured moments in time and space.

These are the maps that best describe many contemporary museums: places which are themselves highlights on other, more urban, maps. Recommended as destinations in city guide books, they promise visitors "voyages" and "trips" into other worlds and times. As Duncan has noted, these are cultural spaces "marked off and culturally designated as special, reserved for a particular kind of contemplation and learning" that assumes other social and economic boundaries. Once we enter the museum and traverse the boundaries that marks outside from in, chaos from known, we are inevitably provided with another map that will guide our trip in words and /or images. These remind us that spatial arrangements here are no accident and contain narratives of their own.

Perhaps the most immediate spatial distinction to be found on these maps is the distance that separates the presentations of Euro and Native Canadian histories and cultures. Inevitably these are to be found on different floors or in different wings of museums; with boundaries open, if at all, only for European excursion into Native spaces. The Smithsonian Museum in Washington presently houses Native American history in an entirely different building. Native Americans can be found in the Natural History Museum, other Americans in the Museum of American History. While the provision of a separate history for Canada's First People may be considered an indicator of respect for a distinctive culture, and perhaps even as an unwitting support for self-government, I would argue that this practice of presenting these two cultures as having no common history and no common future acts to depoliticize and deny Native Canadians a role in current national restructuring.

Consider the floor plan of the Glenbow Museum's third floor. Here, the brochure suggests, one can witness what appears to be the inevitable consequences of the "unfolding" of Western Canadian history. However, as the floor's introductory text hints, it is in fact two different histories, one of which seems tagged on as a historical afterthought.

Step back in time and trace the colourful history of Western Canada. The journey begins with the first explorers and fur traders, then moves to the early days of ranching, thru the dramatic building of the CPR, to the exciting discovery of oil in Alberta. Explore the unique cultures of Canada's Native Peoples through displays of rare ceremonial and religious objects, clothing and an 18 foot tipi.

If one follows the arrows and completes the tour as advised by the brochure, we begin at the fur trade. The earlier presence of Native Canadians is acknowledged in only three of the first six exhibits (from the Fur Trade to the Riel Rebellion), and is quickly dismissed as the country and its two "founding" cultures move into the future. It should also be noted that in these first exhibits, Native Canadian culture is in the process of collapse and decay. Interestingly, cultural erosion is expressed as a loss of spatial control, a loss of a place on geographical maps.

While *Indian Treaties* celebrates alliances between Europeans and First Peoples, the next two exhibits take on a more solemn tone, tracing the loss of traditional land and the movement to reserves (seemingly as a response to the unexplained disappearance of the buffalo): "When the buffalo were destroyed, the Indians were obliged to settled on reserves...reduced to poverty after settling on reserves, many Indians were obliged to beg in order to survive." In the Missionary exhibit another loss, in this case of faith: "Whether Catholic, Methodist or Anglican, most missionaries sought to turn Indians away from their own religion and culture, believing they would find equality with the white, both on earth and in heaven...."

While there is no contesting the reality of these threats and the very real resultant loss, the history of adaptation, transformation, and recovery is denied by its absence. As Fry & Willis have argued in their work on photographs of Australian Aboriginal peoples, these first six exhibits "present appearances which thus produce disappearances" : presences that are marked by absence. In these spaces history as a process of coexistence appears impossible; progress demands the replacement of one people, one time, with another.

The Glenbow's tour continues with a forward moving timeline—through the homestead, railway, and oil industries—to be deposited in the pre-Second World War years. With only one exception (one can break from the path and leave the floor in the ranching exhibit), the spatial configuration reflects the temporal, drawing the visitor through an uninterrupted linear vision of history. However, on leaving the 1930s, we turn the corner to suddenly find ourselves in a non-historic time. There is no sense in the Native Peoples' Gallery of development or evolution as there was in the presentation of Western Canadian history. It would appear that their presence became invisible in the other galleries because they had somehow become trapped here, wherever this may be. Few of these cases, divided by tribal identification, mention specific years or even events. However, we *are* certain that these people no longer exist for they, and their lives, are discussed only in the past tense. The gallery contains a confusing mix of pre-contact and contact era artifacts which comment on the immediate influences of English and French material culture (beads, metal, horses, and guns), but it is an entirely innocuous interaction. With the loss of the temporal structure comes a parallel disruption of the linear historical map. There is no longer a recommended path to follow within these exhibits; no sequential narrative. Here visitors can wander without prescribed method to witness a history that does not "unfold" to any logical and expected end.

While Euro-Canadians have a history marked by progress, Native Canadians have a culture most clearly marked by its fixity. Western Canadian identity is marked by its accomplishments—the railroad, the oil industry—while Native Canadian identity is tied to the region and the land that was inhabited (e.g., *Indians of the North*). This location is an interesting comment on a more contemporary lack or absence, given the current status of First Nations' land claims and the disputation of current Canadian maps. This historical journey, which *begins* with the first explorers, is not history from a Native Canadian point of view, nor from a chronological view of the province's history. The floor's layout reinforces that this is the history of Canada's white settlers, where Native Canadian culture has been inexorably pushed to hang at the end of the exhibit, where it acts as a confusing footnote to Euro-Canadian progress.

The only exhibit that contradicts this is the more recent Métis exhibit, which "tells the story of the lives and history of the Metis people in Western Canada from the earliest days to their present day circumstances". (Unfortunately space restrictions in the permanent exhibit meant that the travelling exhibit's final section on Métis involvement in the constitutional debates of the 1980s was omitted.) This exhibit is in sharp contrast to the others, not only bringing the Métis population into the present with video tapes of individuals speaking directly to the visitor of their own lives, but also discussing the diversity of the population and its relationship to the white world. Interestingly though, it is only the Métis who are able to move into the present in these history museums. At the Canadian Museum of Civilization, the Métis exhibit is included in the larger history of British and French Canadians, while at the Manitoba Museum of Man and Nature they are one of many "immigrant" histories. Aside from this identity crisis, I think it is worth noting that it would seem to be this intersection with white cultures that propels Métis culture into the present. Polarities of authenticity and purity would seem to dictate that Aboriginal Canadians are to be found in the past.

At the Royal British Columbia Museum in Victoria, a particular schizophrenia is apparent in its history floors. As the museum floor plan indicates, this depiction of history begins in the present with "time capsules" of the last five decades. As the visitor moves into the "re-creation" exhibits of earlier British Columbia history (described in the brochure as *Modern History*), he or she travels back through the history of urbanization and industrialization to the fur trade and first contact with Native Canadians, with the same linear vision of history that characterized Western Canada at the Glenbow. Reversal of the usual forward-moving path suggests even more powerfully the inevitability of this particular destination: late-twentieth-century Western Canada. Laid out so that we move back in time, each exhibit, each object, becomes a supporting player in this narrative and evidence of the clear path to this present. The time-line that appears repeatedly throughout the exhibit reinforces this interpretation. We begin here in *The Metropolis* and follow neatly defined and bounded historical moments back to the period defined as *Native Cultures*. Without a known existence before 1675 and ending with the beginning of the Gold Rush in 1850, Native Canadians are again effaced from any contemporary modern map of history. This guide suggests a homogenous world which acts simply as a preface, a moment, in the history of the modern world.

This simple regressive time-line, however, is not the same historical mapping to be found on the floors. After the *Exploration* exhibits (where no reference is made to Native Canadians), visitors have two options: they may leave the floor or take a massive temporal leap to the earliest days of British Columbia, neatly passing over the centuries of Native settlement. What follows *Exploration* is not the expected movement into first contact and a discussion of eighteenth-century Native culture, but an archaeological exhibit entitled *The 12,000 Year Gap* which focuses on the 12,000 years of prehistory for which there are no concrete documents. Here the visitor learns how this prehistory has been pieced together through the careful research of archaeologists. Not surprisingly, it is only the intervention of non-Native science that opens Native history to us.

Following this exhibit, which serves as the boundary between these two worlds, we enter the First Peoples' Gallery, where the regressive time-line has been abandoned and the space structured so as to take the visitor through a chronological progressive history of Native cultures. It remains, however, a history defined by the presence of the two "founding" cultures. Its exhibits are divided into two distinct sections: pre-contact and post-contact history. Again, this is a space and a history marked most visibly by the presence of the French and English. And while I would agree with Clifford when he writes that this exhibit is unusual in the complexity of its treatment of Native history, the transformative presence of Europe in these galleries only more sharply points out the Native absence in the Modern History halls. The land claims exhibit that concludes the First Nations Gallery, could quite logically be seen as an integral part of B.C.'s modern history and lead into, or become a part of, the time capsule exhibits that open the floor. However it remains locked out by the floor's physical layout and the historical boundaries that it reinforces.

It is interesting to note that where dissatisfaction has emerged with these representations, and this is particularly true of museum educators, a potentially more worrisome approach has been proposed: that of universalism. In this context, all boundaries are effaced in the name of what is identified as shared. Many public and school programs now work to emphasize the commonality of all Canadians. It is, I would argue, a colonial attempt to recover the Other, to fill this space by denying all but decorative difference; to reassure ourselves that we can know and understand this Other. It is an attempt to fill this absence with ourselves and our worlds. If one is not the Other, then one is somehow the Same. Difference becomes domesticated. In emphasizing these seeming commonalities (most particularly spirituality and family), contemporary expressions of difference and self-definition can be momentarily quieted.

Hall has observed that in order for one voice, one meaning to be made credible or legitimate, it not only must prove itself authoritative, but it must deny the legitimacy of others. In the colonial museum context, it is contemporary expressions and practices that are being defused and depoliticized. The Native Canadians presented most often in these museums are not those who live outside its doors, but a romanticized people of a mythical ahistoric time, for whom the greatest cost of contact was a change from quillwork to beadwork. But despite, and perhaps finally because of, the fact that this homogenous "they" is defined by lack, this has become for the very large majority of Canadians a reality. Real "Indianness" becomes defined by tradition and technologies now absent. Such exhibits imply that this is the location where the real Native Canadian can, or should, still be found and that those who we may encounter outside its walls or on the evening news are somehow deviations or bastardizations of a pure knowable essence. Change and ultimately the realities of contemporary life are perceived *again* as the *loss* of that culture: deculturation. Denied a place and a voice in institutional histories of Canada, and with those realities that lie outside the museum being systematically silenced within it, the ability to act politically or socially is seriously minimized. If one has never been acknowledged as a participant in Canadian history, how is that a constitutional presence can be found now?

The boundaries created in these maps have served as the constituting frames of identity, fixed and essentialized within spatial and temporal constructs. They work as metonyms, like those historic and tourist maps that use visual images to orient the viewer, substituting a recognizable essence for the whole, conflating and absorbing internal difference. This essence then structures the museum within a primary dichotomy—"here" and "there"—which has been translated into the numerous dichotomies of the museum—"traditional" and "contemporary," "past" and "present," "authentic" and "inauthentic," and ultimately "us" and "them." Gupta & Ferguson argue that this "presumption that spaces are autonomous has enabled the power of topography to conceal successfully the topography of power". Like those familiar maps, museums have traditionally not explored the spaces between centres, or the process of travelling from one hub to another. They have in that sense, like their chapter and plastic counterparts, remained two dimensional. In discussing such dichotomies in the construction of time, Fabian has given voice to their inherent stasis: "Instead of being a measure of movement it may appear as a quality of states; a quality, however, that is unequally distributed among human populations of this world".

MOVING TOWARD THE BORDERS

This construction of the Other is, however, encountering increased resistance, particularly from work in post-colonial theory and practice. This work, which is quickly impacting on the philosophy (if not the permanent exhibits) of museums, sets out to recover the Other: not its lost, pure or authentic voice, but contemporary speech which is historically, socially, and politically situated. Post-colonial theory and practice asks that we question the polarities that have perpetuated this particular representation of the Native Other and to explore the ground that lay between. The challenge to traditional museological thought and practice is asking that we consider alternative spaces, to map out spaces and identities that defy essentializing. These critiques suggest a museum where encounters within these polarities is paramount: a borderland.

Nor need it parcel neatly into zones: precultural, cultural and postcultural. It just could be more often than we usually like to think, criss-crossed by border zones, pockets and eruptions of all kinds. These border zones, pockets and eruptions along with our supposedly transparent cultural selves, are as profoundly cultural as anything else.

Recent councils and meetings of world indigenous peoples have given concrete evidence to the emergence of cultures and nations ill defined by traditional understandings of nation and border. These new maps must also acknowledge for difference within: for spaces within spaces. They also raise perhaps the most frustrating and engaging question communication and cultural studies has encountered: How can difference and distinction be preserved while constructing a common national or international dialogue?

Unlike the margins of colonial maps, borders reflect a *meeting* of two or more cultures. They are spaces where citizens, languages, and customs coexist, necessarily recognizing the presence of one another. Borders are transformative places, where neither here nor there, one temporarily inhabits two realities. These are not, however, idealistic oases of blind commonality. Borders are more often than not places characterized by contestation and friction, by negotiation over identity, and by an acknowledgment of different political and cultural agendas. In our border encounters, we must document our very existence; providing evidence of our allegiances, we define our relationship to others. Here we have the overt recognition that we are, to varying degrees, constitutive of one another's identity.

There is already movement at the borders. In places long marginalized, tribal museums ask that we reconsider constructions of space, history, and academic discipline. Often housed in buildings which once served as residential schools, their stories are inevitably of contact and transformation. Repatriation issues—or the demand that certain ceremonial or sacred pieces be returned to their original owners—have brought with them alternative spaces like the museums at Alert Bay and Cape Mudge. Others like the Woodlands Cultural Centre at Brantford and the Secwepemc Museum in Kamloops have begun to exhibit their own collections in centres which are communal and multi-disciplinary in nature. While much about these exhibit spaces is dictated by the museum discipline, much has been transformed. At the U Mista Cultural Centre in Alert Bay ("U Mista" meaning the state of luck that brings those captured in war home), the potlatch collection is to be found in the simple, open space of the Big House. The collection, repatriated from Ottawa only 13 years ago, literally stands along the sides of the house, leaving a large open space in the centre. The individual pieces are unlabelled, presented in the order of their appearance at the potlatch and free of the glass and cases that marked them as objects of study in Ottawa. The Centre's then director, Gloria Cranmer-Webster saw the importance of the collection not simply in its historical value, but as an impetus for contemporary practices and for its part in the continuing transformation of Kwakw_ is more a symbol than anything else: the symbol of something bad that happened but also a symbol of victory or a battle won". The texts accompanying the pieces set out the history of the suppression of the potlatch and its impact on the Alert Bay community. The narrative here is neither linear nor historical. This is not a pristine timeless world nor simply a preface to a larger history. Here Native and non-Native worlds meet in the past and present. The exhibited objects refuse a strict disciplinary classification weaving their roles as aesthetic, historical, and cultural players through the ongoing life of Alert Bay.

The Kwagiutl Museum in Cape Mudge shapes its space to reflect not the polarities of ancient and modern, but all that stands between. The brochure tells us that "the lofty beam structure of the traditional Big House and the spiral form of the sea snail reflect the evolution of Kwagiutl culture through time." While traditional museum cases and glass have been retained, the space is not divided according to traditional anthropological classification, but according to the family that owns the pieces and the rights to the songs and dances which would accompany them in the potlatch ceremony. Internal understandings of the pieces' genealogy and place in the community here determine the configuration of space.

In these instances where the museum is located on the reserve, the surrounding community is inextricably part of its impact. Clifford notes in his discussion of tribal museums that "[in] a local museum, `here' matters. Either one has travelled to get here, or one already lives here and recognizes and intimate heritage". When asked what role her museum might play for those who live outside the reserve, Linda Jules, director of the Secwepemc Museum, observed:

We have a feeling that if you are going to study Schuswap culture you shouldn't go to Ottawa to study it, you shouldn't go to Victoria to study it, you should come to where the culture sprang up because then you are able to experience the climate and the environment, you are able to experience the community and you can talk to the people. We are part of the culture, you know—we really don't like the idea of studying Native culture in isolation from Native people.

These are, in every sense, border museums, for their histories are indelibly marked by the presence of others.

While smaller tribal museums provide the critical space for local histories, their distances from the centre can also reinforce the marginalization of that history. What then, does the border metaphor suggest for larger non-Native museums? It asks that we turn our attention to the intersections of cultures; moving away from a generalized, yet culturally specific, sweep of history to a more careful depiction of how we continue to produce difference, in all of its dimensions, at those points of contact. "The move we are calling for, most generally, is away from seeing cultural differences as the correlate of a world of `peoples' whose separate histories want to be bridged by the anthropologist and toward seeing it as a producer of a shared historical process that differentiates as it connects it". At borders we are forced to contemplate the mechanisms by which we become a citizen of one place and the Other of another. Museums must, in essence, turn themselves inside out to reveal the distances with which a seemingly singular culture constructs the Other.

The Task Force on Museums and First Peoples, along with recent museum literature, begins to provide a sense of what these borderlands might look like; what meetings will be enacted there. Museums are being asked to consider a representation of history that is marked by continuity, contact, and transformation; where past and present no longer work as isolated and discrete units. Static time-lines, which glorify the past and make suspicious the present, are slowly being abandoned.

For example, at the Royal British Columbia Museum, the final exhibit of the First Peoples' Gallery addresses the history and present status of land claims, while the Canadian Museum of Civilization promises its halls will look to the future of Native Peoples.

Borderland museums cannot be intent simply on recovering the past, but must turn their resources to exploring how that past is constantly being negotiated and redefined in a present and future. The Glenbow Museum, and other institutions, augment slow-changing and unwieldy permanent exhibits with temporary programmes that address current First Nations issues.

However, all involved in this debate are quick to agree that even this perspective on history will be problematic if it continues to be the product of a single cultural voice. The border map must orient its visitor, not with one authoritative interpretation, but with multiple voices and potentially conflicting constructions of history. The Task Force made this diversity of voice its first recommendation: "Museums and First Peoples will work together to correct inequities that have characterized their relationships in the past. In particular the desire and authority of First Peoples to speak for themselves should be recognized and affirmed by museums".

This may, in fact, require that First Peoples also be asked to comment on the histories of Canada's "founding" cultures. As the Task Force further recommends though, these multiple voices cannot remain visitors to, or the illegal aliens of, these borders: "All museums and art galleries with ethnographic or Aboriginal art collections should develop programs which encompass legitimate opportunities and encouragement for the employment of Aboriginal peoples at all levels of their operations".

It further suggests that the multiplicity of voices be extended so as to question the authority of any given disciplinary voice. This will allow museums to explore those traditional mapping techniques that identified art and history as the domain of European citizens and anthropology and artefact as the territory of the native. In the spring of this year, Gerald McMaster mounted an exhibit on the popular construction of First Nations' history and culture at the UBC Museum of Anthropology.

In considering the impact of savage braves, stoic chiefs, Indian princesses, and cigar-store Indians on the consciousness of twentieth-century Native and non-Native Canadians, McMaster's work also challenges the visitor to reflect on the role of this institution in either perpetuating or challenging the on-going meaning of these representations.

The alternative map suggested here focuses both on the history of cultural contact and on the history of the travels of the objects themselves. Part of the process of turning the museum inside out is the inclusion of what Durrans has called a "transactional history."

"This narrow history could be linked not only with wider historical experiences such as explorations or colonial relations but also with earlier uses and presentations of the material by previous generations of anthropologists and curators, emphasizing the value of reinterpreting collections".

If museums are to relinquish a single authoritative voice, they must be willing to reveal the mechanisms by which objects were acquired, classified, and reinterpreted in this new context. As Durrans has noted, it would be excruciatingly cumbersome to do this with each and every object. However, the UBC Museum of

Anthropology has shown, in a spring 1993 exhibit of student work, that it can be done successfully and in a thought-provoking manner on a small scale. During this exhibit, the students targeted certain objects to illustrate the relative nature of interpretation. Small panels asked viewers to consider questions such as how the exhibition context may alter the potential "meaning" of a piece and whether "imitation," or replication, may, in fact, be seen as the sincerest form of flattery.

Finally, the border metaphor further suggests that museums *integrate* these histories in floors and exhibits that explore points of conflict and consensus, revealing the structures of power that mark Canadian history.

This is not to argue that those who occupy the border are not products of unique and specific cultural histories, but to acknowledge that those histories are never isolated. While its name still suggests the exclusions of certain histories, and its exhibits struggle for contemporaneity, the Manitoba Museum of Man and Nature presents a provincial history which reflects upon the *interrelationships* of both the natural world and humankind and of the disciplines of anthropology, history and, to a smaller extent, art.

While their exhibits provide specific histories of peoples and nature, they also acknowledge that important pieces of those histories involve responses to the presence of others.

For this metaphor to be revealing, we must all recognize our presence at these borders and acknowledge systems of privilege that make them operative.

As Hall has argued, identity is constituted *both* outside and within representation: it is a product of many imaginations and discourses. Borderlands ask that we reject the notion of an ethnic or racial difference as somehow structured by a presence and its opposing lack or absence. Further, it demands that we deny normative status to those who only appear to be without ethnicity: the authors of, rather than participants in, multiculturalism. Difference is not denied but is self-defined and amplified to take in those who had occupied the centre. It becomes *inclusive* rather than exclusive. But at the same time, it restores to the homogenized Other variety and multivocality, difference within difference that refuses the single voice narrative of the colonial museum. In the reconstruction of museum maps comes the possibility of a voice directed both inward and outward. While there is no doubt that larger museums will continue to speak of the French and English founding cultures and of non-Native intersections with Native, the singularity of that voice can no longer be assumed. For within the diversity of Native cultures, there are those who wish to speak not simply of themselves but of Others: of those who have until now spoken for them.

3

The Role of Identities and Boundaries in the Contemporary World

Geographers have not traditionally paid much attention to the meanings of boundaries in the construction, organization and reproduction of social life, identities, territoriality and power, but rather have understood boundaries as forming categories of their own and then classified them on diverging grounds. The state-centred system of territories and boundaries largely defines how we understand and represent the world and how knowledge of the geography of the world is produced, organized and used in the reproduction of the nation-state system. This maintains that all individuals should belong to a nation and have a national identity and state citizenship and that the bordered state sovereignties are the fulfilment of a historical destiny. This view has become pivotal in defining not only our world-views but also human identities.

National identity is only one of many, often coexisting and overlapping identities (religious, tribal, linguistic, class, gender, etc.) but it is perhaps the most fundamental in the modern world. Greenfeld and Chirot argue that this identity actually defines the very essence of the individual, which the other identities only slightly modify. States are in a decisive role in the production and reproduction these manifestations of territoriality, particularly through spatial socialization and territorialization of meaning, which occur in many ways through education, politics, administration and governance. This territorialization takes place through physical and symbolic violence, and states everywhere attempt to control, marginalize or destroy various aspects of centrifugal otherness, such as instances of ethnic solidarity or indigenous movements.

Many contemporary discourses have began to challenge the state-centred conceptual narratives during the last decade or so – and to provide new ones in their place. The strongest challenges have emerged from overlapping discourses on postmodern aesthetics, style and culture, the epoch - particularly the socio-economic condition of postmodernity, with its emerging 'flow' rhetoric - and, finally, a postmodern (or rather post-structuralist) understanding of the constructed and contested nature of identities, knowledge and 'truth'. In particular, dissident IR theorists and critical geopoliticians, often drawing on post-structuralist argumentation, have aimed at rendering 'theoretically visible' the constituents of the *territorial trap* - the traditional assumptions of state territoriality and fixed images of the bordered world of nation-states and identities. As Shapiro writes, "The assumption that bordered state sovereignties are the fulfilment of a historical destiny rather than a particular, and in some quarters controversial, form of political containment has been challenged". An increasingly critical attitude exists towards the state and boundaries as categories that are taken for granted, and this can also be seen in a new interest in boundary literature, which seems to be emerging on the basis of both theoretical motives and concrete border cases.

The second challenge for border studies has been more practically based, often emerging from the context of post-Cold War Europe and from concrete efforts to expand various forms of cross-border cooperation. This is linked with a broader context, i.e. the processes of globalization. It is now increasingly being argued that the processes of globalization will give rise to new global geographies and increase all manner of links (cultural, political, economic, informational) across boundaries. This will detract from the role of state boundaries and sovereignty and lead to the de-territorialization and re-territorialization of the territorial system. Boundaries (and nation-states) are comprehended as fading dimensions in socio-spatial transformation rather than fixed physical lines.

Researchers in many fields are engaged today in evaluating the changing roles of state, identities, sovereignty and boundaries, and in extreme cases their disappearance. Much of this discourse is linked with ideas of globalization, but scholars are not unanimous about this phenomenon and its effects on global-local relations and on boundaries. In any case, the new rhetoric reflects changing global links, and boundaries are increasingly being understood as symbols of a past, fixed world that will be replaced by a more dynamic one. Accordingly, this process will reduce the roles of the sovereignty and identities of states and therefore also challenge national identities and boundaries. Ohmae, for instance, declares that "in terms of real flows of economic activity, nation states have *already* lost their role as meaningful units of participation in the global economy of today's borderless world".

Many authors point out that the state will still be the major context in which we organize our lives in the future, and it is crucial to note that territorial states are now simply operating in a new, global context. Hirst and Thompson in particular remind us that despite the rhetoric of globalization, the bulk of the world's population live in closed worlds and are "trapped by the lottery of their birth". They maintain that states remain sovereign, not in the sense that they are all-powerful or omnipotent within their territories, but rather because they police the boundaries of these territories.

This chapter will continue from the arguments set forth by Hirst and Thompson and by Anderson. Its argument will be that the debates on globalization, de-territorialization and re-territorialization have raised serious questions for border scholars, but the idea of a boundary has been understood rather vaguely in these debates. Instead of repeating much used arguments showing how nation-states and boundaries are disappearing, the aim of this chapter is to scrutinize recent theoretical discourses presented in social and cultural studies and on this basis to suggest some new perspectives for boundary studies. The current confusion on the roles of boundaries is easier to understand if we consider the roles of boundaries as *institutions* and *symbols*. This helps us to realize the increasingly complicated meanings of boundaries and the fact that the same symbolizing element may have variegated meanings for different people in different contexts. It is obvious that the arguments provided by the extreme globalization theoreticians have also reflected the traditional meanings of boundaries, interpreting them as fixed, absolute, almost material entities. Nevertheless, one of the major challenges is to note the fact that boundaries are contextual phenomena and can vary from alienated to co-existent, or from interdependent borderlands to integrated ones, to employ the concepts of Martinez. This variation may be seen even in the case of single boundaries when they are analysed in a historical perspective.

Boundaries are institutions, but they exist simultaneously on various spatial scales in a myriad of practices and discourses included in culture, politics, economics, administration or education. If some of these practices and discourses, e.g. in the fields of economics, foreign policy or identity, happen to change, this does not inevitably mean the disappearance of boundaries. It is portentous to note that the meanings of sovereignty and territoriality are also perpetually changing, implying that territoriality is not just a static, unchanging form of behaviour for a state.

We will look here at three challenging themes which seem to be arising in the field of contemporary boundary studies, and will develop an approach that identifies boundaries as complicated social processes and discourses rather than fixed lines. Firstly we will discuss the discursive construction of boundaries and the role of narratives in this process. This is linked with the relation between boundaries and identity, the second theme. Thirdly, we will consider the links between boundaries and power.

Even though this chapter is mainly theoretical and conceptual in its aims, each of these perspectives will be illustrated by using concrete examples. These examples concern the Finnish-Russian border area, but they also draw on broader contexts, particularly the EU, to shape the contemporary meanings of this area. The

Finnish-Russian border is a good example of various forms of de-territorialization that have occurred since the collapse of the rigid East-West dichotomy, and also shows that it is essential to consider the multidimensionality of borders and approach them contextually. A longer historical perspective, beginning from the period when Finland was an autonomous state within the Russian Empire (1809-1917) before gaining its independence in 1917, shows the importance of understanding boundaries contextually. During the autonomy period the border was very much an open one and there was a great deal of cultural and economic cross-border interaction. Using the categories of Martinez, this may perhaps be labelled as an interdependent borderland. When Finland gained its independence the territorial strategy of the state changed radically: the border became an *ideological* one, a much used example in textbooks of political geography, and there was a minimal amount of interaction across the border – it was a typical alienated borderland. Furthermore, the border itself became a decisive symbol in the Finnish national identity, since it distinguished Finland from the Soviet Union, typically represented as the Other, the Evil One. After World War II Finland had to cede more than 12 percent of its territory to the Soviet Union and the border became a very strictly guarded line. Finland's position in western geopolitical images also changed, so that where it had been classified in the western bloc before World War II, it was represented in textbooks of political geography after the war as an eastern European state. This was very much based on the changes in the country's international geopolitical position that followed from the pacts that it was forced to enter into with the Soviet Union. The Finnish state adopted a very cautious foreign policy, and all cross-border trade was organized very formally at the state level.

After the demise of the Soviet Union this strictly closed boundary between a small, western capitalist state and the leading socialist state changed rapidly and became much more open to all kinds of flows. It is still strictly guarded on both sides, however, illustrating coexisting territorial strategies that nation-states may practice. Finland's entry into the European Union at the beginning of the 1995 has changed the meanings of this boundary still further, since it is now the only border between the EU and Russia. This fact has given it new functions and meanings that actually operate on spatial scales larger and smaller than the state. The former is accentuated by the forecasts of those Finnish social scientists who claim that during the next decade Europe will be a federal state and that the European Economic and Monetary Union (EMU) is the first step in that direction. This would imply a very radical change in the territoriality of the state. On the other hand, concrete cross-border spatial planning and development projects are now occurring on a sub-state scale, which again 'transcends' the former territorial exclusiveness of the border.

BOUNDARIES AS NARRATIVES AND INSTITUTIONS

Jean Gottmann pointed out that political and economic interests are combined in a complex way to form a trilogy of territory, population and governmental organization, and he reminded us at the same time of the power of symbolism, values, beliefs and ethics. This points to the point of departure selected for the present paper: that states continue to play a significant role in the popular politics of place-making and in the creation of naturalized links between places and people. The construction of the meanings of communities and their boundaries occurs through *narratives:* 'stories' that provide people with common experiences, history and memories and thereby bind these people together. Somers points out how social life is commonly 'storied'. It is through narrativity that people come to know, understand and make sense of the social world, and it is through narratives that they constitute social identities.

Somers and Gibson write that all people come to be what they are by locating themselves in social narratives, which are rarely of their own making. This is particularly the case with separate generations, which may differ a lot as far as their collective experiences are concerned. From the perspective of this chapter it is narratives connected with the institutions of nation, state and territory that are of vital importance. These are typically linked with ontological narratives – stories that actors use to make sense of their lives as members of social collectives and to define who 'we' are. Boundaries between 'us' and 'others' are critical elements in establishing 'us' and excluding 'others'.

Boundaries are therefore one specific form of institution. The major function of institutions is perhaps to establish stable structures for human interaction and thus to reduce uncertainty and increase ontological security, but they can vary greatly in nature. As North points out, formal rules in a society may change rapidly as a consequence of political or judicial decisions, but informal constraints embedded in customs, traditions and codes of conduct are usually considerably more impervious to deliberate policies. All institutions are perpetually developing and being transformed, however, and the boundaries of territorial communities and the narratives constitutive of collective identities are also constantly changing.

Ashley remarks that the important question is not where a boundary is, but how, by what practices and in the face of what resistances this boundary was imposed and ritualized. This is a strong and somewhat 'non-geographical' argument. We should perhaps point out that while borders are in principle nothing more than lines drawn to demarcate the sovereignty of states, their location may be significant for the fortunes of states in the event of territorial disputes. This is the case also with the history and symbolic meanings of boundaries and how these manifest themselves in the territorial identities of the inhabitants of states and in the iconographies of states.

A boundary does not exist only in the border area, but it manifests itself in many institutions such as education, the media, novels, memorials, ceremonies and spectacles, etc. These are effective expressions of narratives linked with boundaries and border conflicts and serve as references to the Other. These mediums are also the essence of the institutionalization of the border symbolism and perform the key functions of symbolism, that is social control and communication. As far as nationalism is concerned, particularly challenging objects of research are the practices and discourses that territorialize memory and transform it as part of the civil religion. The latter is important in the spatial socialization process of the citizens and occurs most effectively in education.

Education in geography and history in particular typically produces and reproduces the *iconography of boundaries,* that is, the symbols that essentially construct the history and meanings of a territory. This iconography forms an entity that can be scrutinized using many types of concrete material, since boundaries exist in various practices and discourses: in politics, administration, economics, culture or the organisation of ethnic relations. These have both material and textual manifestations (newspapers, books, drawings, paintings, songs, poems, various memorials and monuments, etc.) which reveal and strengthen the material and symbolic elements of historical continuity in human consciousness. Particularly challenging objects of research are maps, which are often the results of deeply institutionalized practices of power and representation. *Geography* is therefore exploited in many senses in these boundary producing practices.

The construction of identity narratives is a contested political process and part of the distribution of social power in society. "Struggles over narrations are thus struggles over identity", write Somers and Gibson. The narrative constitution of identities points to the fact that language is a fundamental element in the nature of identity, where language is understood broadly as including other language-like systems which mean, represent or symbolise something 'beyond themselves'. This is the case with most national symbols and the iconography that is used to communicate territoriality and boundaries. As Smith remarks, "the boundaries of nations and national states may be determined by military, economic and political factors, but their significance for their inhabitants derives from the joys and sufferings associated with a particular ethnoscape", i.e. ethnic landscape. This has become obvious all over the world in places where various minorities have began to raise their voice and where the dominating majorities have aimed at keeping their control in the definition of the relations between physical and social spaces.

Boundary narratives have to be examined in connection with broader national and state narratives. In Finland, for instance, the border with Russia has been an indispensable part of many state narratives since the gaining of independence (e.g. national identity, or links with the West) and it also has a number of material and symbolic manifestations which differ radically from Finland's other borders, with Sweden and Norway. Even though the Soviet collapse has radically altered the roles of the Finnish-Russian border and a total of 26 crossing points over the border have now been opened – six of them to international traffic - the border landscape still includes a strictly controlled frontier zone which can be entered only with special permission.

This zone was established after World War II on the Finnish-Russian border, but no corresponding arrangement exists on the Swedish or Norwegian border. While as many as four million Finns and Russians per year cross the border nowadays and goods traffic is increasing, a similar, very effective border patrol system still exists as during the Soviet period and new, increasingly technical surveillance mechanisms are being introduced. New electronic monitoring systems have been installed which permit more effective governance and control of space. In spite of the increasing flows of people and goods, very much the same system of border signs still exists, including material and symbolic elements from watchtowers, customs houses and flags to barbed wire and uniforms.

All this means that the de-territorialization of the Finnish-Russian border has occurred in discrepant ways and in the context of different social practices. In some practices the border is still largely a closed one and territoriality as control over space is effectively enforced. Customs operations and control over migrants and refugees are very effective, i.e. although the flow of people has radically increased, control over who these people are has increased, too. On the other hand, numerous cross-border planning projects, partly established with the support of EU structural funds, indicate that the formerly almost totally closed border is relatively open in these areas of activity. The Finnish-Russian border is among the largest thresholds in the world as far as standards of living are concerned, and both of the these strategies aim at controlling and governing the situation in the border area.

The narratives attached to boundaries change perpetually along with developments in interterritorial socio-political relations and the internal relations within specific states. One challenge is to study the changing interpretations given to boundaries and how these express inter-state ideologies and links with the international geopolitical landscape. This approach is inevitably historical and non-essentialist: territoriality, boundaries and identities should not be understood as something primordial but rather *situational* and *contextual*.

The Finnish-Russian border provides a fitting example of this contextuality. The meanings of the border have always been historically contingent and contextual, and these meanings have gained varied forms in social actions. While the border is still strictly controlled, the previous forms of territoriality have been changing since the Soviet collapse, indicating de-territorialization of the border, so that Russia is partly excluded from these new territorializations and partly included in them.

Territorial discourses and practices at the state level are now diverging. In the broader context, territorial Finland is part of western Europe and the EU (and now also the forthcoming EMU zone) and speculations on possible NATO membership occupy a significant position in current Finnish society, all of which in a sense constructs an exclusive border between Finland and Russia. On the other hand, Finland has been very active in the EU context in opening links with Russia and including that country in a larger European space.

Finland was particularly active in efforts to have Russia accepted as a member of the Council of Europe. Similarly, current efforts to develop a Northern Dimension in European Union policy have the same aim: to create economic links, particularly with northwestern Russian, in order to prevent environmental problems and to integrate Russia into the larger European space. These links are therefore not merely economic ones but also deep reflections of the aims of security policy elites. In spite of the still strict territorial control maintained at the border, the new spatial planning practices established by the Finnish and Russian authorities are producing new regionalizations that span this border. Thus the border region is now divided into four development zones, Southern Finland-St.Petersburg, Karelia, Arkhangelsk and Barents, each of which has its own problems and its own planning strategies based on cross-border cooperation. Increasing cross-border links are not looked on favourably everywhere.

BOUNDARIES AND THE CONSTRUCTION OF IDENTITY

Boundaries are both symbols and institutions that simultaneously produce distinctions between social groups and are produced by them. Nevertheless, they not only separate groups and social communities from each other but also mediate contacts between them. Borders provide normative patterns that regulate and direct interactions between members of social groups, rules on how to cross boundaries and rules governing the exchange of people, goods and symbolic messages.

As symbols, boundaries are mediums and instruments of social control and the communication and construction of meanings and identities. As institutions, they link the past, present and future together, i.e. they construct a continuity for social interaction. This makes the links between boundaries, nationalism and identity particularly strong. Since identity - or the *representation* of identity - is achieved through the inscription of boundaries, the question of power is essential. Cultural researchers in particular have studied the struggles and symbolic links between social groups, and this question is becoming an increasingly challenging one in a world of voluntary and forced movement and exile. Barth, for instance, puts more emphasis on boundaries than on identity, since the classifications constituting the grounds for identity mean in fact the construction of boundaries. Calhoun points out that though the concern for distinction may be universal, identities themselves are not.

The meanings of boundaries are thus underlined by the fact that identities are produced through boundaries. Identities are often represented in terms of a difference between Us and the Other, rather than being something essentialist or intrinsic to a certain group of people. While identity is based on differentiation, this should not inevitably take the form of opposition, of drawing a hard boundary between 'us' and 'them'. The production of boundaries is linked effectively with the social and spatial division of labour, the control of resourses and social differentiation

Recent studies on the construction of foreign policy discourses, understanding them as boundary-producing practices developed by the state, provide one interesting approach. Campbell, for instance, has examined the relations between identity and difference and how they are exploited in the construction of threats in foreign policy discourses, while the representations of threats serve in turn to secure the boundaries of a state's identity. The Finnish-Russian border illustrates Campbell's argument. The Soviet Union was the Other for the Finns, and before World War II this image held good both at the political level and in the national process of socialization. After the war Finnish foreign policy towards the Soviet Union was very cautious, and both the official 'geopolitical truths' and e.g. the representations of Finland's huge neighbour in national sozialization -school textbooks - became much more neutral. The boundary-mediated interpretations of the geopolitical context thus changed radically. This example illustrates why it is of great importance to examine how state boundaries become a part of the everyday life and the (contested) identity narratives existing in a state. This also makes it possible to understand why various generations living in the same spatial context may have quite different identities – they simply have different spatialized memories.

Boundaries are expressions of power relations. As institutions, they embody implicit or explicit norms and values and legal and moral codes. They are hence constitutive of social action and may be both obstacles and sources of motivation. The Finnish-Russian border is a good example of this duality. During the Soviet period the border areas of both the Finnish and Soviet side became typical examples of alienated borderlands, peripheral areas where all links were directed towards their own national centres. The border is the same today and border patrolling practices are still very strict, but since the collapse of the Soviet Union the border has no longer been a serious obstacle to cooperation, which now takes place across it in forms varying from environmental to cultural and from economic to regional planning projects.

The arguments of (postmodern) globalization theorists and the representatives of IR make it that the spatiality or geographical organization of power is not merely connected with the territorial state but may also 'flow' and manifest itself on all geographical scales. Power should not be understood merely as a commodity to be wielded by agents, usually the dominant social group, in order to control all the places and localities within a given territory. Power is diffused in global networks of wealth, information and images "which circulate and transmute in a system, of variable geometry and dematerialized geography". Power 'flows' in the codes of information and in the "images of representation around which societies organize their institutions, and people build their lives and decide their behaviour".

What, then is 'power' in the case of boundaries? The major challenge for boundary studies is to analyse how the state-centred naturalization of space is produced and reproduced, and how the exclusions and inclusions between 'We' and 'Them' that it implies are historically constructed and shaped in relation to power, various events, episodes and struggles. Therefore one logical object of study is geographical concepts and terms, particularly boundaries, and how they have historically functioned within national discourses. An analysis of the activities of Finnish academic geographers and geography teachers, for instance, has shown that they have done much to shape people's understanding of the national territory through their representations and conceptualizations and that they have also effectively developed diverging concepts and categories to represent the boundary in specific ways. In a word, they have produced geopolitical scripts that have at times been put to effective use by the political and military elites of the state.

Since boundaries are an expression of the power structures that exist between societies, a major challenge for boundary research is to deconstruct such power relations in the form of boundary narratives. Boundaries may therefore be comprehended as flows of power in which memories are transformed into things of the present and future. It is of vital importance to analyse how certain rituals and symbols, discourses and practices of power have emerged, taken their current shape, gained in importance, and affected political decisions. This puts the accent on a contextual, culturally and historically sensitive approach to boundary studies.

Epilogue

"The rise and fall, the construction and deconstruction of various types of boundaries", Oommen writes; "is the very story of human civilization and of contemporary social transformation". This argument lends support to the key conclusion of the present paper: instead of simply accepting rhetorical comments on how boundaries are disappearing in the 'world of flows', boundary scholars should be more sensitive to the changing meanings of boundaries. They also should pay more attention to the contextual nature of boundaries and to the developing of approaches that are based on recent social, political and cultural theory.

Despite the effects of globalization, changing power relations and the meanings of sovereignty, environmental problems and the post-nationality arguments of postmodern theoreticians, the state will apparently continue to be the ideal form of organization for most nations at the turn of the millennium. This argument does not take for granted the much criticized realist viewpoint or the ideas on an anarchical world that exists outside organized states. It is based on the fact that the increasing complexity of the institutional organization and networks of the contemporary world will continue to be mainly organized by the state in the near future. Hirst and Thompson emphasize that the state may now have less control over ideas, but it remains in control of its borders and the movements of people across them. A large majority of the world's people want - voluntarily or by force - to understand themselves as nations or to struggle to create their own sovereign states. It is also obvious that the majority of political, economic and military elites in the already existing states aim to maintain their state and its apparatus in order to retain or increase their own power and symbolic capital or that of their political parties or corporations.

An important challenge for boundary studies is that of searching for new conceptualizations by which to comprehend the changing meanings of boundaries. The latest interdisciplinary literature on boundaries makes it clear that the answers to questions regarding their disappearance are not simple ones, of the either-or type, because boundaries are no longer understood as physical, immovable spatial entities. The questions of context, knowledge, representation and power become crucial. Thus, in addition to empirical case studies on boundaries - which are continually of crucial importance - researchers will also have to develop abstractions to make the multi-dimensional character of territory and boundary building 'theoretically visible'. This will help us to realize that traditional territoriality is increasingly turning into *territorialities*, i.e. more vague, overlapping spaces of dependencies and constellations of power. Hence, where as authors like Ohmae are ready to declare the death of nation-state and boundaries, pointing mainly to economic practices, boundaries still make a difference in the spheres of governance (and also in the governance of economic flows), culture and spatial identities and will also in the future provide interesting challenges for researchers.

BORDERS AND POLITICAL ORDERS

Attention solely to borders between countries is unsustainable in a world in which new regional identities inside states and new supernational ("bloc") identities that group state units are rapidly developing. We want to examine these new kinds of borders, among and between regions, states and blocs whilst at the same time, remembering the advice of Jacques Ancel on linking borders to the units that they enclose. We argue that political developments cannot be explained by the features of a political boundary between two neighbouring countries but rather by the place that the boundary in question occupies as an intrinsic element of the world system. Barrier functions are stronger if the border separates not only two countries, but also two opposing military and/or economic blocs. We hold, like Knight, Murphy, and Newman and Paasi, that border study cannot be separated from identity and territorial questions. Unlike early morphological border studies, there is now much more engagement between students of nationalism and territoriality and those who study borders. As Smith (1981: 187) noted, "whatever else it may be, nationalism always involves a struggle for land, or an assertion about rights to land". In the primordialist tradition of nationalism, the concept of homeland has a central focus. The geographic outcome of national conflicts is frequently new borders, new borderlands and new relations between bordering neighbors. A starting point for border studies, therefore, should be the analysis of identity formation and change, with territorial dimensions as a central theme. Rather than following the primordialist tradition of equating national identity to a specific piece of land based on an historical claim, we see borders as social constructions of recent origin and therefore, place the study of borders into the world-systems tradition of political geography. Though the world-system tradition currently gives little explicit attention to the territorial dimension of political geography, we believe that the world-systems approach offers the opportunity to integrate disparate research traditions in political geography.

World-Systems Theory and Border Study

If the nature of a border depends on state characteristics, which of these are important? What are the state's purposes and functions? How is the nature of the border related to global and international issues? The future of border studies is intimately bound to the attempts of political geography to deal with such major subjects as the world-system, the nature and functions of the state, state-building, nationalism and nation-building, identity and its rapid changes, self-determination and its limitations, as well as democracy and democratization. Borders should therefore be considered simultaneously at different scales from the individual to global; the major concern is, however, likely to remain at the state level.

Borders and the World-Economy

In the modern world-system, economic globalizing forces have impinged to an accelerated extent on localities and states and thus exaggerated claims of the withering away of states can be readily found. About the time of the French Revolution, demarcated boundaries became limits of legal, fiscal, administrative, economic, and political spaces, thus regulating transboundary flows of goods, capital, and people. The increasing openness of political borders in recent decades, led especially by trade, anticipates a move from these "totalitarian" closed borders towards more "differentiated" boundaries. States established different boundaries (sometimes even spatially-different) for different purposes. The regulating function of a border, as a part of its contact function, sorts various transboundary flows and serves as a thin filter. As a result, each social group and each activity has its own "borders" and "frontier zones". For large enterprises, border taxes and formalities play little role, though for local firms they might be very important. As a senior executive of IBM (International Business Machines) stated: "For business purposes, the boundaries that separate one nation from another are no more real than the equator. They are convenient demarcations of ethnic, linguistic and cultural entities".

To an increasing extent, the national border is no longer only a limit to the territory of a state and its waters. The development of communications and international trade has generated national boundaries inside of state territory, as in international airports, around special custom areas, and free economic zones. More lines on the map demarcate economic zones in the oceans. A border space is no longer necessarily stretched along the national boundary. But globalization will never lead to a "spaceless" world or to a world without national boundaries. On the contrary, globalization depends on the partition of space between states, and to the increasing extent, between regions and cities, because capital can circulate only between different legal spaces created within the states and/or regions and with the support of their guaranties. Therefore, the world system needs inequalities and the political borders that perpetuate them, and these borders, in turn, are inconceivable without specific identities legitimizing them. Political boundaries are thus a bio-ethno-social constant of the human society's life, because without membranes, it is impossible to regulate the exchange between the ethnic and/or the state territory and the outer world, protecting this territory from external chaos.

The patterns of global economic relationships are becoming more dynamic and volatile than in the past, while social and cultural structures, including people's identities, change much more slowly and remain one of the most important factors of inertia in world development. The dialectical relationship between "movement" and "iconography" is thereby hindered. In many countries, this is perceived as a threat to cultural and national identities and has the paradoxical effect of reinforcing the barrier functions of borders. However, there are obvious trends towards the creation of a homogeneous global culture that does not recognize borders and identities and which is opposed in certain civilizations.

Borders and the State

Macmillan and Linklater identify three "narratives" of the state: a) the *progressivist* (or primordialist narrative - Kaiser, 1994), which considers the state as a means and a site for realization of one of the basic human rights, self-determination of ethnic political communities; b) the *geopolitical* narrative, or the state as a power-container, viewing the state's activity as managing all affairs within its territorial boundaries so that if the scale of emerging problems extends beyond the borders, the state tries to extend and demonstrate its power beyond them; and c) *the neo-liberal* narrative, emphasizing the problem of scale, that argues that the contemporary state cannot cope with new economic problems, to ensure a satisfactory level of welfare to its citizens, and is increasingly unable to meet the requirements of democratic rule by successfully mediating the effects of economic globalization.

The primordialist view privileges the national basis of statehood, believing that the morphology and functions of national borders depend on the ethnic or political identities of populations on both sides, because there are both stateless ethnic groups and numerous multi-ethnic states. The geopolitical narrative also stresses the problem of identity, though more indirectly, but at the same time focuses on the integral, absolute role of territoriality and accompanying state boundaries. The neo-liberal approach, by contrast, questions the permanency of state borders and political identities and argues that they are eroded by globalization trends. In the twentieth-century, the ideal of a nation-state based on a homogenous ethnic-nation with a common language and culture, certified by the mid-nineteenth century, became legitimized by democratic procedures. The hypothetical nation-state of our time is a specific region with relatively well-defined, internationally recognized boundaries and the political identity of its people is constituted through a unique nationalism.

Nationalism is a specific type of human territoriality and a territorial form of ideology.. The aim of nationalism is to create a national identity that is based on state boundaries. The classic triad of political geography ("nation - territory - state") emerged in the early nineteenth-century at the same time as the appearance in Europe of the nation-state concept. The history of modern France is often used as the best example of the creation of a nation-state "from above", promoting a specific national identity. After centuries of nation-building, France became a great European power only when the majority of its population, independently of ethnic origin, felt their "Frenchness". It happened surprisingly late, only about the 1870s. "France" was constructed because of the economic integration of the national territory by the development of modern roads and railways ("railway imperialism") and the coincidental appearance of national newspapers that helped to build the "imagined community" of France. Political identity emerged only after the system of secondary national socialization had been formed, consisting of the policies of compulsory and universal primary education in all parts of the country, military conscription, and the activity of state functionaries and clergy.

As the example of France demonstrates, the use of a common language is one of the major conditions for the origin of the political and cultural identity. To build on this nascent identity, the state creates its iconography- the system of symbols, images, national holidays, regular parades, festivals, public ceremonies, traditions, and manifestations - that help to cement national solidarity and clarify the perceptions of cultural distinction between the populations on different sides of a state boundary. Iconography also includes a system of national stereotypes, about national history, territory and the place of state in the world, about "natural" allies and enemies, all promoting in turn a geopolitics of national identity. Nationalism looks inwards in order to unify the nation and its constituent territory and outwards to divide one nation and territory from another. National stereotypes necessarily include images of space: regions incorporated into the state territory by the national consciousness get their codes, and many of them became national symbols (like Kosovo for Serbia and Sevastopol for Russia). Sometimes stereotypical territorial representations develop into "territorial ideologies" justifying claims on the ground of theories of "living space".

Negative stereotypes are especially purposefully cultivated when national elites feel a threat to their national integrity and culture; these representations frequently become the key elements of the human territoriality. National and the political identities often play a more important role in the creation of a stable state than the community of race, language, and religion. The famous maxim - "We created Italy, now we have to create Italians" - retains its value for political elites in new states. Without an agreed political identity, the state remains a contingent amalgamation of different cultural or ethnic regions.

National identity, though still occupying the central place in the hierarchy of human territorialities and border-demarcations, may be losing its hegemony at the end of the millenium. Though the "single national identity - single nation-state" equation remains hegemonic in the literature, there is much evidence that individuals carry around a good deal of identity baggage. The concept of "matrioshka" nationalism (named from the Russian dolls that are hidden inside each other) holds much appeal for understanding the post-1989 political developments in former Eastern Europe. In Eastern Ukraine, for example, up to six identities (Soviet, Russian, Ukrainian, and regional mixtures) are layered, liked the dolls, on top of each other. As national, ethnic, regional and local identities overlap but remain "hidden", various political actors compete with each other for adherents, attempting to wake up and activate "sleeping" identities. Internationalization and, in particular, international migrations has led to the growing number of people with double identities, especially children from mixed marriages. Sometimes these identities coexist peacefully even within a territorial community and also in the consciousness of an individual, but sometimes, as in former Yugoslavia, they erupt into intense ethnic conflict. This balanced relationship between two or more identities is subject to rapid change and challenges the existing system of world boundaries.

Continuing Giddens' state as geopolitical container model, Taylor extends the container analogy to four domains and characterizes them in a historical-evolutionary manner. Early modern states were predominantly "power containers", followed later by the state as "economic container" and even later at the end of the eighteenth-century by the state as "national container".

In the past century, the state as "cultural container" has taken on a more significant role. The important point is that the role of the state has greatly expanded over the past 500 years and now incorporates a variety of issue areas.

The traditional state role as provider of defense to its citizens has now been expanded to incorporate a mediating role between locality and the world-economy, to buffer the capitalists and workers from the harsh winds of global economic shifts. The state as container suffers some leakage as a result of pressures from "above" (the global economy and its attendant changes in regional economic fortunes, as well as super-national political organizations like the European Union) and "below" (from ethno-national and regional developments, spurred in turn by changing identities). Long the most logical "spatial fix" to the top-down economic and bottom-up national pressures, the nation-state is now only one of five scales, though still the most significant, in the world-economy. We illustrate these added dimensions in a revised world-system figure.

Border and Localities

National (political) identity is central in contemporary discussions but before nationalization of the state territory, local identity predominated and still persists. Peasants, who constituted most of humanity and rarely moved beyond the direct surroundings of their village, felt primarily or even exclusively members of their "community" and, to a much lesser extent, identified themselves as inhabitants of a historical province or a principality.

The creation of national identity cannot be represented solely as a process imposed "from above" by the central state and its elites who, in the process, ignore and annihilate local differences, whilst promoting the state's political project and rationalizing that it acts in the interests of the whole population. Sahlins argues instead for a two-way process in which local society and social groups play a considerable role in the formation of the nationhood and the consolidation of the nation-state.

In his detailed study of the region of Cerdanya, constituting an integrated natural, economic, ethnic and cultural area in the Pyrenees, Sahlins showed how local dwellers chose their national identity between France and Spain without abandoning local interests, a local sense of place, and a local identity. Rural communities competing with their neighbors for scarce natural resources were always and everywhere hostile to aliens and newcomers, to "others". In border areas, local peasants successfully played on the difference between two notions of sovereignty - the jurisdictional and the territorial ones - and conscientiously manipulated identities in the service of their interests, such as avoiding military conscription during wars. In these areas, national identities were built on the "oppositional model". Imagining oneself as a member of a community or a nation meant perceiving a significant difference between oneself and the "other" across the boundary.

In addition to the world-system - nation-state - locality triad commonly found in political geography, there are two other "intermediate" levels whose structures affect the nature of borders and border areas, though to a different extent in different parts of the world. These additional scales are the regions inside state boundaries and macroregions forming blocs of states.. The analogy of "leaking container" is useful to indicate the hollowing out of the nation-state from above and from below.

BORDERS AND SUB-STATE REGIONS

National identity is eroded by multiple factors inside and outside national borders. The chimera of the nation-state, elaborated in the specific conditions of nineteenth-century Western Europe, implied the creation of a single, homogeneous nation united by common language and common culture, a distinct economy and a specific legal system functioning within clearly-demarcated secure boundaries. This cannot be applied to most contemporary states of the world because of their multi-ethnic and multi-cultural structures and the lack of economic and cultural premises for merging their diverse parts within a stable unitary state. (Contrast the discussions of Western and Third World nationalisms in Hutchinson and Smith, 1994). In many cases, national identity does not mean *ethnic* identity; it would be more correct to use the term "political identity". Many attempts to build a political identity in multi-ethnic countries obviously failed or were stopped at a certain stage by new trends in economic and cultural development. In the Soviet Union, Yugoslavia, Czechoslovakia and Belgium, national identities turned out to be stronger than political ones. Ethnic and linguistic identities stand in contrast to the adopted national identities imposed from above by colonial authorities in many African and Asian countries.

Lots of territorial claims (and contested boundaries) are grounded on the right of nations to self-determination, considered both a liberal ideal and a basic human right. A "nation" can be viewed as a quasi-voluntary association existing on the basis of a changing identity or as a "natural entity" created by nature on the basis of common language and other natural characteristics. It can also be seen as a metaphysical construct emerging naturally or deliberately created out of a set of social representations (images, aspirations and highly selective historical references). Current claims for self-determination and revision of boundaries represent complicated combinations of social representations based on pre-existing ethno-linguistic cleavages and social representations, and the economic and political interests of elites trying to manipulate with identities. Recent electoral successes of the Lega del Nord in Italy indicate that there are few absolutely stable or "eternal" identities and the national (or the political) identity is no more than an element in the hierarchy of territorial identities. In questioning the nation-state model, inhabitants of Northern Italy can ask why they have to fund the poor South from their pockets. Is it only because they and their southern compatriots are Italian? And why is it necessary for all Italians to live in the same state?.

New regional identities are not necessarily constructed as sub-divisions of states. Trans-border regional groupings are evolving in Western Europe and many hark back to anachronistic political forms. The strengthening of supranational bodies in Brussels is going on at the same time as the creation of the so-called "Europe of the regions", where old ethnic and regional identities can be implemented in the policy of decentralization and regionalization. These processes give much larger competence to the regions, whose boundaries frequently do not match existing administrative borders of provinces, departements, counties, etc., but rather match old historical units of the "pre-capitalist" past. Trans-border regions like the famous *Regio Basilensis* get special attention from European planners, and are recognized and endowed with special supranational bodies which can act more or less autonomously from central governments. This trend weakens national borders in relation to the "supranational" or regional, or, more accurately, changes the nature of the borders' system. Europe is crisscrossed by a thick web of former political boundaries, most of which delimit ethnic or regional identities; it was the continent with the newest political boundaries even before the dramatic geopolitical shifts in 1991-1994.

The imprint of earlier borders on the contemporary political landscape is often dramatic long after their disappearance. It is not only minority ethnic areas, such as the German-speakers in Alto-Adige (Italy), that show differences from the national pattern. In a homogenous ethnic population, the legacies of borders are also visible. On such example is Poland, where every post-1989 election has revealed considerable differences in the political patterns in the three historical regions (Western Poland - the so-called "recovered territories" brought under control of Poland after World War II and populated by settlers from Galicia and the former

Polish/Soviet borderland; Eastern Poland - formerly part of the Russian Empire; and the South-East - part of the Austro-Hungarian Empire to 1918). In Ukraine, the strongest national/ethnic identity lies in Western Ukraine, also a part of the Austro-Hungarian Empire and only in the Soviet Union between 1939-1991; it was never part of Russia. If a territorial change occurs, new borders most likely follow the lines of geopolitical ghosts of the past, especially those where linguistic, ethnic and confessional boundaries match old political boundaries.

Borders and Macro-Regions (blocs)

The global economy in the future will not depend exclusively on state boundaries. Globalization processes are creating new identities, especially in Europe where the economic integration process is farthest advanced and a new macroregional identity is forming. The content and development of this new European identity preoccupies ideologists of European integration and the academic community. European identity is still relatively weak and highly variable across the populations of the member states of the European Union, as evidenced by the frequent Eurobarometer surveys on support to the European institutions. European iconography, however, is now being created. The prefix "Euro-" has already become quite familiar for the average European (e.g. "Eurovillage" in Brussels; "EuroDisneyland" near Paris; "Eurostar" for the Paris-London high-speed train; the "European" newspaper, etc.).

Where are the eastern and southern edges of Europe?. Which countries have enough European characteristics to qualify and which fail the test?. It is expected that the barrier function of national borders will now be exacerbated by the emerging geopolitical boundaries. It is not by chance that new nation-states of East-Central Europe vie with one another in their claims to "Europeaness". Due to strict measures against illegal immigration and coordinated customs policy, new barriers are being erected on the borders of the EU and promoted by the Schengen agreement, while political internal borders become more transparent. The long queues of busses and trucks to cross the borders from Lithuania and Ukraine into Poland are a taste of the barrier manifestations that will become more common at the edges of Europe.

A specific kind of border between macroregions is the *critical frontier* distinguished by Boulding. He argued that states protect their interests abroad, but each of them has a unique potential "radius of action", the limit of which is a "critical boundary". The concept is connected to notions of spheres of influence or of vital interests. Obviously, regions of particular sensitivity, "buffer-zones", surround great powers, within which they do not tolerate some actions of other states. The blockade by the U.S. of Cuba during the 1962 missile crisis can be compared with the 1979 invasion of the USSR into Afghanistan. A contemporary manifestation is Moscow's position on the enlargement of NATO into former Eastern Europe. The spatial coincidence of state, bloc and ethno-regional boundaries will enhance the barrier role of specific borders.

In the Western euphoria after the end of the Cold War, it is easy to overlook the relocation of the "Iron Curtain" eastwards to the borders of the former Soviet Union. We argue that coincident borders will show more likelihood to exhibit separating functions. Thus, the post-1989 international borders on the eastern edge of Poland (with the Russian enclave of Kaliningrad, Lithuania, Belarus and Ukraine) will mark the "edge of Europe" if the NATO strategists have their way. This Baltic Sea to Black Sea border is not just a line separating blocs nor an international border but because of the ethnic relocations at the end of World War II, it also marks a cultural-national divide. Traditional Polish-areas to the east are now emptied of ethnic Poles and formerly mixed-ethnic regions are now uni-national. By contrast, territories whose bloc, nation-state, and cultural territories are not coincident, will remain the loci of tension, as in former Yugoslavia. Attempts to make these borders coincident have resulted in large-scale conflict.

Huntington's concept of the "clash of civilizations" is now widely discussed and severely criticized, though Barber and Bennigsen support its empirical premises. Galtung identifies seven major world groupings based on religion and he anticipates that goods and services, labour and capital will flow across borders but *within* the same macro-culture. The so-called "borderless world" is therefore quite limited to states of similar characteristics. The Eastern Christian-Orthodox and Muslim cultural areas in Cyprus, in the Greek-Turkish borderland, in Bosnia and in the Caucasus remain very tense and served as a cleavage along which Cyprus, Nagorno-Karabakh, and Bosnia split. Attention is returning to the line of the "Great Schism" of 1054 in Eastern between Western and Eastern Christianity in Europe which threatens to become a new watershed equally as imposing as the "Iron Curtain". The issue of where "Eastern Europe" begins and "Central Europe" ends has already split the states of former Communist East-Central Europe into candidates for membership in the European Union and NATO (North Atlantic Treaty Organization) - Poland, the Czech Republic and Hungary - and those countries which in the short-term perspective cannot be admitted in these organizations - Belarus, Russia, Serbia and Bulgaria. It is creating a new environment of "us" and "not us".

A MODEL OF BOUNDARIES AND AN ILLUSTRATION

The features of a political boundary between two neighbouring countries should be placed in a wider geo-political context. Shifts in identities provoke the redistribution of functions between borders existing *de jure* (political or administrative) and *de facto* (ethnic, linguistic, cultural or "civilizations"). "*De facto*" borders become transformed into institutionalized borders, and vice versa. It is preferable to call *de facto* boundaries "frontiers" because it is often difficult to identify their precise location; they are rather outwardly-oriented transitive zones of contact between cultures. *De jure* boundaries are, by contrast, lines of "separation, inwardly oriented manifestations of social and national integration, necessary components of sovereignty". To illustrate our argument, we use the case of borders in independent Ukraine providing examples of almost all their types and situations.

Europe, both West and East, is a tapestry of borders. Relict borders sit cheek-by-jowl with well-demarcated lines. The term "fragments' applies aptly both to territories and the lines that enclose them. The history of border changes in the past century should give pause to those whose believe that the era of territorial shifts is over, though the inviolability of international borders is attested by the signatories to the Helsinki Accords of 1975. The mosaic of territorial fragments that is found in Europe, most prominently in East and Central Europe. The main features of the schema, extended from the more local and landscape-oriented models of Haggett and Foucher, are the presence of different types of boundaries and the mismatches between social and economic distributions and the lines that enclose the territories. The schema can be used to illustrate the difficulties inherent in the creation of new nation-states and the historical legacies that further impede regional solutions. Non-overlapping territories and sub-divisions of territorial units hinder any agreements on geographic delimitations and foster inter- and intra-territorial rivalries. We illustrate the dimensions of contemporary border issues with a contemporary example of Ukraine, independent since 1991.

Nation-Building and the System of New Borders in Ukraine

The western border of Ukraine, created in 1939 as a result of the annexation of Galicia and North Bukovina by the Soviet Union, was a frontier dividing two antagonistic superpowers - the German Reich and the Soviet Union. - before World War II. Because of the ideological, autarchic, and closed character of the Soviet regime, this border maintained strong barrier functions and continued in that "frontal" role even after the Soviet Union had moved the "Iron Curtain" westward to the inner-German border. This Western international border of Ukraine not only marks the Ukrainian political territory but indications are that it will remain a strong barrier in a future as a result of the inclusion of Central European countries in the western political and economic system through NATO and the EU.

The "civilizational" border between Western Christianity and Orthodox areas does not match the former Soviet (now Ukrainian) western border. It coincides with the border between major Ukrainian sub-state economic and cultural regions and serves as the administrative boundary between a number of Oblasts (provinces), following the old "formal" boundary which for centuries divided the Russian and the Austro-Hungarian empires. This relict boundary can still be seen in the spatial impress of different housing and town styles in Western Ukraine. The regions of Galicia and North Bukovina were never united with Russia in the same state except a short period before World War II and from 1945 to 1991. This imperial relict border also divides adherents of the Uniate church (created in 1596 by the Brest Union from the unification between part of the Orthodox clergy and the Roman Catholic church) to the west and the rest of Ukraine, which is mainly Orthodox. This ancient "institutionalized" political frontier, now marked by contemporary regional and administrative boundaries, is extremely important for the creation of the Ukrainian national identity and the Ukrainian political nation. Due to the political and cultural separation of Galicians from other Ukrainians and especially from East Ukraine with its large Russian population, ethnic mixture, and blurred identities, there are far greater differences between a West Ukrainian from L'viv and a Russian-speaking Ukrainian from Donbass than between (for example) a Russian from Arkhangelsk and a Russian Cossack from the Don.

Under these "two nation" circumstances, the obvious way to form the all-Ukrainian identity as the basis of the new state was to use the "oppositional" model of identity. Ukrainian politics is torn by a cleavage that concerns the geopolitical orientation of the country to the CIS (Commonwealth of Independent State) or to the West. President Leonid Kuchma was elected in 1994 on a platform of closer ties to the CIS but he received very little voter support in the west of Ukraine. Though there are many forms and traditions of Ukrainian identity, some ideologists of Ukrainian nation-building clearly opted for the oppositional path in developing the so-called "western" geopolitical doctrine.. Its basic tenets are that it is possible to create an independent Ukraine as a new large European state in opposition to Russia, and to develop a system of iconography, myths and social representations aimed as depicting Ukrainians as the sole, direct, cultural and geopolitical heirs of the Kievan "Rus-Ukraine". This heritage marks Ukrainians as more ancient, more civilized and a more "European" nation than Russians. These "myths" or "imaginations" portray Ukraine as a fertile and rich country possessing huge natural resources and controlling key strategic locations, making it both an object and a victim of the claims of neighbouring states (i.e. Russia), and a supplier of the "human material" for colonization of new lands by these "foreign powers" in their imperialist adventures in other regions. Ideologists of the new national Ukrainian identity picture entrepreneurship, thriftiness, honesty, the willingness to care for the environment of everyday life, and peasant individualism as basic features of the Ukrainian national character; they contrast these characteristics to Russian collectivism and laziness. The ideas of the German scholar, Gessen-Tihlmann in the 1934 book "*Peasant Europe*" are used to ground the unity of Central Europe and, of course, the attachment of Ukraine to it by the specific "peasant" character of Central European peoples living in the regions from the Baltic Sea to the Black Sea.

New Ukrainian ideologists challenge the common historical and cultural roots as well as the long-term mutual interests of Russia and Ukraine. They speculate about a late ethnogenesis of Russians, arguing that only Ukrainians are "a true Slavic people", since the Russian nation results from the mixture of Slavic tribes with other ethnic groups. They discuss the unavoidable "Asiatic" backwardness that Russians imposed on Ukraine, as well as the specific historical path of development of the Ukrainian people that was interrupted by the Russian colonization. For Ukrainian nationalists, there is little doubt that their country is the geographical core of Europe, and therefore, an organic part of Central Europe. Moreover, for some of them, their country even belongs to the Western European world. Grushevsky, the first president of Ukraine in 1918 and still a respected historian in independent Ukraine wrote: "...the Ukrainian people belongs to the West European (cultural) circle not only due to historical relationships, which during centuries united the Ukrainian life with the West European one, but also because of the very composition of the national character".

The Ukrainian claims for "Europeaness" would seem over-stretched and unworthy of serious attention if they did not play a pivotal role in post-1991 Ukrainian geopolitics. The relevant geopolitical doctrine can be summarized in Naumann's formula: "Who does not like or cannot be Russian, must become Central European". In other words, formation of the "Central European" (Balto-Pontic) union of states lying between the Baltic and the Black seas, separating "true Europe" from Russia (part of Eurasia or simply Asia), is the only way to avoid incorporation by Russia. For Ukrainian nationalists, the eastern frontiers of Central Europe or Europe pass along the Russian-Ukrainian border. Ukrainian nationalists would like to transform this new border into a frontier between cultural-civilizational macroregions, indicated by the black dots. Success in this endeavor would exclude Russia from Europe, firmly place Ukraine in the West, institute new geopolitical blocs and certify the edge of Europe as the Ukrainian-Russian border.

The neighborhood with Russia is described as pregnant with dramatic consequences for independent Ukraine. A Ukrainian nationalist, Yury Lypa, wrote in 1944 that this region was dangerous because of the future disintegration of Russia, losing all the lands (Caucasus, Siberia and the Far East) beyond its historical European core. Because of the imperial character of the Russian national consciousness, this process would not take a peaceful form but would instead provoke a new geopolitical confrontation. Therefore, geopolitical interests dictate to Ukraine the need to strengthen and carefully protect its eastern border, avoiding any alliances or security agreements with Russia and looking for a union with the West

Nationalism, the "childhood disease" of a new state, can have very clear and palpable implications for the regime and functions of the Ukrainian boundaries and border zones. Geographers from L'viv, in fact, contest the whole system of Ukrainian borders, including the Ukrainian-Polish one, arguing that are "unjustified" and that they were unilaterally imposed on the Ukrainian people by Russian (Soviet) authorities. These writers stress that vast areas of the neighbouring Russian oblasts, including such large cities as Taganrog and Novy Oskol, as well as a large part of the Russian North Caucasus, of Krasnodar and Stavropol regions should be ceded to Ukraine, justifying this position by quoting the results of the 1926 Soviet census on mother-tongue use.

Ukrainian nationalist mythologists wish to transform the eastern border to a "true political" boundary by strengthening the army, the national police, border guards, and the security service, instead of maintaining "mythical transparent boundaries". Ideologists of an accelerated nation-building believe that "civilized" relations between Russia and Ukraine are possible only when Russia gives up its imperial ambitions. It is believed that the state of Russian-Ukrainian relations is *a priori* the responsibility of Russia.

As a new state, it was natural that Ukraine initiated the first border restrictions and introduced custom and border controls with Russia shortly after independence in 1991-1992. Ukraine wants to demarcate the Russian-Ukrainian border as soon as possible and invests large amounts from its state budget in border infrastructure. The system of border posts of Ukraine will be as dense as one per every 20 kilometres of the boundary (the ratio on the former Soviet boundary), rather than just control of selected major roads and railways crossings. As we observed in the Donetsk (Ukraine)-Rostov (Russia) border zone in September 1996, the staff of Ukrainian customs and border guards posts is two to three times more numerous as the corresponding Russian side. For Ukrainian leaders, the eastern border is important not only as a protective barrier around the national economic space but also as a major political and ideological symbol of independence.

Borders and Regional Identities in Ukraine

Ukraine is a country with significant regional economic and cultural disparities. The possibility of federalism as a new state structure was widely debated in Ukraine up to the time of the adoption of the new national constitution in June 1996 but was eventually defeated by a coalition of parliamentary deputies from the centre and the west of the country. Ukraine is commonly divided into four major cultural regions - East, South, Centre and West. The East and South regions have been colonized and settled by Ukrainians and Russians since the late eighteenth-century. Ethnic Ukrainians make up two-thirds of the total population of the South, where the cities are mostly Russian-speaking; in the East, Ukrainians are about 50% of the population in the Donbass, the main industrial region in the country. The Crimean peninsula with its predominantly-Russian population (67%) represents a particularly difficult case. The most serious problems for nation- and state-building in Ukraine are created by these sharp cultural and historical contrasts between East and West.

Though about half of the population in both the Donetsk and Lugansk oblasts of the Ukrainian Donbass are Russian, the majority, including a large share of ethnic Ukrainians, reported Russian as their first native language in the 1989 Soviet census (68 % and 63 %, respectively). Russian still remains the dominant language of education and of the media in the region, even after Ukrainian independence. Before 1991, there were no schools in the city of Donetsk (more than 1 million inhabitants) where Ukrainian was taught as the first language. By 1996, the ratio of Ukrainian newspapers in the total number of regional and local newspapers' titles was only 9.8%. Most people in Donbass easily understand both languages. The version of Ukrainian spoken in Central and East Ukraine considerably differs from the Ukrainian of the Western part of the country, where more than 80% of the population consider Ukrainian as their mother tongue.

The spatial division of labour strengthens the sharp cultural divide between Ukrainian regions. Eastern Ukraine is heavily urbanized and industrialized, while West Ukraine is still rural and agricultural. Donetsk Oblast is one of the few regions that has traditionally made a net contribution to the state coffers: the oblast still maintains this status in 1997. The Donbass however maintains a very traditional industrial structure with a very high proportion of workers and output concentrated in the coal mining, steel industry and heavy machine-building.

Donbass and Eastern Ukraine have always had particularly strong economic relations with Russia and with neighbouring regions across the border. Due to the ethnic mixture and local job and family migrations, transboundary contacts are very intense. According to a poll in Rostov (Russia) in 1994, 45% of respondents declared that they had relatives or close friends in neighbouring Ukrainian Donbass districts; the same is true for border Ukrainian Oblasts. 80 to 90% of the voters of Donetsk Oblast in 1994 supported the principle of Russian as a second state language to Russian as well as the federalization of Ukraine. In April 1996, 85.8% of respondents in Donetsk were against privileges for any language. In January 1997, however, Ukrainian was declared the only language of official communication in the Donbass.

This peculiar local socio-economic situation exaggerates regional interests and regionalism and explains why any attempt of the Donbass regional authorities to establish stronger cooperation with neighbouring Russian regions is perceived with suspicion by Kiev. Regional and local authorities at all levels try to mitigate the consequences of the transformation of the former administrative border between Russia and Ukraine inside the former Soviet Union into an international political boundary. The governors of 14 regions of Russia and Ukraine and the city of Sevastapol (Crimea) created the "Council of Leaders of Border Oblasts of Russia and Ukraine". They have adopted many resolutions asking national leaders to undertake urgent measures for rapprochement of the two countries. Their major success was the signing in January 1995 of the intergovernmental agreement about cooperation between border regions but they are strictly limited by the larger geo-political context, especially the state of relations between Kiev and Moscow.

Grass-roots Ukrainian nationalism is strong only in Western Ukraine, especially in Galicia. For the rest of the country, the "oriental", or the "pro-Muscovite", doctrine predicated on close and friendly relations with transparent borders with Russia remains a real alternative to the "Western Ukrainian" doctrine but often overlooked by national ideologists anxious to make a "Yugoslavia in reverse"

The Ukrainian experience of recent years supports the notion that there are *no* "eternal" national identities, as the primordialists claim. Identities sometimes change in the course of a few months. About three-quarters of Ukrainian voters in a March 1991 referendum asserted their loyalty to the Soviet Union but in December of the same year, almost the same majority voted for Ukrainian independence. Most voters in Eastern, and partly in Southern and Central, Ukraine hoped to avoid the threat of famine, which was real at the time in neighbouring Russia. The ruling

Ukrainian communist political elite feared both the return of conservatives to power in Moscow (restoring a highly centralized state) and unpredictable Russian democrats who could deprive the Kievans of power. Thus, the opposition to the "others" living in "hungry Russia" and, of course, to the "others" from the culturally-alien and poor republics of Soviet Central Asia quickly coalesced. Paradoxically in Crimea, the identity changed very soon again back towards Russia as most Crimeans supported separatist forces and candidates during local elections after 1991.

Borders and Localities in Ukraine

At the level of locality - the every-day experience in Taylor's terms - the transformation of "de facto" frontiers into "formal" boundaries, or shifts in the status of a boundary, instead of maintaining "mythical transparent boundaries can cause dramatic problems. A simple example will suffice to illustrate the Ukrainian-Russian case. The two district (*rayon*) capitals, Chertkovo (Rostov oblast in Russia) and Melovoye on the Ukrainian side, with populations of 11,000 and 6,000 respectively, was one township with a common railway station, communications and public services, including secondary schools, hospitals, ambulance, sewage and water, and even a common cemetery. Parts of both Russian and Ukrainian local industrial plants were separated after 1991 by customs and border guards as was the system of health and veterinary control. Local people, working for a long time on the other side of a transparent border, are now officially treated as "foreigners", receiving salaries in a foreign currency and have become subject to two different legislations at home and at work. Locals on both sides of the border blame central authorities in Moscow and Kiev for the border difficulties, claiming that political elites in the national cores worry only about "national interests" and ignore local needs. Local districts (*oblasts*) are shown by the light.

Ukrainian territorial and identity developments, the study of borders needs to be broadened from the local level to incorporate geopolitical relations with neighbouring states and with large blocs. As a world-systems perspective holds, conditions at the local level are determined by the wider economic and geopolitical contexts, with the national government as mediator in some places and as active protagonist in other regions. National identities are frequently ill-formed and complemented by a variety of identities at other scales, based on mixed ethnic loyalties. Identities can also shift under rapidly-changing political and economic circumstances, especially as a reaction to perceived improvements in quality of life. Shifting identities may provide geopolitical breaks, usually along former political, administrative and cultural boundaries. Therefore, current political boundaries are only one element in the contemporary world system of borders and cannot be considered *in vacuo*. The Ukrainian case is important because of the lessons that it holds for the future of East-West relations and the building of future blocs in Europe. As Western Europe moves towards more transparency in territorial divisions, the situation in East and Central Europe is increasingly marked by more barriers.

THE FUTURE OF BORDERS

Transformations of identities as a result of changes in the world system deeply affect the functions of national borders. Lord Curzon was the first to distinguish between frontiers of separation and contact. In fact, every geographical boundary (not only political or administrative) combines these functions in different proportions. Physical and material flows, transfers and interactions ensuring social reproduction now shape the nature of national boundaries. At the *fin-de-siecle,* territorial expansion is no longer considered the primary means of increase state influence as adherence to international norms and avoidance of force become requirements for full membership of the international community. The quality of human resources, the "innovativeness" of economy, and capital investment are more important elements than the possession of deposits of mineral resources or fertile lands.

While the dominant discussions concerning problems of "integrating", open, peaceful, well-delimited and demarcated, and internationally-recognized borders concern borders in Western Europe and North America, these make up only 8% of the total length of world land frontiers. Historically, during the allocation and the delimitation of borders, local populations' needs and feelings were ignored. Even in Europe, only 2% of political boundaries established in the twentieth-century up to 1989 resulted from plebiscites. About 42% of the total length of land boundaries in Africa represent geometrical lines (parts of parallels and meridians, equidistant lines, arcs), imposed by colonial powers. About 20% of current world boundaries were drawn by British and about 17% the French.

Territorial disputes are still a part of geopolitical reality and cannot be excluded in the foreseeable future. Though the efficiency of internationally-recognized procedures of peace-making and peace-keeping has increased, international legislation alone can now hardly put an end to bloody territorial conflicts, as, for example, in Nagorno-Karabakh or in Bosnia, and the use of coercion by the international community is highly questionable. Borders *per se* rarely cause war, but rather structure the opportunities in which conflicting behaviour is more likely to occur. Weak small states usually have longer boundaries with respect to their territory and population and are less able to influence their neighbors. War spreads when there are more interactions between neighbouring states: a state with a warring neighbour was three times as likely to be at war as one that did not have a bordering state at war. Guerillas, for instance, in the southern part of Africa in the 1970s and the 1980s often had their bases on the territory of a neighbour state, increasing the risk of the diffusion of warfare.

Nationalism and the unlimited right to self-determination obviously contradict the principle of the state territorial integrity and are the main factors undermining the value of both realist and liberal/neoliberal approaches to territorial disputes. A pessimistic scenario expects the disintegration of states with high degrees of ethno-political tensions (a scenario for Europe in presented in Kolossov and Treivish, 1998), producing a total revision of the existing system of countries and the redistribution of functions between current national boundaries and old *de facto* frontiers. The most pessimistic version of this scenario can be gauged from the assumption that all 800 ethnic groups of India and all 250 ethnies of Nigeria, as well as numerous other ethnic groups in Third

World countries will demand territorial self-determination. Social modernization (industrialization, urbanization, and the augmentation of the level of education) can stimulate outbursts of nationalism, as they accelerate nationalism of intellectual and political elites and, later, of large masses of population. The result is increased competition between various indigenous and non-indigenous groups for control over the resources of the homeland and of high-status jobs, as shown by the experience of the former Soviet Union.

It is very important to define the riskiest section of the world-system of borders and frontiers. Most likely, the most sensitive are the frontiers between highly industrialized and less developed countries, Muslim and Orthodox countries/ regions, and in the Third World. The frontier between Western and Eastern Europe (the West-Christian and the Orthodox-Christian worlds) can also become dangerous, if the EU and NATO succeed in expanding eastward without appropriate guarantees for the countries of the East and the South-East of the continent, in particular, Russia. A new security arrangement in Europe contrasting NATO-Europe with a Russian-dominated security zone might dampen hostilities within the blocs but magnify the probability of confrontation between them. As we have argued in this chapter, the concentration of political geographers on (nation)state borders has limited the options for examining the effects of economic globalization and emerging cultural identities on new territorial delimitations. Central questions in the new limology must be the measurement of cultural and political gradients across new geopolitical, regional and local frontiers.

BORDERS AND POLITICAL GEOGRAPHY

Borders have provided perhaps the most enduring research object in the tradition of political geography; the history of border studies is as long as political geography itself. Already the first major text, Friedrich Ratzel's *Politische Geographie*, published in 1897, included a survey of the functions of borders and he took some steps to develop the terminology of border studies. In his organistic thinking borders were an expression and measure of state power. States were 'living organisms', thus reflecting the social Darwinist *Zeitgeist* of the late 19th century. Respectively, all 'vigorous states' try to expand in spatial terms while declining states contract to physically easily defensible land contours. After the horrors of World War II borders maintained their position as research objects, being now often understood as empirical categories, material 'border landscapes' related to given state territories or functional spaces rendering possible – or not – economic and social interaction.

Border studies witnessed a major revival in the 1990s. This was related to several international events and tendencies, such as the collapse of the ideological divide between the capitalist and communist blocks, the acceleration of the 'globalization', and the development of information and communication technologies. In Europe the deepening integration and the EU's active tendency to lower the borders between member states motivated scholars. National security has been closely related to borders but the 9/11 terrorist attacks in the USA gave a new boost to this idea and security related border studies and also partly twisted the scale of such studies by bringing on stage new supra-state dividing lines such as the much criticized Huntingtonian idea of the "clash between *civilizations*".

As to the academic impulses behind the new interest in border issues, a crucial element was the rise of post-modern and post-structuralist thinking in social and cultural sciences. New theoretical literature both expanded and 'homogenized' conceptual views that border scholars adopted in various fields. Borders were now understood as social constructs rather than being naturally given entities. Critical or 'dissident' IR scholars challenged the state-centric assumptions of realist IR theory and questioned the self-evidence of such divides as inside/outside, self/other or domestic/foreign that were typically exploited in the maintenance of the discourses on 'national security'. New IR studies looked at how such national moral spaces – made possible by the ethical borders of identity as a much as by the territorial borders of the state – were often constituted by leaning on images of threat and enemy in foreign policy.

The emerging post-structuralist, post-modern, feminist and postcolonial language was soon adopted by critical geopolitics scholars and keywords such as power, discourse, and de- and re-territorialization soon appeared in their vocabularies. The representatives of critical geopolitics were greatly influenced by the dissident IR theory that was interested in discursive practices. The key tenets of dissident IR inspired critical geopolitics scholars who were from the first beginning interested in the geopolitical dimensions and ideologies hidden in foreign policy discourses. The first major books in the field, Simon Dalby's (1990a) *Creating the Second Cold War* and Gearoid O'Tuathail's *Critical Geopolitics,* also draw on this theoretical basis but both took also further steps to develop the theoretical language of critical geopolitics. Especially ÒTuathail strove to contextualize his account into the history of power-knowledge relations and their spatialization in geopolitical thinking and, against this background, to develop new conceptual ideas.

As to border studies, these books were at the same time both intriguing and paradoxical. The paradox was that while both books were crucially related to the issues of *boundedness,* that is the real and imagined lines that bordered and ordered political life, and, further, while both of them scrutinized how these lines manifests themselves in foreign policy discourses, or in the definitions of the State, territory and the Other, contrary to the accounts of some dissident IR scholars, these books did not include theoretical discussion on borders that would somehow bring the new themes of critical geopolitics into a dialogue with the long tradition of border studies. Concrete borders and border contexts thus seemed to be, in a way, too prosaic and material to become topical in the early accounts in critical geopolitics that were dealing with wider themes, such as foreign policy discourses and that leaned on textual strategies when looking largely at different texts.

The aim of this chapter is to make sense of the previous paradox by asking questions such as what was the role of 'boundedness' and borders for early critical geopolitical thinking, what were the key sources of inspiration for this thinking and how the choice of certain perspectives– and the neglect of others – led simultaneously to neglect the *theorization* of borders. 'New' border studies that emerged gradually paralleling critical geopolitics, took inspiration partly from similar sources as critical geopolitics scholars but built also on other premises to theorize borders and power as part of production of territory and territoriality. Neither did new border studies and critical geopolitics match at first. Later, especially after the turn of the millennium, critical geopolitics and border studies have become partly fused.

This chapter will look at these themes in seven sections. At first it will scrutinize how the works of early critical geopolitics tackled with the issue of *boundedness* (rather than theorizing *borders*). Secondly, it will reflect the rise and characteristics of new border studies that are increasingly interdisciplinary. This section will also discuss some research themes that have been studied by border scholars inspired explicitly by critical geopolitics. Then the role of borders in the making of territories is discussed. The next section looks at the role of maps in bordering. Then the meanings of borders in everyday life and how critical geopolitics has tackled this issue are scrutinized. This is followed by a discussion on current and future challenges in borders studies that will especially problematize the one-sided view on the 'location' of borders on border areas alone, an issue that was almost self-evident, given 'fact' in the tradition of border studies but which is increasingly problematic in the current relational world of interactions. Finally, some conclusions are drawn.

CRITICAL GEOPOLITICS AND THE ISSUE OF BOUNDEDNESS

Early studies in critical geopolitics leaned on a number of sources of inspiration that were related to the boundedness of social life. The general idea of the roots of social and political distinctions, that were present, for instance, in Bachelard's and Said's key texts, motivated political geographers. Dalby, for example, draw on Said's thoughts to develop his ideas of the Other and otherness that he then used to study empirically the security discourses and images of 'Soviet threat' in the writings of the members of an influential political lobby organization in the USA, the Committee on the Present Danger (CPD). Many conceptions developed by critical geopolitics scholars closely resonated with "dissident IR" studies, where researchers had scrutinized critically how the dividing lines between inside/outside are constructed in the context of state and sovereignty. This theme was soon theorized also by political geographers (the best known conceptual analysis related to this issue is John Agnew's idea of territorial trap).

Yet some IR scholars had reflected the issue of bordering even more explicitly. They analysed the meanings of boundaries mainly in the context of foreign policy discourses, relating borders to *boundary-producing practices*. Particularly important was Ashley's comment that accentuated foreign policy not merely as behaviour across boundaries but rather as a "specific sort of boundary producing political performance". Ashley suggested that this political performance – taking place in a historically carved out social space – has important effects such as the constitution and reaffirmation of socially recognizable boundaries separating fields of practice on a global scale. Later Ashley (1989:311) draw explicitly on poststructuralism when reflecting the roles of the boundary that the state patrols and marks and that separates the total 'other' from the total 'same'. He wrote how "Displacing the state, poststructuralism puts this boundary in doubt. The boundary itself is never simply there, poststructuralism knows. It is always in the process of being marked, transgressed, erased, and marked again. The questions to be asked are not: Where is the boundary? What marks the boundary? ...Instead, the sort of question to be asked is ... a *how* question. How, by way of what practices, by appeal to what cultural resources, and in the face of what resistances is this boundary imposed and ritualized".

Another IR scholar David Campbell leaned on this idea in his *Writing security*. Campbell was interested in the relations between identity and difference and how they are exploited in the construction of threats in foreign policy discourses. The representations of threats, for their part, are often used to secure the boundaries of a state's identity. He suggested that foreign policy needs to be understood as giving rise to a boundary rather than acting as a bridge,

"Foreign policy shifts *from* a concern of relations *between* states which take place *across* ahistorical, frozen and pregiven boundaries, *to* a concern with *the establishment of the boundaries* that constitute, at one and the same time, the 'state' and 'the international system'

Many geographers adopted Ashley's idea on foreign policy as boundary producing practice that seemingly both directed the choice of research topics and the conceptual basis in critical geopolitics. Dalby followed Ashley's lead and wrote that "Geopolitics is about that ideological process of constructing spatial, political and cultural boundaries to demarcate the domestic space as separate from the threatening Other; to exclude Otherness and simultaneously to discipline and control the domestic political sphere". While discussing 'boundedness', Dalby did not reflect more deeply the idea of border in relation to existing border studies and how these studies could be developed further in the new research framework that accentuated discourse, power and practice. This is somewhat surprising since new perspectives clearly forcefully challenged and claimed to radically broaden the ideas of borders that were simultaneously set forth by political geographers, such as "boundaries as human creations are an expression of territoriality, *reflecting a basic human need to live in a bounded space*".

The representatives of critical geopolitics thus followed the pathway opened by IR scholars but actually did less to contribute to *border studies* than IR scholars. Neither did all of them agree that geopolitics is a boundary producing practice. Indeed, 'Tuathail commented on Dalby's post-structuralist idea that geopolitics is a boundary producing practice whose 'essential moment' is the exclusion of the Other and the inclusion of the same. He argued that Dalby's view essentializes geopolitics within the terms of an identity politics narrative and is a reductionist reading strategy of foreign policy texts that allows one to read off the production of otherness from foreign policy texts. 'Tuathail suggested that in producing Otherness geopolitical actors are not only specifying a dangerous external Other beyond the territorial borders of the state, as Dalby seemed to imply, but that these actors are also projecting an image of their own subjectivity and its Other and respectively the Other is not only "a beyond" but "a within", a threat not only from abroad but also within domestic and personal sphere. Tuathail's conclusion was that reading geopolitics-as-spatial-exclusion solely in territorial terms limits other possible productive readings of this suggestion.

However, two years later Tuathail and Dalby were largely on the same track in their introduction to an edited volume, *Rethinking Geopolitics*:

"it [critical geopolitics] pays particular attention to the boundary-drawing practices and performances that characterize the everyday life of states. In contrast to conventional geography and geopolitics, both the material borders at the edge of the state and the conceptual borders designating this as a boundary between a secure inside and an anarchic outside are objects of investigation. Critical geopolitics is not about `the outside' of the state but about the very construction of boundaries of `inside' and `outside', `here' and `there', the 'domestic' and the 'foreign' "

They referred again to Ashley, Walker, and Campbell to support their arguments, and accentuated that "geopolitics is already about more boundaries than those on a map, for those boundaries are themselves implicated in conceptual boundary-drawing practices of various kinds.... The boundary drawing practices we seek to investigate in this volume are both conceptual and cartographic, imaginary and actual, social and aesthetic".

Rethinking Geopolitics included two articles that took the idea of border further by analysing how borders have been exploited in the geopolitical national identity construction. Rygiel analysed these processes in the case of Turkey and Bonura discussed boundaries on a more theoretical level when looking at the geopolitics of nation and culture.

The same lack of deeper reflection of "border studies" and the idea of border characterizes many publications at the beginning of the 1990s. While 'boundedness' was thus an implicit or at times even explicit theme in publications, their authors did not simply pay attention to simultaneous border studies. This neglect of can be understood only in relation to wider theoretical, interdisciplinary academic backgrounds that were major sources of inspiration to early critical geopoliticians *and* to the dominant features of the long, empiricist tradition of border studies. This tradition clearly did not provide similar theoretical inspiration as the emerging post-modern and post-structuralist theories regarding social and political life and the discourses and power relations hidden in all kind of texts (written texts, maps, images, etc.). Political geographers thus looked beyond the disciplinary boundaries but neglected perhaps the potential of their own tradition. The comment by John Agnew is probably telling of the *Zeitgeist*. In a book review he wrote how border studies had long been one of the most torpid sub-fields of political geography that seemed largely oblivious to theorizing about geographies of political identity and the spatialities of power. New interdisciplinary perspectives, raised by new academic generation of political geographers and the old political geographic thinking on borders simply seemed not to match.

One of the few explicit references to the tradition of border studies was put forward by Dodds, who states, again reflecting the more theoretically oriented *Zeitgeist* that "Given the tenor of much of the recent work in critical geopolitics, it might seem strange to propose a return to the study of boundaries". Yet his return was not to re-theorize borders but to accentuate, in the spirit of the then ongoing debates in media studies, philosophy and dissident IR, how old apparently fixed political spaces seemed to be outdated in the dynamic world of all kinds of interactions. The challenge to develop border studies thus remained while at the same critical geopolitics scholars expanded their ideas of boundaries to such issues as state- everyday life or masculine-feminist relations.

Perhaps the strangest feature in the rapid rise of critical geopolitics and its leaning on dissident IR literature was that IR scholars continued their life largely as if there were no critical geopolitics at all, i.e. they very much ignored the works of critical geopolitics scholars. *Challenging Boundaries*, a 500 page long volume edited by Shapiro and Alker, for example, included only a couple minor references to critical geopolitics. And if critical geopolitics scholars did not cite, use and develop border literature produced by political geographers, neither were the emerging critical geopolitical perspectives familiar among political geographers working at the same time. A fitting illustration is the edited collection *Political Boundaries and coexistence* based on papers of a border symposium organised in Basel, Switzerland in 1994. This book includes almost 50 articles on borders but there is not a single reference to critical geopolitics literature. Critical geopolitics and border studies where hence still travelling forward in different trains.

THE RISE OF BORDER STUDIES

In spite of the fact that the early work in critical geopolitics did not pay particular attention to the re-conceptualization of borders, ignored this issue, regarded earlier accounts of borders as examples of a fixed world view, or leaned on the general ideas of border suggested by IR scholars, a lot happened simultaneously in border studies that began to mushroom in political geography, anthropology, literary criticism and sociology. Often publications were located in two ideological extremes: for few scholars borders were *passé* in a new borderless world, for some others they were perpetually fascinating objects of research.

To take but a few examples from various fields, the disappearance of state borders was proposed by globalization propagandists like Ohmae and partly followed by some IR scholars like Luke who was excited about the rise of transnational trends, 'informationalization' and the rhetoric related to all kinds of flows that inspired many scholars during the 1990s.

For Luke, "flows are decentering, despatializing, and dematerializing forces, and they work alongside and against the geopolitical codes of spatial sovereignty"... "the flows create new transnational communities that are blurring the old geographics of 'them' and 'us', 'I', or 'friend' and 'foe' in new informational modes if ideography, technography, demography, or plutography".

Also sociologist Levine suggested that major developments in the social world are weakening the claims of national boundaries, whereas another sociologist Oommen tried to show how new boundaries do not replace the old ones but rather they tend to co-exist.

Philosopher Balibar, for his part, scrutinized the historical contingency of state-nation relations and problematized the production of people, national belonging, 'fictive ethnicity' and ideal nation. He discussed the role of 'translators' (politicians, writers, journalists) in the creation of national languages, as well as the roles of family and schools.

Also Balibar emphasized the roles of borders for identities. Anthropologists, who had a long tradition in border studies looked now critically at the relations between state and nation and the territorialization of national identities. Feminist scholar Yuval-Davis reflected emerging asymmetries related to borders, such as the gendered and generation-based features of de-bordering and re-bordering.

On the basis of new heterogeneous theoretical literature and empirical approaches on boundaries, four themes seemed to be important to political geographical argumentation: a) the suggested 'disappearance' of boundaries in the post-modern world, b) the role of boundaries in the construction of socio-spatial identities, c) boundary narratives and discourse, and d) the role of different spatial scales of boundary construction.

These forced to re-think the classical political geographic question on the relations between borders and territories. New interdisciplinary but internally somewhat contradictory literature on boundaries made soon clear that the answers to the questions regarding the persistence or disappearance of boundaries are not simple either-or type, because boundaries were no more understood as mere physical, static and immovable spatial entities.

For most borders scholars the issue of a borderless or bordered world was more complex and respectively questions of power, knowledge, representation and context became crucial in reflecting and understanding of borders and boundedness. The challenge was now to develop abstractions to make 'theoretically' visible the dimensions of territory and boundary building.

BORDERS AND THE MAKING OF TERRITORY

Political geographers have recognized the role of borders for (state) territory and territoriality for a long time. Sack, for example, argued that borders are crucial in the making of a territory and in the exercise of territoriality. He suggested that circumscribing things is space or map does not itself create a territory. Territory is related to control and certain delimitated areas become territories only when their boundaries are used to affect behaviour, resources and power by controlling access. This is most obvious in the case of international state borders where border-crossings are policed and controlled very effectively and practices related to state sovereignty, such as admitting citizenship are crucial in this process. Yet Sack did not relate his theoretical discussion on territoriality to the political geographic ideas of borders. Border was for him a fundamental but largely given element of territoriality.

Paasi attempted to bring together his earlier theoretical work on the institutionalization of regions/territories, the issue of spatial scales, and power relations, and respectively analysed the construction of territories, and the making of borders as both institutions and symbols. His study on the Finnish-Russian border follows a geohistorical approach which accentuates the contextuality of borders and the need to relate their making to both wider international context, nation-building process and the everyday lives of ordinary people. The idea of the institutionalization of territories led him to conceptualize boundaries as a phenomenon that are 'located' not only on edges but are 'spread' around the territory, in diverging institutional and discursive practices and that the perpetual making of the territory (represented as the creation of "us" or "we") can actually extent outside of the territory. Paasi integrated the dimensions discussed by cultural theorists and IR scholars and showed that both 'we' and 'the Other' can be both 'here' and 'there', dividing lines between these socio-spatial elements may be fuzzy – an idea suggested also by Tuathail. This inevitably complicates the idea of making national bounded spaces on the basis of categorical othering and the distinctions between 'us' and 'them'. This issue is increasingly significant in a world characterized by immigrants and refugees that often "transport" symbolic boundaries from one cultural context to another. In analytical terms, the symbolic construction of space, territoriality and borders are based on a dialectics between two languages, the language of *integration* and the language of *difference*. Whereas the language of integration aims at homogenizing the contents of collective spatial consciousness and experiences, the language of difference strives to distinguish this homogenized experience from the other.

By looking at the construction and historical contingency of the Finnish-Russian border, this work showed how boundary making was closely related to foreign policy discourses and but also to certain prosaic forms of banal nationalism that entered everyday life and were present in media discourses and school textbooks. This led to a theorization of *spatial socialization*, i.e. the process through which individual actors and collectivities are socialized as members of certain territorially bounded spatial entities and through which they more or less actively internalize collective territorial identities and shared traditions. Respectively 'othering' and the construction of images of threat, for instance, occur in many forms that are related to daily lives of citizens. Moisio has shown how geopolitical images of order and threats to security have been crucial in the Finnish identity project and related boundary construction.

Maps, territory, and bordering

One important theme raised by critical cartographers was the relation between power and cartography, an issue that is crucially related to the 'bordering' themes raised by critical geopoliticians and by IR scholars. Paasi leaned on Wood's and Harley's works when analysing the discursive roles of cartography and maps in Finnish geopolitics during World War II and scrutinized their role especially in the making of borders. He also showed how human bodies, especially female bodies, are often used as allegories of the nation so that bodies become 'maps', in a way mixing spatial scales. Later the power of maps in the making of territory and borders has motivated several scholars who have grounded their work in critical geopolitics. Berg and Oras studied post-Soviet

Estonia and how this 'new' entity was written on the world map in diverging boundary producing practices. Other examples of studies inspired by critical geopolitics are Herb's analysis on the territorial strategies that were in use in the making of national identities in Germany and Culcasi's study on the geographical construction of Kurdistan. Herb looked at the period when there were two

'Germanies'. In the initial situation both governments claimed to represent German national identity but this changed gradually and both states developed their own strategies in identity work. The border between the two states was a crucial element in this work. Culcasi's study, for its part, analysed the U.S. journalist cartography to look at how it represents the geopolitical conflict in Kurdistan. She found out that cartographic representations did not only reflect social and political narratives but also constructed and communicated subtle and blatant positions towards Kurds and Kurdistan. All these studies were explicitly using discursive perspectives and leaned on the ideas developed within critical geopolitics.

BORDERS, EVERYDAY LIFE AND CRITICAL GEOPOLITICS

'Tuathail and Dalby made a division between formal, practical and popular geopolitics that all are related to the spatializing of boundaries, dangers and geopolitical representations of the self and other. At the turn of the millennium some critique was raised against the dominance of formal and practical geopolitics research perspectives and the related 'geopolitical remote sensing' approach that looked at boundary producing practices from a distance and largely through official texts, that is by not paying attention to the geopolitical issues, problems and struggles, affects and emotions in the *context* of everyday life. Feminist scholars have argued that the exclusive focus of critical geopolitics on texts – as opposed to the embodied and the everyday – left it open to charges of elitism and academic distance. This critique emerged partly from theoretical grounds but one concrete background was the lack of the local (ethnographic) studies and the lack of deeper knowledge of the contextual features of political cultures. The importance of studying the meanings of borders in everyday life is obvious since borders provide most individuals with a concrete, local, and powerful experience of the state, for this is the site where citizenship is strongly enforced (through passport checks, for instance).

Paasi had brought together depth interviews and participant observation and leaned on ideas from visual anthropology to study local experiences and meanings of borders and combined them with a broader societal analysis of the production of space and scale. Later Megoran has developed ethnographic, focus group-based and participating methods in a series of articles were he leaned on the theoretical ideas of critical geopolitics and brought this literature into a dialogue with border literature. He analysed how a critical geopolitics of danger emerged in the context of Uzbekistan-Kyrgyzstan boundary dispute and claimed that more cross-cultural work is needed in the world where western narratives tend to dominate border studies. Similarly Ó Tuathail's long-term project on Bosnia has aimed at developing the conceptual and methodological basis of 'localized geopolitics'.

Also Sharp had made claims on the need to take the perspective of critical geopolitics beyond the formal boundaries of the state. For her this meant the analysis of the products of popular and media culture. These can be effective boundary producing artefacts and are useful in the analysis of gendered dimensions of geopolitics. The research materials she used were the popular American magazine *Reader's Digest* and its changing perception of the Soviet Union and communism between 1930 and 1945, and post-Cold War American movies, for example. Similarly political cartoons have motivated research in critical geopolitics. Cartoons can be effectively used both to create geopolitical imaginaries and borders, as well as to deconstruct them. This perspective continues e.g. in studies that have scrutinized the so-called Mohammed cartoons and the cultural dividing lines and conflicts associated with them.

Going beyond the lines

The increasing border crossings, all kinds of mobilities, post 9/11 security-related control mechanisms of travellers and refugees and the simultaneous diversification of border studies have led to a situation where scholars have started to ask where borders actually are located. While Paasi's work on the institutionalization of territories expanded the traditional idea of border from being a mere line between territories and by accentuating the location of borders all round territories in discourses, symbolisms and social practices, this idea has gained new ground in literature. There seem to be two main strands of thought where 'bounded spaces' are challenged: relational thinking (and the related topological idea of space) and 'borders are everywhere' –thesis.

The first of these ideas is closely related to network-based thinking (e.g. actor network theory). Relational thinking sees bounded spaces generally as politically regressive and suggests that territories should be seen as open networked or topological spaces of social relations. It may be argued that contrary to the current vibrant theoretical and empirical research on the meanings and functions of borders, relational thinking has been more general and normative. Relational thinkers have not studied concrete state borders but have rather reflected and challenged their ontological roles as products of modernity.

The "borders are everywhere" thesis is related to the Balibar's ideas that have gained currency during the last ten years or so. He suggests that borders have perhaps not disappeared but have rather become so diffuse that they have transformed whole countries into borderlands. New technologies of border control that have been developed in the post 9/11 world to prevent terrorism, for example, do not locate merely on border areas but may exist literally 'everywhere': at airports, in shopping precincts, in streets, and even in other states. Such complexity and networking becomes clear in the homepage of UK border agency, for example, which is now global organization with 25,000 staff operating in local communities, at UK's borders and across 135 countries worldwide. These new landscapes of control constitute something that can be labelled as *technical landscapes of control and surveillance.* These landscapes are monitored by increasingly technical devices that have gained importance in the post 9/11 world. This may simultaneously strengthen bordering in a society, be constitutive of social, cultural and political distinctions between social groups and also contribute to the making of 'calculable territories' that each state tries to produce and reproduce to govern space and population.

These tendencies have also forced researchers to expand the concepts of security that have by tradition characterized border studies. Feminist scholars have defined security beyond classical binaries – such as inside-outside or same-different – and thus also challenged the militarized, bounded version of security "which posits *an* identity which needs protection from the danger posed by a different external other". Feminist scholars have reminded how also other scales than that of the nation-state have to be studied in critical geopolitics. Indeed, the body, nation and global are seen now indicative of the same processes rather than as separate scales. Hyndman has discussed how people's bodies are often construed as 'territories' in conflict situations and how, for instance, in civil wars they may become sites of public violence on which the symbolic construction of the nation and its boundaries occurs.

The new interest in the (mobile) bodies and security has given rise to new conceptual perspectives in current border studies. Amoore, for example, speaks about 'biometric borders' which are, on the one hand, related to digital technologies, data integration and managerial expertise in the politics of border management; and, on the other hand, to the exercise of biopower such that the "body itself is inscribed with, and demarcates, a continual crossing of multiple encoded borders social, legal, gendered, racialized and so on". Biometric borders have motivated border scholars to study new increasingly technical security practices in such networked places as airports.

However, borders are simultaneously typically rooted in historically constructed, contingent practices and discourses that are related to nationalist ideologies and identity narratives, that is *discursive or emotional landscapes of social power* that often draw on banal forms of nationalism. The persistence and almost universal power of such nationalist landscapes is related to the observation that only 3% of the world's population resided in a state other than the one in which they were born. While physical borders may at times be significant symbols and institutions, the 'location' of the national(ist) border is therefore not only in the borderland but rather in the wider manifestations of the perpetual nation-building *process* and nationalist practices. The roots of these manifestations are contextual and have to be traced back to the histories of these practices and existing iconographies. A lot of emotional bordering and 'othering' may be hidden in flag or independence days and other national celebrations, military parades, international sports events, nationalized and memorialized landscapes and other elements of national iconographies. These practices may 'stretch' across borders in both time and space and can be ultimately very international.

It is important to recognize that the role of the state is also changing. It is increasingly the case that traditional self-other and friend-enemy distinctions between states in foreign policies are surpassed or at least paralleled by practices and narratives related to geo-economic rivalry between states. Such narratives may accentuate the openness of borders simultaneously as cultural identity narratives maintain ideas of the boundedness of the state. This shows, as Taylor has earlier suggested, that the practice of territoriality may take simultaneously different overlapping forms.

Conclusion

Earlier accounts on the evolution or 'development' of border studies have accentuated the historically contingent nature of such studies and that each generation of scholars seems to create their own vision of what is relevant and topical. The role of generations challenging traditional thinking has been recognized also more generally in science studies literature. New developments of theory and research practice reflect not only institutional developments in academic fields but also wider academic and societal contexts. This tendency can be seen, for example, in the rise of positivist, humanist, behavioural or Marxist geography.

The origin of critical geopolitics can also be understood as a rise of a new generation of scholars in political geography, a generation that was drawing effectively on interdisciplinary, mainly post-modern and post-structuralist literature. Its representatives used actively interdisciplinary conceptual ideas to develop their disciplinary thinking. They leaned particularly on the influences from IR, and soon constituted a visible 'community of circulating ideas' when citing widely each other's publications.

In terms of border studies the start was much slower. At first critical geopolitics scholars seemed to be happy with the general border ideas that they adopted from IR literature. In particular, Richard Ashley's idea about foreign policy as boundary producing practice motivated critical geopolitics scholars interested in foreign policy practices. Gradually the idea of the border itself gained more attention and became an object of theoretical endeavour.

Yet it is difficult to say, to what extent new ideas reflected exactly "critical geopolitics" which itself had developed to a heterogeneous set of ideas and perspectives. Increasing attention was now paid to how geopolitics exists in popular forms and further how it may modify everyday life in certain contexts. Feminist scholars have simultaneously challenged the 'self-evidence' of militarized, bounded versions of security and the ideas of fixed, linear borders.

The language used when discussing boundaries also partly changed. The ideas of borders, boundaries, borderlands, border-crossings and transgressions of borders that the representatives of various disciplines used, were increasingly employed in a metaphoric sense so that they did not inevitably refer to the material border contexts of states that political geographers typically had dealt with.

New interest in *boundary producing practices* gave rise to studies analysing the practices and discourses in which hegemonic ideas representing certain forms of 'boundedness' are produced. This led to an analysis of the images of threat,

danger and, more widely, foreign policy practices. Such studies may actually be separate from concrete state borders that political geographers have scrutinized by tradition, yet be highly significant. Think, for example, the Cold War "macro level" dividing lines between capitalist west and communist east or the later, much criticized, abstract dividing lines between 'civilizations'.

This chapter shows that, as far as concrete state borders are concerned, there is no specific single approach to borders that could be labelled as such as 'critical geopolitical'. Rather the perspectives developed gradually in critical geopolitics seem to inform current border studies in many ways by raising new questions, by opening new research materials and concepts. Thus these perspectives may help to re-direct and develop border studies. Perpetual 'updating' of border studies will hence be a major challenge in a world where accelerating globalization, integration, economic competition and new images of security threats characterize the operations of states and economic blocs, and where the mobility of human beings and their border-crossings are crucial elements of the international human landscape.

4

Security as Boundary Function

The discipline of International Relations has recently witnessed a number of attempts to redefine "security" in innovative ways. Unfortunately, barely can an agreement be said to exist on the direction in which security studies should be heading. Even more, almost every single author seems to adopt an individual definition of "security." Is the concept to relate to the state alone? Is state security of the same quality as personal security? Answers to questions such as these vary widely. In addition, concepts like "insecurity," "risk," "danger," etc. are used freely with either no analytical distinction being established at all, or at best in a highly arbitrary manner. We propose that a lot of the confusion surrounding the conceptualization of what "security" means can be avoided by not treating it as an independent object or field of study, but rather by linking it to larger-scale developments in social systems, thus also taking advantage of the rich conceptual approach that has been developed by modern systems theory – yet remains unused in IR theory.

I would like to take the concepts of "societal security" and "securitization" as a starting point, which in the current literature come closest to a concept that links the study of security to developments in the wider social world. Most prominently, these concepts have been developed and elaborated by what has become known as the "Copenhagen School," especially in the works of Ole Wæver and Barry Buzan. For the purpose of introduction, the main ideas as developed in the context of this school can be summarized as follows:

- next to state security (the issue that students of international relations/international security have mostly dealt with), issues of "societal security" need to be accounted for in order to understand an international order that is no longer defined by one dominant form of conflict;
- an issue is an issue of societal security if a society perceives it to constitute an existential threat to its identity;
- for an issue to constitute a threat to a society's identity it is necessary that society perceives/constructs the issue as such ("securitization"); this also implies that a society can "desecuritize" an issue, i.e. cease to perceive it as a threat; and
- at the most basic level then, "security" is a speech act; to study security therefore means to study "a particular set of historical discourses and practices that rest upon institutionally shared understandings".

These ideas have been successfully applied to take a fresh look at issues as diverse as international migration, European integration and regionalism. Not only have they provided new concepts to tackle the notion of "security," but have helped to alert students of international affairs to the intricate links that exist between the maintenance or failure of order(s) and issues of "identity," thus fostering the further introduction of a theme into the discipline of IR that has come to preoccupy many of the social sciences. This in turn has contributed to the discipline becoming much finer attuned to some of the fluidity underlying the categories of "nation" and "territory" that still constitute the main fabric of the current international system.

Be that as it may, in spite of its contributions to the new roads of inquiry just mentioned, the Copenhagen School has been criticized for "freezing" the notions of "identity" and "society," allegedly not giving due respect to the insight that identity "is not a fact of society," but a process. While it is certainly not the case that the constructed nature of "societal identity" has gone unnoticed by the group, it indeed seems prone to refer to a certain, more or less fixed construct of "identity" in order to be better able to handle the fluent attribute of "security".

While the differentiation of the notion of security into process terms, securitization and desecuritization, has a lot to offer in terms of a fresh look at issues of peace and conflict in the context of a changing international order, the criticism is legitimate that such an analysis, if it wants to explain change in the meanings and practices of "security" cannot start from the assumption that societal identity and state identity, as its reference points, are fixed. We here encounter a far-reaching problem that continues to plague all social sciences. However, IR as a discipline that only recently encountered the dynamization of its theoretical approahes (in constructivism, postmodernism, ect.) seems to be affected in particular. Therefore, some general remarks on this problem seem to be warranted here.

Trying to explain process solely through process will always remain a futile exercise. One needs to arrest categories, draw boundaries and build frames in order to establish "mental maps" that relate process to something which, at least temporarily, has to be taken as fixed and stable. Thus one cannot hope to come to terms with a process like "securitization" solely by relating it to a process like "identification."

In the analysis of security, no less than in the rest of the discipline and in fact much of the social sciences - and especially in its "critical" part - it seems to have escaped the attention of analysts quite regularly that such a process of drawing lines and establishing boundaries is inherent in their thinking, as well as the world that they study. However, neither the "rigid mind" that only thinks in terms of fixed entities and categories surrounded by clear boundaries, nor the "fuzzy mind" that respects no boundaries and thinks only in terms of process can expect to be able to make sense of things "as they are," yet explain change. What is needed to explain a world which is full of turbulence is, in the words of Eviatar Zerubavel, a "flexible mind." This means to respect the need for boundaries and categories, yet recognize "that any entity can be situated in more than one mental context." It means to accept the constitutive role that boundaries play, thereby enabling perception and meaning, yet to avoid seeing boundaries as merely enclosing.

Following this understanding of a necessary duality of fluidity and fixation even in the analytic categories we use to make sense of world politics, I propose that the concept of "security" is able to unfold its full explanatory power if seen not as either process or as a state of affairs, but as a boundary-function. Such an argument tries to preserve the analytic richness of the notion of "securitization" without accepting the main shortcoming of its analysis as developed in the context of the Copenhagen School — namely the fixed nature of its notion of "societal identity." Contrary to other critics, such as Bill McSweeny, I do not want to argue at all, however, that this "rigidity" regarding societal identity is due to a lack of understanding of the processual character of identity formation (and reproduction) on the side of the Copenhagen School. It rather seems as if the conceptual rigidity of this type of "security studies" is to blame for the fact that "identity" is taken to refer to "society" in the first place.

If one, on the one hand, does not want to make an outdated and oversimplifying claim that the world consists of clearly and rigidly demarcated societies (i.e. that societies are basically congruent with the territorial state), then the usefulness of the notion of an identity of "a" society becomes highly dubious. If one, on the other hand, comes to accept that bereft of territorial attachments or primordial groundings, the only appropriate definition of "society" is that it is that which includes, reproduces and forms horizons for social communication and that therefore today only world "society" can legitimately bear the name as the highest-order social system that includes all other social systems and communication, then the interplay between concepts that refer to "society," concepts like "security," "identity" and "order," are in need of reexamination.

The first and maybe most important consequence of such a change of focus is then to question the givenness or continuity of the territorial character of these reference points. If "societal identity," "societal security," etc. cease to be meaningful analytic categories because the idea of the whole of "society" becomes an unstable reference, then one is forced to spell out more clearly which part of (world) "society" it is to which the identity, or security processes referred to pertain: the social system, the political system, the military system, various national, ethnic, or others groups?

To embark on such an effort does not promise to result in a new grand concept of "security." Quite to the contrary, it entails quite a substantial multiplication of realms to which the term could possibly be applied. What it does promise, however, is to help shed light on some of the common traits which legitimize why such a variety of concepts and practices can claim to be about "security"; yet it also does not reduce "security" to a conceptually overstretched reference point which explains everything yet nothing at all. In a larger theoretical context, it promises to contribute to a better understanding of the continuing evolution and transformation of "the (Westphalian) state", the international political system and the role that security plays in it — and vice versa. And, last but not least, it does not promise but at least sincerely rests on the hope that it can make a small contribution towards vaporizing some of the unnecessary communicative barriers that the discipline erects around the various notions of "security."

The questions that need to be asked in order to establish the analytical framework in which "security" is seen as having an important function for every social system. The sketch some approaches to deal with these questions: first, by deriving the meaning of security as a boundary function from some tenets of modern systems theory; second, by scrutinizing the relationship between "security" and "identity" and especially the role of "state" and "nation" in this respect; and third by distilling a refined meaning of the terms "securitization," "desecuritization" and "asecuritization" from this analysis.

Questions on "Securitization"

Analysis starts with differentiation. Any analysis of processes at work in the framework of world society has to start by acknowledging the latter's character as being differentiated into functional subsystems, with individually varying evolutionary status. In modern systems analysis, this is accommodated by breaking down world society into a multitude of more or less developed social systems. Relating "security" not to one, but to all of these social systems seems only logical, yet also seems to be the issue most fervently disputed in security studies. Indeed, some scholars want to preserve the usage of the term for purely military issues (i.e. the military system), while others are afraid that the logic of these issues might unduly distort thinking about other issues through the usage of the term. Yet, to conclude from that fact that security is a function in the military system, and that it should only be used in this context is as absurd as it would be to conclude that the term "system" should only be applied to one system. The concept of "identity" as well cannot be exempted from being examined in its differentiated nature. It will in fact be one of the main tasks of this chapter to elucidate some of the intricate relationships that appear when identities and securities are taken together in their variety. It is in referring to the processes underlying this variety that one can approach the important questions that have to be asked in this regard.

What does it mean to say that an issue becomes an issue of security or is "securitized?" In terms of modern systems theory, "security" first of all means a security of expectations. "Expectation" here is to be understood in a very basic way as a cognitive relation to the future. A certain security of expectations is the sine qua non for system stability. It is required for and achieved through the formation of identities. It is created at the system boundary by "filtering out" communication from an (infinitely) complex environment and then processing it according to the system's own operational code (system language). In this sense security, or, better, securitization forms a basic boundary function of social systems. Every social system has to create a security of expectations in order not to be overwhelmed by an infinitely complex and chaotic environment. For that reason a system needs to, in fact is defined by, the establishment of boundaries that allow it to reduce complexity. It is now obviously the case that not every operation of reducing complexity upon the entry of communication into the system is actively perceived by the system or parts of the system as a potential "threat." Certainly, securitization involves a reduction of complexity, but not all reduction of complexity necessarily involves securitization. The question then is when and how do issues become "security" issues proper, i.e. issues that are "securitized" in the sense that they are perceived to constitute a threat to an identity in and/or of the system? How do processes of identity-formation and identity-reproduction fit in the picture, given that these processes are dependent on and supportive of border-processes of reducing complexity? If we want to gain an understanding of "securitization" that does not freeze one reference point, i.e. (societal) identity, but can account for identity's processual character too, we have to able to explain why some issues are more "prone" to being securitized than others and why the repertoire of issues and their "proneness" to be securitized differs from system to system.

Proper questions in this regard may be, for example, why it is that European Monetary Union is more easily constructed as a potential threat to national identity than other measures in the context of European integration that intrude into people's daily lives; why is it that the death of one U.S. soldier on another continent is perceived as a matter of national security while hundreds of homicides in the District of Columbia are not, etc.? What follows is not an attempt to give the only possible answer to difficult questions like these. It is, however, an attempt to scrutinize them in such a way so as to be able to achieve a more broader understanding of the process of securitization, an understanding that is less reliant on the notion of a fixed "societal identity" — or, for that matter, any other inappropriately "fixed" point of reference — and thus applicable to a greater variety of cases.

SECURITIZATION AND THE SECURITY/INSECURITY CODE

There is no security without insecurity. Since the meaning of one of these terms is only established in relation to the other, it is impossible, indeed meaningless, to have one without the other: "A structureless chaos would be absolutely insecure; only that would be secure. Basically, the concepts of security and insecurity have no meaning for such a state. Through the differentiation of expectational structures, this state is replaced by a combinatory interplay of relatively secure or insecure positive and negative expectations". Security is about introducing a stability into expectations that would otherwise be unstable (i.e. disappointment of expectations would be the rule). In his 1996 presidential address to the International Studies Association, Dennis Bobrow reflects on this fact by treating security as primarily being about coming to terms with "complex insecurity."

Such an approach illustrates that security and insecurity need not be considered as facts, but can be treated as poles or "ideal models." This becomes especially clear in relation to social systems. As ideal types, neither absolute insecurity nor absolute security can exist as real states of a social system (or, for that matter, any other system, as safety experts are well aware of). Bobrow seeks to illustrate this state of affairs by comparing insecurity-security to illness-health: "The metaphor of disease, illness, and decline implies that we come to terms with insecurity as an unending stream of threats and imperfect strategies".

If security is referred to as a boundary function of social systems, then "securitization" means a process that is somehow involved in the reduction of complexity in order to increase the security of expectations in the system. By no means, however, does the operation of securitization mean that "something" which is insecure is turned into "something" which is secure. As succinctly pointed out by the Copenhagen School, "securitization" as a "speech act" is more about implanting something into the meaningful realm that is defined by the security-insecurity difference (that is why there is only "securitization" and "desecuritization," but not "insecuritization").

In spite of the central place that this process of securitization occupies in the analysis, it is nonetheless very important also to be precise about what it actually means to say that something is meaningful in terms of security/insecurity. The notion of "threat" is highly unspecific in this regard and it seems more appropriate to start by pointing to the sources, the raw materials so to speak, that lend itself to securitization and that can be distinguished accordiung to two fundamental categories: risk and danger. The "risk concept indicates a complex state that, at least in modern society, is a normal aspect of life". While both risk and danger are basically about the anticipation of (possible) future loss, "risk" is about a loss to be attributed to the system's environment, "danger" refers to future loss as a consequence of a decision taken by or in the system. How do these concepts relate to security? Is it safe to say that the more risk and danger processed by the system (i.e. "securitized issues"), the "higher" the level of security in it?

And that the higher the level of unprocessed risk and danger, the higher the level of insecurity? Quite obviously not. In fact, any attempt to answer these questions must in the end remain futile, giving the essentially processual character of security. There are no "levels of security," and being secure or insecure is not an attribute of an identity or a system.

Rather, certain kinds or levels of complexity are identified by the system as risk and danger. And it is exactly when complexities are observed by the system and translated into its own code (i.e. the moment that the communication/information crosses the system's boundary), that "securitization" happens.

Of course, this as such does as yet say anything about why some issues are securitized and others are not. Nonetheless, it is known that in operatively closed, complex social systems this involves observation, either self-observation or the observation of the difference between system and environment. "Security," then, cannot possibly be about "eliminating" risk, but rather about enabling the (observing) system to successfully process it: "Security as a counterconcept to risk remains an empty concept on this constellation, similar to the concept of health in the distinction ill/healthy. It thus functions only as a reflexive concept".

Social systems, then, abound with security and insecurity. Some expectations or sets of expectations are more secure than others. It is important to reiterate, however, that "securitization" is not a process in which expectations that have been insecure become secure. "Securitization" is the process which makes it possible (and necessary) for the system to process a perceived risk or danger with the reflexive device of "security" - or, more correct: with the reflective device that is constituted by the ideal-type distinction of security-insecurity. Bearing security's quality as a reflexive device in mind does help to get a fuller understanding of particular systems in question and also why it is that some issues are securitized and others are not.

Although set in the complex language of systems theory, it is worth quoting Niklas Luhmann's elaboration on the link between system quality and security/insecurity at length:

The time that is measured chronologically is still the most secure one: no matter what happens, it continues on. At least one condition of insecurity [i.e. condition for having expectations that can be disappointed at all; M.A.] is absolutely secure. Time and security/insecurity are different dimensions, and this difference can be used to steer the selection of expectational structures. Even organic life develops anticipatory systems by means of it, selecting indicators in the present (which is all that is available) that will correlate more securely with changes in the future and can thereby prepare for the future without "knowing" it. Meaning systems consolidated this technique by forming expectations and giving these structural, that is, connective value.

If this is possible, the insecurity can finally be "voluntarily" accepted and enhanced. All evolution seems to rest on massing and amplifying insecurities. This principle of amplifying insecurity is repeated in sociocultural evolution and in the decisive interpenetration of entire human beings into the social order. One must treat human beings as if they were reliable and at the same time secure expectations against disappointment. One can form riskier expectations if one can guarantee that disappointments remain tied to specific events and do not trigger accumulations that would endanger security. Viewed in this way, evolution is an ever-new incorporation of insecurities into securities and of securities into insecurities without an ultimate guarantee that this will always succeed on every level of complexity".

The idea of a connection between a system's evolutionary stage and the interplay of security-insecurity will become very important when the possibility of desecuritization is addressed. First, however, it is necessary to take a closer look on how "securitization" works and why it is that some issues are securitized and others are not. This is where it becomes necessary to inspect the Copenhagen School´s definition of security once again: "Societal security is about situations when societies perceive a threat in identity terms". Following the preceding thoughts, it can now be spelled out in greater detail what identity is about. Identities are means to stabilize expectations over time. The trick is to relate expectations "to something that is not an even, that is, cannot in the strict sense itself be expected". It is important to be clear about the notion of "identity" at this point. "Identity" simply refers to a common reference point for expectations, not the same kind of expectations. When we refer to identities in the context of (world) society, we do of course refer to identities that are the reference point of expectations that emerge in the context of various social systems. It is by no means necessary that an "identity" serves as a reference point for expectations emerging from but one social system. Thus, for example, "national identity" can serve as a reference point for expectations that are generated in the political system as well as for expectations that are generated in the economic system; and this does not imply, by any means, that once an identity is formed the expectations referring to it would cease to emerge from and remain embedded in different, operatively closed systems (in fact, this example helps to clarify one of the main points of modern systems theory, i.e. that autopoietic systems are "open" in spite of their operative closure).

If security is about identity, then one could think that it is those communications that become "securitized" upon observation by a social system ("at the system's border") that relate to expectations that refer to an identity. In order to see if this conclusion forms a useful proposition to analyse the relation between security and identity, however, it is necessary to see what it actually means to say that an "identity is threatened." To shed further light on this question, I will now briefly summarize and then elaborate and extend the account that the Copenhagen School gives on this question.

What Is an Identity and how Is It Threatened?

When Ole Wæver introduces the concept of "societal security", he is clearly aware of the need to provide a sharper circumscription of the vague term "society." However, after inspecting many uses of the term in social and political thought, he comes up with something that very closely resembles its "classical" meaning: society is defined solely in relation to the state. Given such a broad and pervasive notion of "society," the reference points that it can relate to must also be broad enough to be able to support the great variety of expectations that refer to it. That is why the "identity" of a concept like "society" can only arise in concepts like nation and religion. Alas, while societal security is about society, the nation is the preferred point of reference for constructing identities in modern societies; hence most studies of societal security find themselves winding up as studies of "national security" (i.e. in relation to national identity).

Wæver correctly identifies "the nation" as "a circular reference to an empty spot". But this also holds true, if not more so, for society. The uneasiness regarding the question of identity in relation to "society" is expressed in the difficulty of attaching societal identity to any particular feature that may be said to characterize "a" society. This operation works for society probably even less than it does for "nation" or "culture."

"Society," or what we used to associate with this term for quite some time, has a multiplicity of identities as it is composed of many systems with and supportive of a multitude of different identities. That such a by and large meaningless notion as the identity of a society is preserved so as to constitute a meaningful frame of analysis for security, is arguably largely due to the fact that the Copenhagen school as yet does not go the full way to acknowledge the processual core of the security idea. Rather than deal with securitization as an important, indeed indispensable function of highly developed and diverse social systems, "security" remains a "property" of units. This is not to suggest that the Copenhagen school would be on the wrong track from the very beginning of its enterprise. However, its analysis proceeds on the ground of a tacit understanding that there is no such thing as a society's identity and what it boils down to is the identity of states and nations: "State and nation offer symbols and identities which both attract individuals seeking expression and outlet for their insecurities, and reproduce the political conditions that are one of the major sources of personal insecurity".

It is in indeed true and essential for a meaningful understanding of security to acknowledge that the state and the nation (or a "combination" of both) offer points of reference which provide identities for various social systems as well as for individuals. It is very important to stress, however, that the way and the processes in which identities are constructed in a symbolic way do account for the differences regarding the production of security to a considerable extent. This is the case especially since the production of security is more properly described as a symbolically mediated processing of insecurities rather than, as could be thought after reading the quotation of Buzan in the preceding paragraph, individuals "dumping" their insecurities on to symbols and identities. Acknowledging that "what we can study...is the processes producing security concerns", Ole Wæver has done extensive work on the way that the process of European integration has to proceed in order to avoid its securitization, i.e. a European identity coming to be perceived as a threat to national identities. Starting from the insight that is also advocated here, namely that "most identity will need complex, multidimensional systems to make sense", he explores how the discursive spaces of (national) societies - as the realm where meaning (and, hence, identity) is constructed - are conditioned by various layers of discourse. Thus, to explore the question of the compatibility of European integration with national identity, i.e. trying to avoid a "securitization" of the former, it is necessary to see how the self-perception of a "society" vis-a-vis "Europe" and concepts of Europe emerging therefrom are structured by and cannot escape the horizons set by the very first layer of "domestic discursive structure". This first layer, which conditions discursive possibilities at the second and third layers, is shaped according to the basic relation of state and nation in "domestic society," a relation that is usually regarded to oscillate between the ideal models of the French Staatsnation and the German Kulturnation. The basic argument is that "European stability requires two kinds of compatibility that it is in each of the major countries possible to construct a narrative of state, nation and Europe that makes sense in relation to the national tradition of political thought. And then when we in this way get Europe in the plural, that these different Europes are compatible".

I do not want to take odds with Wæver's analysis in this respect at all; quite to the contrary, it seems to be among the most sensitive and theoretically innovative current analyses of European integration. To elaborate the horizons of meaning structured by the interplay of nation and state (as, to paraphrase Wæver, circular references to empty spots) does however not suffice to gain a more general understanding of the interplay between securitization as a border function of social systems and the category of "identity." Appropriate though the analysis may be in the case of European integration, the notions of "state" and "nation" are far too unspecific as to provide an insight to the question how it is that some issues are more prone to securitization than others upon their observation by a social system. What an analysis of the kind that Wæver conducts provides is insights on why a specific issue is securitized in the context of highly specific social subsystems (most prominently the French and German political systems). Yet there is even more to be gained by looking at how something becomes a security issue for an identity. However, to further approach this question, it is first of all necessary to see how a concept like "nation" came to occupy the "central place" to which identities could refer, yet remain an "empty spot" at the same time.

Historically, an ethnic consciousness and an "ethnic identity" built thereupon have usually been contingent upon a relatively high degree of communication and interaction among the individuals of a group. In spatial terms, ethnicity as a constantly reproduced feature of individual and collective identity was certainly of the most intensive character on the local and maybe on the regional level, whereas it depended on an elite understanding (e.g. the nobility) to have ethnic or ethnic-like commonalities carried much further. The evolution of modern societies necessitated and effected a profound change in the meaning of ethnic identity, especially by introducing the concept of the nation. No longer a matter of elite consciousness, the nation became a melting pot of various ethnic identities and has managed to become a reference point for ethnic identity while being largely divorced from direct, locally bound interaction and communication (thereby supplementing modern societies with fiction-like elements of community). This abstract and intangible nature of the nation itself may on the one hand explain its durability in the process of modernization; while local contexts are penetrated and transformed by the global, the nation still provides orientation points for ethnic identities where (especially in Western culture) the local and regional level are only good or more folcloristic stuff. On the other hand, its abstractness and remoteness from local or regional specifics makes nationality the perfect choice for identity-construction projects where these former specifics by themselves would hardly lend themselves to legitimize a clear or even violent distanciation from the other.

This fluent character of national identity is also clearly visible when looking at its relation to the construct of ethnic identity. Witness the present-day United States, where it has become basically impossible to construct an "American" ethnic identity. Whereas this is perfectly possible and common in France or Germany, the U.S. has witnessed an upsurge of projects of constructing ethnic identities along purely racial lines; these retain a necessary connection to national identity, but this connection is not sufficient for the construction of an ethnic "American" identity. A similar argument is made by Eisenstadt and Giesen when they point out that collective identity is never fixed and given, not even in the sense of a "fixed construction" which uses myths and narratives of origin as legitimizing reference points. Rather, collective identity crucially depends on flux: it can "fulfill its 'function' only if the social processes constructing it are kept latent", from which follows that one has to "reconstruct the process by which latency is achieved and by which the fragile social order is considered to be the self-evident order of things". What is it therefore that preserves the fixation of everyday thinking as well as theorizing in the social sciences on reference points such as "state," "nation," or "society," while on the other hand rendering their identities impossible to spell out?

"Collective identity is produced by the social construction of boundaries". However, it is important to remember that the mere construction of boundaries does not "necessarily entail a process of inclusion and exclusion". Also, the social construction of boundaries is a necessary, but not a sufficient condition to produce a collective identity. Rather, what is on either site of the boundary needs to be symbolically coded in order to mark the difference as a positive difference, in contrast to the boundary, which only allows a difference to be perceived in negative terms. These symbolic codes can be grouped into various "layers." The most basic symbolic codes form "original references" which over time are extremely immune to change; change is not impossible, but highly unlikely. In as far as "primordialism" would refer only to these codes, one could easily grant validity to a primordialist perspective even from a social constructivist point of view. These original codes are the differences between kin and akin, hierarchy and equality, parents and children etc. What a collective identity "is," however, will for the most part depend not on differences between the utilized "original references," but "in the special way they combine and interfuse the 'them and us' distinction with other distinctions like 'sacred and profane', 'parents and children', etc.".

Supplementing this first major type of codes for constructing collective identity are a second and third type. The second major code is the civic code, which "is constructed on the basis of familiarity with implicit rules of conduct, traditions and social routines, that define and demarcate the boundary of the collectivity. It links the constitutive difference between 'us and them' to the difference between the routine and the extraordinary". A third major type links the constitutive boundary between us and them to a particular relation of the collective subject to the sacred. Eisenstadt and Giessen describe how, building on these codes, German national identity is constructed as a cultural code that achieves latency by categorizing and thereby basing itself "on an essential tension between the profane sphere of politics and economy and the sacred sphere of morals, aesthetics and culture". Drawing on the extensive anthropological work done on these issues, one can further clarify these processes by taking note of the fact that the symbolism used to mark boundaries is very often not expressed in a highly visible manner, but "part of the meaning which we intuitively ascribe to more instrumental and pragmatic things in ordinary use – such as words". Indeed, sometimes contents are so unclear that categories only exist in terms of their symbolic boundaries. Such seems exactly to be the case with the nation, in relation to which a lot of people share its symbols, but do not attach the same meanings to them.

Put in different terms, if people form a national community, whose boundary is defined in terms of a shared relation to symbols such as flag, anthem, historic events and myths, their commonality is not established by virtue of the way that people form their identities in relation to these symbols. Such a view would inevitably lead to an account which sees collective identity to be constructed as the sum of its parts. It would quite obviously be wrong, however, since people do not relate to these symbols in the same way, i.e. attach the same kind of meaning to them.

This means that a shared relation to symbols is as important in constructing a collective identity as is the latency of this shared set of symbols. Thus, a collective identity is not sufficiently understood as a shared relation to some symbols (to which others supposedly do not relate). Rather, with a view to the equally important aspect of maintaining latency in this specific resource of codes, a collective identity is better understood as a shared form of processing differences between those that share these symbols and the rest of the world. Kulturnation and Staatsnation do not point to combinations of state and nation as historically constructed and variable identity-cocktails. Both express different modalities of processing differences (between shared set of symbols and other symbols as well as between specific ways to retain the latency of the body of symbols and other such ways). This does not lead to an account that would be incompatible with that presented by Wæver on the issue of European integration. However, having differentiated the category of collective identity much further than the Copenhagen school, it is now possible to see more clearly how "threats" or even "existential threats" to identity can emerge, i.e. how it is that some issues are more prone to securitization than others. How can "an identity" be threatened? By endangering the successful continuation of its construction (and continuous reconstruction), its prime task of stabilizing various expectations, its ability to cluster a number of symbols to form a referential point for various expectations yet keep the meaning of this point latent. This means that a system which uses this point of reference (in its self-description) will securitize an issue exactly when it interferes with the possibility of a continued successful processing of differences by the means of utilizing the tension between a symbolic repository and its latency. An issue becomes a security issues if it interrupts the system's ability to process differences.

In order to employ this very general description for the study of specific processes of securitization, it is necessary to take account of the fact that the requirements for processing differences and the construction of identity vary significantly not only from system to system, but especially also between different evolutionary states of the same system.

On the one hand, for example, the European political system can be seen as a highly complex social system which is so far developed that its main problem has become its own cognitive and systemic complexity. It processes differences at this high level of complexity either discursively in the highly connective structures and processes of "multi-level governance", or even generatively by excluding systemic properties from the system, thus reducing system complexity and creating (proto-) boundaries for new systems. Following the argument made above it would seem that in order to successfully stabilize expectations at this level of systemic evolution it is necessary to keep up the tension between a very subtle and diversified set of symbols (probably much less in the form of institutions nowadays than increasingly in the form of the intrusion of these symbols into everyday life) and a highly elusive and underspecified idea of "Europe" that is structurally similar to, but much less mythically condensed than most national identities. In this case, and basically supporting Wæver's argument in this respect — "securitization" would for example occur if an attempt were made to give the "idea of Europe" a more fixed and definite shape, thus possibly tying symbols to fixed meanings they do not and cannot support, because as "latent" symbols they are also claimed as reference points for the construction of a "national" identity.

On the other hand, a social system in its early stages of evolution would securitize different issues. Thus, for example, a balance-of-power-system between states that has just developed some kind of structure and only rudimentary differentiation along processual lines usually has to process differences by introducing norms (international law) that guarantee a security of expectations. At this level of systemic evolution, "identity" consists of a tension that is upheld between various symbols (treaties etc.) of the law and an ideal or mechanism of law enforcement intrinsic to the idea of law, but practically non-existent. Thus, for example, "securitization" in such a system happens to everything perceived as upsetting this balance, for example by trying to tie international law to an effective law enforcement mechanism.

Such a formulation of the function of securitization in relation to identity of course warrants a great deal more of empirical work, or a re-reading of some empirical work. Nonetheless, before moving on to describe how this interplay of security and identity in complex social systems translates into the analysis of "new" or "changing" forms of statehood, the conceptual argument can be driven one step further by more precisely defining the meaning of securitization and desecuritization in the context of systems-theoretical thinking.

Systems Evolution: Desecuritization and Asecuritization

How does an issue, once securitized, become desecuritized again? Having linked the function of securitization to the evolution of the social system in question, it is now possible to state more precisely the process of securitization – an issue becomes not necessarily securitized if it intervenes in an "identity-driven" processing of differences in the system, but primarily if it does so at unconsolidated levels of complexity of the system in question, i.e. levels of complexity the system has to deal with "actively," so to speak, and not as routine. In today's European Union, the European Court of Justice is arguably not a frequent source of "securitized" issues, because the court operates at a level of normative integration that has long been surpassed by the evolution of the European legal and political systems (and, one should add, because the national judicial systems have by and large successfully managed to include the European layer of European jurisdiction into their own self-description). While the processing of normative differences in and through the European Court of Justice has for a time now been a quite routine affair, it could only produce issues prone to securitization if it chose to address questions on the highest level of system complexity (if it were to rule, for example, on what a European identity is).

It is then quite clear what "desecuritization" would mean in this context. An issue becomes "desecuritized" by system evolution, i.e. if the system ceases to deal "actively" with the complexity at whose level an issue got securitized. This leads to a seemingly marginal, yet important difference to Wæver's account of desecuritization processes: "Détente, as negotiated desecuritization and limitation of the use of the security speech act, contributed to the modification of Eastern societies and systems that eventually made possible, via sudden desecuritization through a speech-act failure, the radical changes of 1989". Given the account of the connection between securitization and system development outlined above, one would phrase this differently and take the process of détente as a strong indicator that the East-West-system had developed into one in which the reference point of identity had changed from one of antagonism to one of common destiny, heavily desecuritizing some issues which are operational only in reference to processing antagonism. Put in this way, the observation may not be that utterly different from Wæver's. It does however relieve it of the the burden of having to tie systemic change to interactions ("speech acts"). This means that in the case given by Wæver one cannot speak of a "desecuritization through speech-act failure"; the speech-act failure is rather an indicator of desecuritization through system evolution. That account also sheds light on the notion of "asecuritization." The notion of "asecurity" was developed by Pertti Joenniemmi to account for the fact that the Baltic Sea Region as a qualitatively new way of organizing political space, alternative to or defying the logic of territorial statehood, was characterized by a total absence of any securitization logic. "Region" is here understood as a "regionality," a new form of organizing political space, not as a territorial, but a functional agglomeration. While it would certainly be incorrect to regard the Baltic Sea region as a system without any function of securitization, it is certainly correct that it has established a different system where before the logic of the state and state security had dominated political space. In the context of regional cooperation in the Baltic, this could be read as a highly complex system having "emitted" some of its functions regarding the organization of political space, these functions creating boundaries of a different system of regionality. This system became "asecuritized" in the sense that its properties were no longer meaningful on the security-insecurity scale of the preceding system. This does not mean that there would cease to be any "security-logic" in the new system, just that it is an entirely different one.

However, there is another connotation of the idea of "asecurity" that can be distilled from the conceptual linkage between securitization and system evolution. "Generative differentiation," defined as the exclusion of a system property from a highly developed social system — thus as to reduce system complexity and thereby create the boundaries of possible new (quasi-)systems — can also result in an "asecuritization" of a different kind. Whereas "asecuritization" was just seen as a process to which the newly created (quasi-)system was subject (by not being subject to the "mother systems'" securitization functions any longer), "asecuritization" might as well refer to the highly developed social system undergoing generative differentiation. "Asecuritization" would then mean that it is securitized issues that are shed from the system's self-description as a result of processes of generative differentiation. Such issues cease to be security issues for the system because as issues they are now exempt from the system's self-description and rather form part of the system's environment. In a sense, of course, this is also "desecuritization." However, since it comes out of a process that changes the contours of the system in that it leads to a creation of a new system, it seems but appropriate to refer to this process as "asecuritization."

I will now illustrate how this framework of analysis that combines insights from modern systems theory with newer studies on the concept of "securitization" in international relations can usefully be employed to study change in the concept of "the state," first in conceptual terms, then by taking as a case the "privatization" of security through the privatization of policing.

WITHER "STATE SECURITY?"

The changing meanings of state, security, state security versus societal security and the relation of all to "identity" currently receive a significant amount of attention in international studies. Rarely do studies dare to go beyond an analysis that includes but two dimensions, the categories in one of which are ususally thoroughly fixed. Be it that "society" is fixed and "securitization" is liquefied, or be it that "security" is fixed and the "societal" construction of threat seen in a processual manner (as in most contributions in Katzenstein, 1996). Utilizing some tenets of thought taken from modern systems theory carries no promise to provide an overall remedy and be able to analyse all important dimensions of the issue in question and address them in their processual character. It may be enough, however, if it simply adds to the possibility to break down some of the fixed categories of other approaches into pieces — pieces of which then at least some can duly be treated as processes.

Regarding "the state," it is two distinctions that can be introduced immediately. Though they may seem to be of a marginal character at first glance, they reveal tremendously altered views of various processes in the course of their analysis. The first of these distinctions, both of which in their obviousness barely even warrant attention in modern systems theory, would be to differentiate between the various operatively closed social systems, an overlap and coupling of which is usually very unspecifically called "the state" (i.e. political system, legal system, economic system, etc.). The second distinction would be to pay attention to system-sub-system relationships (e.g. international political system-national political systems). The consequences of introducing these distinctions to the analysis of "the state" can briefly be introduced and used as a springboard in order to ask how the state has changed in relation to its "security function."

The State and its Systems

To illustrate the distinction between system and sub-system, one could, for example, reserve the usage of the term "security" for the function that allows a "national" political system to preserve its operative autonomy and its system boundary. This seems to be the meaning of "security" that during the years of the Cold War was by and large undisputed in "security studies." In current discussions on the "new" meanings of security, two trends prevail in attempts to redefine the term. More orthodox contributions basically do nothing else than accept that as a result of the sudden disappearance of the East-West-conflict the environment of national political systems has become more complex; "the state" now faces dangers from international terrorism, environmental hazards, social conflict.

Others, such as the Copenhagen School, try to alert to the fact that it may rather be that it is the referent object of security that has changed. To introduce a simple system-subsystem distinction into the analysis means to show that these two lines of thought are by no means exhaustive and that indeed the "new security agenda" may in fact not only be about new security issues for a political system or security issues for a system other than the political system, but for the international political system as a whole. It may not be "the state," but the "world of states" which needs to modify its boundary-function of securitization in order to cope with the increasing risk that is generated by other systems but that cannot be handled by these systems.

However, the system-sub-system distinction can only be useful if taken together with the second distinction — that between different social systems. Almost as a rule in the analysis of international relations, various social systems are usually collapsed indiscriminately into "the state." While "the state" or a certain "model" of statehood (i.e. "Westphalia") may serve as an important, even outstanding reference point for some systemic identities or identities in systems, reference to it very often obscures underlying distinctions between different systems or system-sub-system-distinctions. In contrast, introducing these distinctions as well as the notion of system evolution not only leads to new perspectives on the changing "nature" of "the state," but also on the changing "nature" of "security."

From this perspective, it is indeed correct that most misunderstandings of security are a direct outcome of misunderstandings of the role of the state in a changing world ; it is even more correct to add, however, that the misunderstandings of the role of the state in a changing world are a direct outcome of misunderstandings of the evolution, coexistence and coupling between various social systems. Thus, for example, given the existence of an international political system in which all states are embedded, "all states are states."

Even the qualifier "quasi-state" — meaning that the state is "sovereign" in formal terms (and that usually means: recognized as such in an international context), but lacks "real control" of a developed Westphalian state (e.g. control over entire territory) — does not deprive a state in question of its statehood. Quasi-states "are" states, given that we can deem the presence of a functioning political system as sufficient to assume the existence of "a state." This is however the place where the reference to ideal models such as "Westphalian state" is indeed very misleading, because we then tend to assume that only those states "are" states that (i.e. their political systems) are most highly developed in relation to this ideal model (that is states whose political systems are functioning according to the same standards).

Yet, it would be nonsense to conclude from the fact that various groups fight for territorial control in Afghanistan and the absence of a functioning "state apparatus" that there is no political system. Afghanistan's political system has not developed beyond a first-stage social system that fulfills the prime system function of territorial demarcation by adjusting to the problem of different authority claims on the same territory by constitutive wars; yet it is a political system. And the fact that a multitude of political systems in various evolutionary stages exist in world society does not at all alter the fact that most of them are not autonomous, but sub-systems of the international political system, bound into the latter's operative logic and exerting an influence on its evolutionary status.

This duality of political systems being characterized by their evolutionary stage and their embeddedness as sub-systems in the international political system also accounts for the difficulty to come to terms with what "security" means. According to the argument made above, what becomes securitized depends on the kind of complexity that the system is primarily dealing with.

The matter gets even more complicated if we are dealing with different levels of complexity, and thus different border/securitization functions - on systemic and sub-systemic levels. Although certainly not holding out the promise of leading to generalized forecasts about what the "nature" of security is going to be in the future, these differentiations have to be taken into account in explorations of its change. And indeed it seems that slowly they are taken into account; thus, in a recent chapter on the military and state-formation in the Middle East, Keith Krause concluded, "the quest for security in the developing world cannot be understood without reference to the process of military development, the insertion of new states into the global security order and the state-building projects that new regimes have embarked upon". Although certainly not based on modern system theory, this quotation very well expresses the conclusions that can be drawn from the conceptual argument made here. The only difference being that the latter would claim explanatory power beyond the developing world (or in fact see the whole world as developing), beyond a too narrow focus on "military" development, and beyond the idea that it is all about new and original events. Thus Krause should read more like: "the quest for security in world society cannot be understood without reference to the process of system evolution, the insertion of 'states' into the 'world of states' (sub-systems into systems) and the project of complexity-reduction that various systems have embarked upon."

State Security and the Public Peace

Of course there is no way of asking if the state either "looses" or "gains" power (vis-a-vis society, transnational actors, NGOs), or if it changes its "nature" (becoming "post-Westphalian," for example). There is no "either-or" involved here. What there is one question of "power-gains" or "losses" that may arise between various social systems, but not in relation to the symbolic reference-point that serves to construct identities of or in (some of) these systems. And there is another question of changes of the systems themselves, i.e. either system evolution or generative differentiation (in highly developed, autopoietic systems). As argued above, such generative differentiation can be seen as a case of "asecuritization" of the "expelling" system, if the property excluded from its self-description was securitized in the system. And such has happened, or is happening, to quite some highly developed political and judicial systems, with immediate repercussions as to what the notion of "security" can mean in relation to them — or, for that purpose, what it can mean for "state" and "society."

If the "Westphalian model" is about "sovereignty," then it is also about a process — the "norms of sovereign control develop through the practical resolution of international issues which must first be politicized [i.e. processed by the political system]". If it is fair to say that the evolution of state sovereignty as the central distinguishing feature of the Westphalian model involved the consolidation of the state's (or: the political and, partly, the judicial system's) monopoly on the legitimate use of power on a certain territory and, as suggested by Thomson, on the control over extraterritorial violence, then a challenge on this monopoly/control means that what "state sovereignty" entails is changing.

Such a change may come as a result of system devolution; in highly "developed" political and legal systems, it is more likely to be an indicator for further system evolution through generative differentiation. Thus, one could argue that places like South Central L.A. and South East Washington D.C. are indicators for the emergence of such new systems. In a more radical interpretation, they may even be seen as being excluded from the political system's self-description as being based on territory, thus forming "new" extraterritorial spaces within the geographical borders of a sovereign state. In this sense they would have not only ceased to belong to the system by forming a new (quasi-)system, that however still does operate according to the modern "guiding difference" par excellence, functional differentiation, but would be on the way to form a system that differs radically from existing social systems by beginning to function on a new "Leitdifferenz." In such a case, these new systems would not only belong to the environment of other social systems, but become "non-addresses." However, in a less radical interpretation, these areas would be characterized more by the fact that the functional systems that set the framework for interaction in these areas use codes and mechanisms that formerly were part of, regulated and securitized by, other systems. While these developments are about genuinely new ways of controlling people in relation to territory, they are not only restricted to locally limited developments, but indicators for the direction of overall change of "the state". In fact, as Didier Bigo notices, the "delinking of territory and control...generates very significant practical and symbolic alterations which affect concepts of sovereignty, power and its day-to day exercise". This change is most clearly epitomized in a much more wide-spread phenomenon that can be summarized as the "privatization of security": a "multiplicity of legitimate arms-bearing, institutionalized centers of coercive power - witness university police - as well as the relative powerlessness of many government units".

At first glance, this may be seen as a decline or erosion of "public security," the political system's "monopoly" on the legitimate use of force, etc. However, primary indicators like public police being outnumbered by private police in many countries do not sufficiently describe the phenomenon. First of all, the resurgence of private policing has to be seen against the background of its earlier demise. As can be seen in the U.S. case, the railroad and mining companies' policing practices arguably led Congress to seek a strengthening of state policing not because of "power" issues, but because public policing was intrinsical to a concept of public peace that made up part of the symbolic repertoire that allowed to construct a collective "state identity".

If there was to be any role for private agents, it was not as police sustaining a private conception of peace. The only acceptable roles for them were as guards which assisted private entities in a very limited way to protect life and property as an expression of self-defense or self-help". However, the resurgence of private policing, especially in the 1980s, did not seem to threaten public peace in the way it seemed to do so before. This is mainly due to the fact that the political system´s self-description had changed considerably by the 1960s and 1970s. Shearing convincingly argues that this is very well expressed in an influential RAND study from this era. "The image of private policing as private armies challenging state authority was replaced with one of private policing as just another industry providing services to the public", without the RAND-report even raising the question of civil liberties. The growing importance of private policing has to be primarily understood in the context of changing self-descriptions of various social systems, in the sense that the notion of the public peace they relate to has been altered. In addition, one also has to take account of the qualitative change in public policing itself. As policing is no longer monopolized by public police, it experiences identity-crises. In the most "advanced" countries in this respect, the U.S. and Canada, the legalistic (police officer as law officer) and professionalist (police officer as public servant) self-perceptions of police give way to "communitarian" self-descriptions. In that process, community policing ceases to be perceived as a program, but comes to be seen as a guideline for all policing. It is indeed no longer possible to describe this as a weakening of public versus private policing as the difference becomes more and more blurred – public police begin to charge fees for some kinds of protection and "moonlighting" police officers work additional jobs as security guards but retain their authority of public police invested in them in personam while performing private policing.

It is of course possible to describe these developments as genuine transformations of "the state," its "weakening" or "strengthening"; however, this is not the question. The question to be addressed to such phenomena as community policing or community mediation is not whether they expand or limit things like the "state's control over conflict resolution". Rather, it is a question if a particular political system in question is still the same as it was before. And it isn't. Quite to the contrary, to deal with its increasing complexity as a system it has in processes of generative differentiation excluded some system properties from its self-description as a system: "In effect, central government is, in this field of policy as in several others, operating upon the established boundaries which separate the private from the public realm, seeking to renegotiate the question of what is properly a state function and what is not". This means that parts of what before was clearly seen as "public peace" by a political (and legal) system whose function was to uphold this system is simply not considered to be part of that public peace any longer. "The normality of high crime rates in late modern society has prompted a series of transformations in official perceptions of crime, in criminological discourse, in modes of governmental action, and in the structure of criminal justice organizations". Some sorts of crime are simply shed from the political system's description of the public peace; a range of minor crimes are "desecuritized" in the sense that they simply do not pose a threat to "society" any longer. This is reflected in the fact that police agencies are more and more evaluated "by reference to internal goals...rather than by reference to social goals such as reducing crime rates".

Put in the context of the previous argumentation: since "desecuritization" occurred through the political system, excluding a part of the public peace from its self-description, this development can be described as "asecuritization." These asecuritized issues can not be transformed to be non-securitized from one day to another, they are too firmly designated as "security" ("the speech act"). "Asecuritization" simply means that these issues cease to be securitized in the political system— they will probably continue to be treated as securitized issues in the new systems that they form (or that take them up). However, as they enter/constitute a new (quasi-)system, they transform from stumbling blocs in an old system in which they had been securitized because they where perceived to interfere with the "identity-driven" processing of differences in a system at an unconsolidated (here: highest and not consolidable) level of complexity, to building blocks in new (quasi-) systems. What does this mean for "the state"? First of all it means that the political system has changed. And it is only here that a question of weakening or strengthening could be asked: has the political system be strengthened or weakened in its capacity to influence the context parameters in which the legal, economic etc. systems do operate and define themselves? What no answer to these questions can put in doubt, however, is that as a point of reference, "the state" retains its function for the political system and as such does not change as long as it continues to serve as an efficient reference point for the construction and reconstruction of collective identity, necessary to stabilize expectations in the system.

SECURITY'S FUTURE

In has been argued that the privatization of security entailed a changing definition of the public peace that pointed to evolutionary processes in modern social systems. The argument I have tried to make is that modern systems theory can profitably be employed to analyse changes in various realms and that it can do so in a way that can deal with the elusiveness and flexibility of concepts like identity and security, without reducing them to catch-all concepts. If this is a call for increasing the complexity of seemingly simple social concepts (which simply aren't that simple), it is also a call for constantly situating the development of these concepts in relation to larger-scale trends in world-society. Thus, for example, the privatization of policing has to be seen against the background of a militarization of law enforcement and the assumption of more and more policing functions by the military. While in this case the privatization of policing points to an evolution of individual political systems, the latter developments point to a blurring of lines between individual political systems and the international political system.

To bring down a conceptually broad argument to the strategic confines of disciplinary debate — in the latter's terms, to make the present argument means to argue for an extreme "broadening " and a "narrowing" of security studies at the same time. On the one hand, it means to broaden the security agenda. I use modern systems theory to describe how security is a boundary function of every social system. I propose that seeing security as such a function and thereby to be dependent on the character and especially the evolutionary status of functionally differentiated social systems allows us to tackle the complexities in today's world in the complex way that is adequate to them, not reducing security and other concepts to grand schemes which in the end explain nothing at all.

On the other hand, however, this also means to narrow, or better: shrink, the security agenda; not by placing a lighter conceptual burden on "security," but by removing its glamour. We do not study security in and for itself. We study security as a function of certain social systems. And as such a function, "security" is first of all a reflexive device. A reflexive device for the system in question, but also for those who observe these systems.

5

New Dimensions: Shifting Borders, Boundaries, and Sovereignty

Crimea has been incorporated into Russia, and Ukraine is fighting to keep whole. Iraq is devolving into a state in three parts, and the new "Islamic State" stretches—at least for now—across the borders of Syria and northern Iraq, while the Iraqi Kurdish regional government pushes forward with independent energy exports through Turkey and discussion of a referendum on independence.

Scotland's unsuccessful referendum for separation from the United Kingdom undermined immediate prospects of independence for Edinburgh, but the closeness of the vote—55% no, 45% yes—will further devolve power from Westminster and change the relationship between Scotland and the UK.

The Spanish government has vowed to use the "full force of the law" to block November's scheduled Catalonia independence referendum, but either the vote or early regional elections could intensify separatist sentiment not just in Catalonia, but also among Spain's Basque population and plausibly elsewhere in Europe.

In Afghanistan, contested election results, insurgent momentum, and an abundance of not-quite-aligned interests of external actors have heightened the potential for persistent political unrest. Across the long-lamented Durand Line dividing the

Pashtuns of Afghanistan from those in Pakistan, the Pakistani government and military are in the midst of a violent offensive to regain control of its North Waziristan province from Tehrik-e-Taliban Pakistan militants.

In East Asia, the possibility for unification or conflict along the tense border on the Korean Peninsula looms over the region, as does intense concern over the near daily incursions of contested air defense zones and maritime borders and boundaries from the South China Sea to the Kuril Islands in northeast Asia.

From Erbil to Edinburgh, Kabul to Khartoum, and from Donetsk to Damascus to the Diaoyus, the dimensions of the international system—the Westphalian concept that nation-states have sovereignty over their territory—are being challenged in stark and destabilizing ways. Challenges within states and contested borders between states ensure that shifting borders and boundaries will play a critical role in driving competition, crisis, and potentially conflict in the 21st century. Emerging de jure and, more importantly, de facto dimensions of the international system have important implications for security, intelligence, and defense communities across the globe as well as for businesses seeking to effectively operate and expand in a complex and fluid world.

NEW STATES AND STRUGGLING SOVEREIGNS

Changing borders and boundaries are not a new phenomenon. Most tend to think of maps as inviolate and certain, but the dimensions of the international system have changed dramatically over time and are frequently ill defined. The disintegration of pre-World War II empires, gradual redrawing or contestation of colonial boundaries, and formation and collapse of the post-World War II Soviet empire have ensured significant changes to the world's political geography in the last seven decades. However, current and emerging challenges to modern maps are different. They are not primarily the result of a singular "big bang" in the supra-structure of international geopolitics, such as the end of World War II or the end of the Cold War.

The changing maps of the early 21st century are the result of the interplay of a series of disruptive forces that have gathered momentum in the last two decades. These include globalization; the prevalence of information technologies and the impact of social media to redefine the meaning of community; weapons and capability proliferation; demographic shifts; environmental degradation and resource competition; crime and corruption; and ethnic, sectarian, religious, and linguistic identity trumping state identity, among others.

These forces are interacting to erode Westphalian concepts of sovereignty and statehood and increasingly separate historical and cultural "nations" from the political "states" to which they belong. The result is growing disparity—in wealth, values, primary self-identity, culture, opportunity, and access—between countries' political and economic centers and their peripheries.

As The Guardian commented about the Scottish independence movement on September 5, it is not that the significant risks of independence are not known, but rather that they are not as troubling as enduring "two increasingly intolerable burdens": a growing disconnect in values between "left-leaning Scots" and the British government and an inability to access and affect policy that reflects their differing values. Add in generational shifts in attitudes and the potential for exploitation of North Sea natural resources and it is no surprise the margin was so close.

Connections to external actors seeking to leverage struggling sovereigns for geopolitical gain frequently amplify and complicate these border-shattering dynamics. Russia's annexation of Crimea and continued destabilization of Ukraine have relied on Russian material support and the creation and furtherance of a narrative that stressed nationalist and historical links among Russia, Crimea, and eastern Ukraine in an effort to destabilize Ukraine, challenge the European Union and NATO, and reassert Russian influence in Eastern Europe.

The effects of environmental strain and degradation—damaged crops, eroding coastal areas—are increasingly posing uncomfortable questions of sovereign governments seeking to assess and balance the growing possibility and potential burden of climate change-induced mass migrations with humanitarian imperatives. In June 2014, the Immigration and Protection Tribunal of New Zealand granted asylum to a family from the Pacific island of Tuvalu to immigrate to New Zealand due to the threat of rising sea level to their home island. The tribunal's decision was narrowly interpreted, according to the Washington Post, and is not an endorsement of climate change as a compelling justification on par with political persecution for asylum seekers to come to New Zealand. However, it highlights the difficult decisions and sovereign challenges that many governments throughout the world will face as the combined effect of a global population of over seven billion people and the erosion and disappearance of island or coastal land masses drives migration across and within borders.

Today's challenges to the Westphalian system are also distinguished by their seeming ubiquity. Challenges to government control and political demarcations are no longer restricted to "failed" or "failing" states. They are being felt, and in some places strongly—Ukraine, for example, as well as in Xinjiang, Hong Kong, and Tibet, in China—by Western and modern Asian states thought to be stable and in possession of strong state institutions and identities.

For example, the United States' struggle to reconcile two competing views—red state versus blue state—of what the republic is, what it represents, and how it should behave has led to a hamstrung and divided polity. American institutions are likely resilient enough to avoid collapse, secession, or internal conflict, but the current political stagnation has a deleterious effect on national discourse and federal government effectiveness on critical issues, including immigration and the management of a porous border with Mexico. Political divisiveness has also contributed to uncertainty about military force structure and capabilities to project US power and pursue US security interests, all primary functions of an effective sovereign.

Ceding influence

Attempts to devolve control or, at the very least, effective influence from central sovereigns to more emergent "true places" governed by sub-state—and in some cases, non-state—actors are generating a range of behaviors and shared sovereignty arrangements and calculations on the part of central governments and those that challenge them

Few more striking or emblematic examples of these increasingly prevalent behaviors exist than Lebanon. In 2006, the Lebanese government remained neutral in a 30-day war fought almost entirely within its territory—a war that killed thousands of Lebanese citizens and displaced hundreds of thousands more. The decision was an acknowledgement of the accommodation the Lebanese government had reached with non-state actor and Iranian- and Syrian-linked Hezbollah.

In order for Lebanon to ensure continuation as a viable place on the map—a viability that is currently threatened by an ongoing political crisis fueled by a highly sectarian political system and spillover of sectarian tensions and violence from the conflict in Syria—its government ceded control of a portion of its territory in southern Lebanon to a non-state actor with its own robust military capability and political and societal traction.

Other more formal acknowledgements of the increasingly delicate balance being struck between central sovereign authority and social and political groups on the periphery of the state are being explored throughout the world. In India, decentralizing pressures have led to the establishment of four new states since 2000, including the formation of India's 29th state, Telangana—carved out of territory in Andhra Pradesh—in June 2014. The new Telangana state raises several immediate governance questions for both Telangana and Andhra Pradesh, which will share the state capital of Hyderabad for the next decade. It also raises longer-term questions about the next states that could be created and what additional segmentation of the Indian polity means for the world's largest democracy.

Autonomy for the Kurdish regional government in Iraq has tested the ability of the Shi'a-led government of Iraq to exercise key instruments of sovereignty, such as exports of strategic resources and control of populations and territory in northern Iraq, especially as Iraqi security forces have retreated in the face of the Islamic State summer offensive. Kurdish autonomy has held implications for Iraq since it was first negotiated in 1970, but the growing assertiveness of the Kurdish government in operating increasingly independently of Baghdad could change the nature of the relationship between Iraqi Kurdistan and the Iraqi government once the current political and security crisis abates. Actions such as the movement of Kurdish forces into Kirkuk and occupation of oil-rich area west of its regional border after the withdrawal of Iraqi security forces are likely to shape a new starting point for post-conflict autonomy negotiations.

Iraqi Kurdistan autonomy also has implications for the Kurds' neighbors, especially Turkey, which is in the midst of a significant demographic transition that is changing the nature and depth of Turkish government engagement of Kurdish groups both in Turkey and across the region.

Not all accommodations and shared sovereignty environments are entered into willingly by governments, of course. Indeed, many are resisted quite intensely, though not always effectively. The proliferation of military and dual-use items has allowed more actors to affect strategic and operational environments and for more robust military challenges to sovereign forces. For example, according to the BBC, since 2006 more than 77,000 people have died in drug-related violence in Mexico, as the government seeks to exert or regain control over significant portions of the country from drug cartels, which are competing violently with one another for control over parts of Mexico's sovereign territory and the citizens and resources residing there.

Another severe and urgent example of contested sovereignty is seen in the range of armed conflicts taking place across the Middle East and North Africa—especially in Libya, Syria, Iraq, and Yemen. Each of these conflicts constitutes a perfect storm of several of the most intense forces driving internal challenges to boundaries and sovereignty: deep and historic sectarian tensions, religious extremism, weak institutions and poor governmental leadership, the influx of arms to both state and non-state actors, and the influence and interventions of outside actors seeking to extract geopolitical gain.

These conflicts have important and immediate implications for the future political geography, geopolitical competitions, and ultimately security and stability of the entire region. Most notably, they present existential challenges to Iraq, Syria, and Libya, all countries that could devolve into political entities with different contours as a result of the fighting and expose political vulnerabilities and fragilities of many other states across the Middle East. Regional armed conflicts also demonstrate that borders cease to be an effective constraint of crises once they start, especially in an environment in which external actors are supporting elements challenging state sovereignty and coherence.

These examples are stark but also reflective of the broader challenges that governments throughout the world are facing to their sovereignty, societal stability, and established borders. The new—if unofficial—dimensions of the international system will soon demand new maps that acknowledge that the boundaries and borders to which we have grown accustomed may no longer reflect the location of the world's "true places."

Contested boundaries

Erosion of Westphalian concepts of sovereignty resulting from competition within states is not the only way in which borders and boundaries are affecting our current geopolitical environment. Competition between states seeking to exercise exclusive control over contested territory is also shaping the future dimensions of the international system and creating anxious environments that lend themselves to miscalculation and sudden, accidental escalation.

This issue is of acute concern in East Asia, where bilateral and multilateral disputes persist over the South China Sea, the Senkaku/Diaoyu Islands, Ieodo/Suyan, Takeshima/Dokdo, Sakhalin Island, and the Kuril Islands. All of these disputes have critical elements in common: they are primarily maritime in nature; they are the result of claims by multiple states holding frequently maximalist territorial positions; and the contested borders sit across key shipping lanes, fishing locations, or areas of presumed abundance of natural resources.

China's rise as a regional power and its unfolding competition with the United States, in particular, but also Japan and other states in the Western Pacific, are motivating increasingly assertive challenges to the status quo in East Asia. The unilateral placement of the Haiyang Shiyou 981 oil rig well within Vietnam's exclusive economic zone near the contested Paracel Islands in May 2014 was the most provocative of a series of moves designed to assert control over territory—basically the entire South China Sea—covered by China's "nine-dash line" claim. Ongoing island reclamation activity in both the Paracel and Spratly island chains will provide China with landing strips and expanded harbors from which to further pursue historical claims to the nine-dash line territory. Such perceived provocations have also generated growing concern among other claimants, particularly Vietnam and the Philippines, as well as extra-regional actors in the United States and Japan, over both China's maximalist objectives and unilateral approach to pursuing these objectives.

China, of course, is not the only actor in East Asia that is pursuing its territorial claims, nor are all territorial disputes in the region between China and its nervous neighbors. According to an IHS Jane's Defence Weekly report from April 2014, Russia is in the process of enhancing its military presence on the Kuril Islands and Sakhalin Island—both claimed by Russia and Japan—while Japan's normalization of its defense and security policy has explicitly focused on reinforcing and exercising capabilities designed for the defense of Tokyo's claims in the East China Sea.

Two types of technological development are also intensifying border and boundary disputes in East Asia. New and social media-fueled hyper-nationalism in northeast Asia is driving harsh and escalating rhetoric, provocative actions, and, critically, zero-sum thinking about the full range of regional contested border and boundary issues. This thinking constrains political alternatives for moderating foreign policies; reduces domestic political incentives for engagement and compromise; and accelerates decision-making timelines.

In addition, new technologies that enhance precise demarcation of the maritime borders of most concern in East Asia can also contribute to geopolitical tensions by eliminating ambiguity over borders. Asian states have leveraged the utility of ambiguity in the past to avoid bilateral escalations. Enhanced clarity about boundaries can serve to incite rather than dampen tensions, especially when they intersect with newly enmeshed and new media-fueled nationalisms and resource competition. Overlapping territorial claims are likely to prevail in this environment, a dynamic that can contribute to miscalculation, crisis, and conflict.

SECURITY AND INVESTMENT IMPLICATIONS

Struggling sovereigns and contested boundaries will have direct consequences for national security and defense communities throughout the world as well as for corporate enterprises seeking to safely, responsibly, and effectively operate in complex and fluid geopolitical environments. Three implications seem particularly relevant to both national security/defense community organizations and private companies.

Border and physical security

Because borders and boundaries are increasingly challenged and porous and, as a result, frequently do not contain crises geographically—the Arab Spring, for example—nations are focusing more assets and resources on securing borders and ports of entry to the greatest degree possible. Similarly, companies operating in unstable or insecure areas are vulnerable to fast-moving physical security threats to assets, personnel, and corporate interests, especially those companies supporting critical infrastructure and natural resource development.

The result is growing demand among both public and private sector organizations for a novel suite of command, control, communication, computer, intelligence, surveillance, and reconnaissance (C4ISR) capabilities previously most commonly associated with defense requirements.

Unmanned and autonomous systems, remote sensing, cybersecurity, sophisticated command, control, and data integration systems, and effective security training, among other capabilities, are in demand to help monitor borders and fence lines, mitigate risk, track threats, and collect vital operational intelligence.

New dimensions, new maps

The development of new or more robust analysis about, and monitoring of, both possible fault lines within states and communities of interest and the networks that connect these communities to other at-risk states or localities are critical in understanding and responding to environments in which challenges—violent or otherwise—to current control of territory or resources are increasingly likely.

Network, influencer, and nodal analyses are especially useful for both public and private organizations seeking to identify pathways of crisis contagion. Effective application of these tools allows enterprises to develop a nuanced understanding of tribal, social, business, and influence networks within and across at-risk geographies. Assessing online influencers—given the important role that globalization and information technologies play in current border challenges—is also key to identifying and potentially influencing networks of interest.

IHS leverages social media monitoring tools to perform analyses of social media activity during and in advance of sovereign crises. For example, our team retroactively examined over 3.5 million tweets—about 10% of the total potential data set—posted in the month before and during large anti-government protests across Turkey in late May and early June 2013. IHS assessed this data to develop an understanding of general sentiment, geo-locate especially intense pockets of sentiment, and assess the most influential social media centers of gravity during the protests, which communities cohered around them, and how they connected to other online influencers.

Social media intelligence (SOCMINT), especially in conjunction with a more in-depth analysis of network links and fault lines, provides enterprises with valuable indicators and warnings of changes in the intensity, trajectory, pace, and geographic focus areas of unfolding challenges. These types of analyses can also allow national security and corporate entities to better influence or, as in the case of extremist, criminal, or weapons proliferation networks, disrupt operations and decision making in these networks to protect assets, infrastructure, and interests.

Anticipating 'sudden' shifts

Shifting borders and boundaries raise the possibility of fundamental and potentially sudden shifts in political, geopolitical, and security landscapes. Companies and national security and defense agency strategies, interests, and assets may be compromised, threatened by, or vulnerable to shifts in control of territory and resources, which can subsequently constrain strategic and operational alternatives and force these communities into uncomfortable or undesirable alternatives.

For the private sector, contested, uncertain, or newly drawn borders or newly acquired or lost resources (human and physical) can not only affect the physical security of personnel and assets, but also have implications on tax and contract regimes, regulatory and administrative environments, payment terms, and other critical elements affecting operational efficiency and business viability. For example, the growing tendency toward absolute claims of sovereignty and eschewing of multilateral dispute resolution mechanisms in Southeast Asia, in particular, can complicate the ability of a range of commercial companies—transportation, shipping, energy, infrastructure—to finalize deals "without prejudice" in which sovereignty can be put aside.

Predicting the exact timing, dimensions, and trajectories of these shifts is exceedingly difficult. Even when risks are identified, crafting effective responses is difficult. However, both private sector and national security organizations can benefit from incorporation of enhanced strategy and decision-making support tools and capabilities that can help organizations anticipate plausible security, political, geopolitical, and business risks associated with shifting and contested borders. These capabilities can also help organizations develop strategies and operational solutions for mitigating these risks when they arise.

Advanced and alternative analytical techniques—such as scenario planning and tabletop gaming—can help offset uncertainty by openly incorporating it into planning and decision-making processes. These tools are designed to posit and explore alternative environments and challenge core assumptions, such as the sovereignty and efficacy of central governments, buttressing risk mitigation strategies. Full incorporation of effective alternative analysis techniques can help decision makers identify and monitor signposts that specific challenges and risks are more or less likely to come to pass and develop hedging strategies designed to respond to crises as they unfold.

Originally developed and implemented most intensively by national security planners—notably Herman Kahn, who frequently employed the methodology to determine pathways to, and outcomes of, nuclear conflicts in the 1950s—scenario planning has been utilized extensively and increasingly by corporations, most famously by Shell to help navigate the challenges of uncertain oil markets in the 1970s. A December 2012 survey of 77 European multinational corporations performed by Rene Rohrbeck of Aarhus University and Jan Oliver Schwarz of Germany's EBS Business School found that implementation of "strategic foresight" methods was becoming more widespread and that these methods were believed to add value through enhancing corporate capacity to perceive, interpret, and respond to change, precisely the types of capabilities required to anticipate significant shifts in control of territories and resources.

GLOBALIZATION, THE INFORMATION REVOLUTION, AND THE ISLAMIC STATE

The interaction of globalization and the information revolution is playing an important role in shaping sovereign challenges in the early 21st century in at least three ways.

First, globalization and the information technologies that support and enable it facilitate proliferation of advanced commercial, dual-use, and military technologies, providing more and better capability to a wider range of sub-state and non-state actors. Conflicts across the Middle East and North Africa have been fueled in part by the influx of new weapons through licit and illicit means as well as shadowy connections to external patrons

Second, the perception that globalization has created winners and losers is amplifying centre-periphery tensions within states.

Third, and most important, the information technologies and media that facilitate globalization also allow for enduring cross-border and diaspora connections and the coherence, hardening, and promulgation of ideologies and narratives—be they ethnic nationalist, extremist, nihilist, or something else entirely—that build momentum, credibility, and justification for tests of status quo borders and boundaries

For example, the Islamic State has engaged in an active, advanced, and effective new and social media strategy that was an important element supporting its rapid and unexpected advance across northern Iraq over the summer of 2014. The Islamic State live streamed the execution of Iraqi soldiers in June 2014 as well as its advance through Iraq—which was abetted by the collapse of an Iraqi army fully aware of the fate that awaited those who resisted the Islamic State—demonstrating the futility of resistance to the Iraqi army as well as the glory of victory to potential recruits.

Kurdish population growing faster than ethnic Turks

Turkey, like much of the rest of the Middle East, is in the midst of significant demographic shifts that are likely to have implications for the country's societal, economic, and political future and highlight the significance of Kurdish cross-boundary links with Kurdish populations in Iraq, Syria, and Iran (which is itself confronted by historic drops in fertility rates).

According to Turkey's official statistics organization, TurkStat, the country's population growth rate reached an all-time low of 1.2% in 2012, while the fertility rate for all of Turkey stayed below replacement levels. However, all 10 provinces with the highest fertility rates in 2012 were in eastern Turkey, where Kurdish populations are highest, while fertility rates in the rest of the country were significantly below replacement levels.

These trends suggest that by the middle of the 21st century, the Kurdish population in Turkey will grow in both an absolute sense and as a markedly larger proportion of the Turkish society, its workforce, and its pool of military recruits.

Such an important demographic shift is already having—and will continue to have—implications for Turkish policies toward both its Kurdish minority and the large and linked Kurdish populations across Turkey's borders in Iraq, Syria, and Iran.

BOUNDARY ANXIETIES: BETWEEN BORDERS AND BELONGINGS

Watching the Queen of England's Jubilee celebrations on a television set in Germany qualifies without a doubt as one of those 'weird global media events' which networked communications bring to us with increasing regularity. Since their defeat at the hands of the British in two world wars, and alongside other historical processes, particularly those of nation-state formation which decisively put to rest the last vestiges of feudalism and effectively abolished aristocratic rule, Germany it seems has developed a compensatory passion, bordering closely on fetishism, for the English Monarchy, and in particular the Queen who sits at its throne. Hence the Jubilee celebrations that unfolded over a number of days of activities in London, not only outside Buckingham Palace, but in many places and sites across the British Isles, were covered by the German media in close and meticulous detail.

Over four days it was possible to watch the live coverage of the music-concerts, the suburban street-parties and the Royal Family's appearances at numerous locations during the celebrations. The Queen's every movement was closely tracked, including her many changes of dress and outfit, the mood of the crowds was assessed and registered, and the constituent parts of the Commonwealth procession dissected and analysed in terms of their (in)adequate displays of national character and image. But even without the assistance of the precise and comprehensive German news commentary, the sheer sight of those thousands upon thousands of Union Jacks being waved in the Mall that long weekend in June brought home the realisation that the expiry date of the symbolic terrain of the nation-state — the flags, the anthems, the nationalistic fervor — notwithstanding the entity of the nation-state itself, seems, at times like this, a long way off indeed. This was simply one of the many spectacles of the 'perverse perseverance of sovereignty', as one of the other articles in this issue so succinctly puts it, which we are increasingly seeing in this contemporary context supposedly defined by the 'withering away of the nation-state'.

At that moment, from my location in a country that is very much one of the primary movers and shakers of the project of European integration, it was very easy to understand the reasons England announces so intransigently that it may be 'in' Europe, but it is not really a part 'of' Europe. As the crowds sang Land of Hope and Glory and the bands played God save the Queen, this small island defiantly announced to the world the nature of its national character and continuing independence 'from Europe', and at the same time the nature and definition of its continuing sovereignty. In Germany, surrounded by friends who regularly comment that the introduction of the common European currency, the Euro, has made them feel optimistically a part of something bigger than the nation-state from which they, as yet, continue to draw their citizenship, something which they acknowledge is rather ambiguously called 'Europe', or 'European culture', this display of nationalist chauvinism, and I think it is fair to call it that, seemed like a short, sharp reality check.

This display also made me think about that geo-political space called 'the new Europe' and its ability to offer some a transnational mode of being and belonging and the promise of overcoming the violent legacies of the nation-state, while at the very same time this space undergoes a process of effective border fortification and cultural homogenisation through the introduction of new EU anti-immigration legislation and amendments, and the popularity of extreme right-wing political movements demanding an ever more repressive and exclusive 'Fortress Europe'. On the one hand, it made me think of the *Aussiedler,* the ethnic Germans who are returning to Germany in the wake of unification, after their ancestors settled hundreds of years ago in Eastern bloc countries such as Russia and Poland, and who, in many cases, are confronted with their uncertain status (persecuted in the Soviet Union, and unwanted in Germany) and who, being neither Russian but not really German either, are condemned to float like ghosts in the borderlands of (national) identity. For many of these Russian-Germans, the category 'European' offers a legitimate form of belonging, and a way out of the impasse of an identity solely conveyed by nationality. On the other, though, 'the New Europe' as it is currently taking shape—closed, bounded and restrictive—seems to offer little refuge to the growing numbers of asylum-seekers arriving unwelcome at borders, living in refugee camps, facing often-violent forced deportations and expulsions and who, if they are lucky to have their claims for asylum actually heard and processed, must live with the alarming rise in racism and xenophobia taking place in all European cities. And finally, this somewhat perverse celebration during this mild European summer, made me also think uncomfortably of other perverse demonstrations of 'sovereignty', 'territorial protection and integrity', 'national pride and interest' closer to home, in Australia: the Tampa crisis, the detention-centres in remote locations, the so-called 'Pacific Solution'... The ironies of being an Australian teaching at a German university, specifically in a cultural studies program called Euroculture, a program directly concerned with the process of Transnationalising Europe, of taking Europe beyond the Westphalian model of sovereign power into a more open and ecumenical political future, were not lost on me either.

The French media theorist Jean Baudrillard once argued that Europe can no longer be understood by starting out from Europe itself. From my position as an Australian, located simultaneously both in and outside of Europe, this chapter seeks to explore the transformed roles and meanings of the 'border' and 'boundary' in the post-national order of Europe. It also considers the re-negotiation of inclusion and exclusion along lines of race and culture in the 'new Europe' and the current boundary anxieties taking place across the continent as it is transformed from one of colonial emigration to one of post-colonial immigration. The current crises taking place across nearly all the major cities of Europe are motivated it seems largely by the fact that the 'others' against which Europe has been traditionally defined are now inside its borders. In the present context many of the groups who were defined and racialised as 'non-European' are now in Europe and not only challenging the 'fictive ethnicities' of the nation-states in which they live — states historically premised upon the fiction of a national identity grounded in ethno-cultural homogeneity — but also by claiming the identity of 'European' at the same time as they maintain diasporic and transnational communities which reach beyond and outside of Europe, are also creating new configurations of identity and potentialising new powers of citizenship.

If Europe's historical position of dominance is inextricably linked with the processes of colonialism and imperialism through which it negotiated with the rest of the world, then this increasingly deterritorialised cosmopolitan space within its borders poses a potent challenge to many of the assumptions upon which these processes were founded. This contested space then, has the potential to actually contribute to the project Dipesh Chakrabarty has called 'provincialising Europe'. The post-national order of Europe, configured as a space where questions of identity, belonging, culture, language and representation must be articulated together in complex ways, has the potential to dismantle the singular concept of world-history in which Europe has a monopoly on the idea of the modern and on the political forms of modern sovereignty. While this approach appears at first glance unrealistically optimistic it is underscored by a certain pragmatism the realities of the current moment force us to confront. What is at stake here is how countries respond to and deal with the increasing difference, diversity and cultural heterogeneity within their borders. This crucial issue is also an ethical question: how do nation-states, founded historically on the premise of unity, commonality and sameness respond to the multiplicity of ethnicities and identities within their cities. The most fundamental issue at stake here then is about how Europe might move beyond the nation-state model of sovereign power. This model, which depended on a well-integrated social and political order, the grounding of the national community in a specific, delineated territory, and the effacing and assimilation of differences, cannot respond to the transnational complexities of the current moment of globalisation. Yet, in the present climate, the 'new Europe' appears to be simply reproducing the political and ideological machinery of the nation-state at a supranational level. In this situation, the role of borders and boundaries in enacting modes and inclusion and exclusion in the European sphere take on a primary significance.

From Imperialism to Empire

Over the last few decades, the globalisation of cultural and economic exchanges has undoubtedly intensified: the growth of communications systems, the globalising logic of capital, and apparatuses of command and control have linked the world into a complex whole, a dense matrix of mobility and circulation. This period of globalisation—a process involving a nexus of political, economic and cultural changes linked to the growth and spread of communication and transportation technologies, has redefined the relations between the nation-state and the forces of capital, transformed communities, and profoundly reshaped the connections between place and culture. With the current acceleration of globalisation, political and physical boundaries no longer serve to delimit the nation-state's 'natural' borders: the nation simultaneously exists and disintegrates amidst transnational allegiances and contestations, information vectors and flows of capital, cultures and labour power, and the generally increasing movement, both 'legal' and 'illegal', of people around the world. Inter-state and supra-national structures, along with a pervasive neo-liberalism, all short-circuit the legitimacy and autonomy of the nation-state.

In their recent project, *Empire,* Michael Hardt and Antonio Negri trace these global patterns of social organisation and describe the emergence of a new global form of sovereignty that gradually encompasses the entire world within its expanding, flexible frontiers. This new form of sovereignty is not tied to the system of modernity and to the territorial nation-state which very much existed at the core of this system, but to a new supranational and deterritorialising regime defined by constant flows of movement (of money, technology, people and goods) along global circuits of production and exchange. Against the territorial centres, borders and boundaries of nation-states, empire establishes an apparatus of rule and a spatial totality that modulates its reach and extension over new and different markets, spaces and identities, incorporating and using all within the expansion of its imperial command. The passage to Empire, they argue, emerges in the wake of the demise of the nation state along with the social and political principles upon which it was based and the nationalist ideologies of exclusion, division and containment it supported. Yet, as Hardt and Negri state, the 'decline in sovereignty of nation-states, however, does not mean that sovereignty as such has declined'. But before I go on to consider the Europe Union as a supranational space within the framework suggested, it is worth considering the political form of the nation-state, its role in European colonialism, and also the way in which this state-form was both exported by Europe, and became the geo-political normative premise by which Europe interacted with 'elsewhere'.

Outside Europe

The modern nation-state is characterised by three distinct elements: territory, peoples, and sovereignty. Over recent decades the meanings of the three terms have undergone considerable permutation and they no longer map so easily or neatly onto self-evident realities. As Hardt and Negri argue, the territorial boundaries, highly-integrated spaces of national identity and identification as a means of legitimation, and the political and military technologies of sovereignty defined by the modern system of nation-states were fundamental to European colonialism and economic expansion:

> Imperialism was really an extension of the sovereignty of the European nation-states beyond their own boundaries. Eventually nearly all the world's territories could be parceled out and the entire world map could be coded in European colours: red for British territory, blue for French, green for Portugese, and so forth. Wherever modern sovereignty took root, it constructed a Leviathan that overarched its social domain and imposed hierarchical territorial boundaries, both to police the purity of its own identity and to exclude all that was other.

In one most definitive sense, Australia is an historical product of this universalising project of European modernity and colonial expansion. It is a settler society and immigrant-based country, produced from successive waves of migration and settlement, from trade and colonialism, from the exploitation of both human and natural resources, and from entangled and overlaid vectors of mobility and movement. Despite the substantial non-European migration to Australia since the 1970s, mostly from South-East Asia, Australian culture and its peoples are 'demonstrably European', the product of a European-derived society and heritage.

Mainly as a result of this resolutely international past, and the legacy of a civil war between the white European settlers and the indigenous inhabitants, a war that has yet to be fully acknowledged and recognised as such, narratives of national culture and identity have become a salient site for working through the ambiguities, ambivalences and repressions that will consequently adhere to any proposed model of nationhood or national 'home'. Nations are narrated, and Australian identity has historically been played out according to the shifting narrative demands of a white, European self. Yet unlike more conventional forms of European nation-building, Australian national identity has had to negotiate a difficult path through two related yet opposing demands: enunciating difference—from the British Empire and more generally the Western World (Australia has always had a strong, though unrealised, republican tradition)—while simultaneously claiming sameness, unity and commonality (through an assimilation policy which stressed not only white identity but often also European identity, and in its guise as the White Australia policy excluded Asians and other 'non-whites'). White Australia carries with it this heritage of double displacement: a history of displaced Europeans who are neither wholly displaced nor wholly European, struggling to achieve settlement in an inhospitable land in the Antipodes—a geographic site already constructed as a semi-mythical space of imaginary longing and displacement—by various means that have included the violent displacement and dispossession of others.

An export of the project of European modernity, Australia constructed itself as a site of democracy and civilisation. Like all instances of European civilisation, however, this image is incomplete. In reality, it was founded on exclusion and repression, a historical process realised through regimes of brutality and inequality.

The land that the European explorers declared *Terra Nullius,* meaning literally, empty, vacant land, was actually far from empty: the traditional owners of the land were the many language groups within the Indigenous population. But it was already occupied in another way too: founded on the cultural and political assumptions of European colonialism, it was impossible for this land to exist outside of the principles of European modernity even if it was a space outside of Europe. As first a settler colony, and later as an independent nation-state, Australia was positioned firmly within the framework of European imperialism and reproduced its values and also its ideologies: namely, the universalisation of the nation-state as the most desirable form of political community. This is of course the political form whose unity can only ever be predicated on the imposed assimilation, containment, even eradication, of difference and complexity, of 'minorities', 'migrants' and 'foreigners', by the establishment of an imagined community that must be maintained through the performative work of nation-building, and through constantly-rehearsed anxieties of national identity, and also through the policing of borders.

Given it's geographical location, and strategic and economic position in the Asia-Pacific region, a European cultural identity for Australia now seems a strange misnomer. At the same time though, to define Australia as a European country forces one to negotiate Australia's anomolous geographic and ethnic position in an Asia-Pacific region which also continually reminds it that it is not Asian. Not only must Australia work through what it actually means to be South of the West, but also South of the East. Perhaps then, to recognise Australia as a European society is also to recognise its provincial qualities and limitations. This recognition has significance that extends far wider than Australia's borders however: it is simultaneously, a recognition that 'the West' is no longer simply European or European-derived. Modernity has become global.

But what do we actually mean when we talk about 'Australia', 'Asia', 'Europe' and the 'West'? After all, these sites are not natural entities but historically produced, homogenising categories which reflect the assumptions of the systems in which they were first created. As Ang has pointed out, the very idea of distinct, demarcatable regions of the world originated within a Eurocentric system of geographical classification, which then circumscribed in an asymmetrical relationship Asia and the East's negative *difference* from the West. As one Japanese theorist Naoki Sakai has recently pointed out, the West, is 'a name which always associating itself with those regions, communities, and peoples that appear politically and economically superior to other regions, communities and peoples'. Europe, likewise, is not just a geographical site, it is also an idea: an idea inextricably linked with the origins and myths of Western civilisation and indissociable from the haunting and violent encounters with its colonial Others.

These processes of conquest, colonisation, and empire formation, the settlement by Europeans of other parts of the globe, of nationalism and nationalist struggles, decolonisation and postcolonialism, constitute the terrain on which Europe constructed itself and its others. It is very much against this background that the current transformations in the global economic and political order are taking shape. And, it is against this backdrop that the 'new Europe' is emerging. But what exactly is this 'new Europe'? What can this Europe mean? Is there such a thing as Euroculture? Is it possible to speak about a European identity? What points of identification can it offer to its peoples? Nothing is less certain. It is though these very questions that address exactly how it is that Europe is to come to terms with the forces of globalisation that are reshaping the contemporary world system, and what kind of state-formation and identity it is that Europeans are imagining for themselves in this new world order?

FORTRESS EUROPE

Since the signing of the Maastricht Treaty in 1992, in and around the 'new Europe' we've seen a resurgence of nationalisms, along with the intensification of popular as well as institutionalised racism, and genocidal campaigns of ethnic cleansing. Since 1992, we've also heard much about a new space of collective belonging and identification, a transnational Euroculture able to transcend and also unite national particularisms and local and regional identities. The sense of being European has been invoked. But what does this mean exactly? Is there a difference between thinking of oneself as a "European" (a label once synonymous with that of being a white coloniser of nonwhite people's territories) and of being a member of an as yet unrealised European state or nation or people?. Like all identity categories, the category of European is slippery and difficult indeed. It is not a natural, unchanging category; it is a discursive nomination articulated by a range, of diverse, sometimes incompatible, discourses. It is subject to change and contestation and it has been mobilised, historically, in different ways to suit different political agendas. As Etienne Balibar has pointed out, until the middle of the 20th century, the principal meaning of the term 'European' refereed to groups of colonisers in the colonised regions of the world.

So, what kind of identity for Europe? The language of official Euroculture is significant here. The discourses we've seen so far have emphasised cohesion, unity, integration and security. A new European order is imagined in terms of an idealised wholeness, boundedness and containment. Conceived in this sense, difference is always problematic, a threat to coherence and integrity. This model of identity belies an inability to imagine Europe as anything other than the nation-state writ large. Some have suggested that focus should be on what have been called European 'core values'. A typical shopping list could perhaps include: democracy, private property, the market, Roman law, renaissance Humanism, Christianity, individualism and rationalism.

A number of solutions to the lack of a common European culture have also been proposed. There has been a concerted attempt to produce an overarching European identity that can articulate with the official identities of existing nation-states and also with the emergent identities of regions, a model of supra-national identity that can compete with the powerful appeal of national identity. The idea of an integrated Europe 'a common

European Home' emerged to express cohesion, community and 'unity from diversity' as the European Community struggled to build a coherent trading bloc. Although this was an attempt to create a new space of identity and interaction that could articulate identification across a number of scales (local, regional, national, transnational), the European House soon began to appear as simply 'Fortress Europe': closed, exclusive and bounded.

The supranationalist quest for a new Europe forces us however to rethink the nation-state, along with the system of modernity it both belonged to and represented. It may be a little premature to proclaim the withering away or disappearance of the nation-state, but it is certainly changing, and definitely in crisis. But, in the light of the old and new nationalist sentiments we hear every day, what exactly has changed? One of the defining characteristics of the nation-state and its nationalism was its racial and ethnic homogeneity, its insistence on integration and equilibrium. Yet with the increasing movement of people, communities and cultures through immigration and diasporic networks of labour, we now live in a world where all traces of homogeneity seem to have disappeared. The massive flows and migrations of people around the globe have not only redefined place-based identity, but have led to deterritorialised connections and attachments to multiple places, where people's lives transcend and are translated across specific boundaries and identities.

The history of the nation-state is one of territorial integrity and the 'invented traditions' of an imagined identity and unity. Yet national cultures and sovereign claims to national destinies have never been ethnically pure or able to successfully erase differences. What's more, this always already heterogeneous nation-state form is now being compounded by one of the largest, voluntary and involuntary mass migrations. In Europe, countries which are already the sites of diasporic spaces and transnational cultures that bypass the nation-state, are becoming inextricably 'multicultural states'. These changes have transformed Europe from a continent of emigration into a continent of immigration, an epochal change that has introduced an unprecedented cultural and ethnic heterogeneity—ethnically, religiously, culturally, linguistically— throughout European space. Many of the groups who existed historically as the Others against which Europe defined itself and who were previously racialised outside Europe, are now literally in Europe.

What we are seeing then are new forms of social organisation and new kinds of identity formation in the weakening of nation-states. Alongside the formation of new transnational political and economic entities and networks, therefore, there is then a corresponding transnationalism in the formation of identities and loyalties among various groups who do not regard the nation as the sole or principal source of identification. These go hand in hand with the formation of new solidarities (human rights groups, environmental groups, counter-globalisation movements) and new notions of citizenship. Major cities, as Saskia Sassen's work has demonstrated, have emerged as sites not only for global capital, but also for the transnationalisation of labour and the formation of transnational identities. The transnational encounters and connections and diasporic communities and cultures found in most global cities today, break the binary relation of 'minorities' and 'majorities', 'locals and 'foreigners' and are sustained in hybrid historical junctures.

So, economic globalisation promotes the flows of footloose transnational capital as well as strengthens the control of financial networks and corporations. But the same forces also produce increasingly deterritorialied transnational communities, cosmopolitan public spheres, and potentialise new powers of citizenship. The territorialising forces of colonialism and neocolonialism are now, in a sense, inverted, with the reverse flows of deterritorialised populations — mobilities driven to a great extent by political or economic necessity—disturbing the fixed identities of places and spaces. Transnationalism, therefore does not simply refer to the globalisation of markets and capital and transnational elites, but also to social and cultural relations which flow through transnational spaces. This 'transnationalism from below' as it has been called, is concerned with the social spaces and everyday practices of ordinary people as their lives transcends national boundaries and intersect with and are formed within the cultures of at least two nations. The complex cultural and political allegiances and politics of identity emerging from these disjunctures, however, is far from a simple happy hybridity, straightfoward fusion or cultural relativism. It is entirely a product of cultures and histories in collision and confrontation. We can consider the phenomenon of the Russian-Germans, which I mentioned at the start of this chapter, as another example which highlights the complexity of experiences of identity and belonging in the present period. These ethnic Germans from Eastern Europe are 'returning' to Germany in the wake of unification and the end of the cold war. The ancestors of these people settled several hundred years ago in Russia in response to an invitation to fill labour shortages, but were then persecuted as 'aliens' and 'foreigners' by Stalin, with many deported to camps in Siberia and central Asia. They say they are returning to their homeland. Yet many speak antique German dialects, and many others only speak Russian. Many return puzzled to find that actually-existing Germany is not like they imagined, and that they are not always welcomed back 'home' by their fellow German citizens. One German woman from Kazakhstan, arriving at Frankfurt airport, declared 'We are in heaven'. Another young woman however, complained (in Russian because she speaks no German) 'I thought I was coming to Germany ... Instead it's Turkey'.

This situation not only highlights the changing discourses of foreignness in Germany and the different ways the 'outsider' has been defined, but it also reveals the myths of origin and identity ('blood, soil and frontiers') enshrined and called into being by the nation-state. The predominant term conventionally used to denote the 'foreigner' was that of *Gastarbeiter.* This term has now largely disappeared from both official and popular discourse and has generally been replaced by the opposition between Germans and*Ausländer.* This term functioned largely as a synonym for the group most often assumed to be at the furthest cultural distance from Germany - the Turkish. In recent years, a further distinction has been made between *Ausländer* and *Asylanter* (asylum seekers). The arrival of Germans from the eastern 'new states' has further complicated these hierarchies of difference. Many locals feel increasing levels of resentment towards these*Aussiedler* who, unlike Turkish-German residents, can claim their 'blood tie' to German ethnicity and thus are immediately granted citizenship.

Thus we can imagine these new identity formations, this new cosmopolitanism of sorts, as a contested space that both reinforces and challenges the traditional divisions and hierarchies of the national order. We must not forget, however, that over the last few years the processes I've just been describing have been matched by the disturbing rise of ugly and chauvinist nationalisms, fundamentalisms of all kinds, and increasing xenophobia. World-wide, we are seeing more and more so-called 'tough measures' to deal with the 'undocumented': people without identity papers, asylum seekers, refugees, what Fanon so aptly described as the wretched of the earth. In Italy, Berlusconi pushes for new anti-immigration legislation; in Germany and Austia we hear the constant complaints about *Uberfremdung,* too many foreigners; in the Netherlands, politicians are campaigning on anti-Muslim, zero immigration campaigns. In France of course, we have seen the recent elections where the National Front, though defeated, gained one of the highest votes ever recorded by the far right. Everywhere we hear the rhetoric of 'swamping'. What is being asserted here is a defensive, cultural exclusiveness and fundamentalism, an aggressive assertion of places and nations as origins, as the sites of primordial identity and belonging. However nations and places, have never been closed, bounded and stable. Perhaps, as Marc Auge puts it, the reason why immigrants worry settled people so much is that they expose the relative nature of certainties inscribed in the soil.

The various fundamentalisms and nationalisms around us today, are of course racist and xenophobic, but they also have to be understood as the social and political protests of newly marginalised groups against the dominant political and economic order that excludes them from full participation in social life. Our contemporary theories and analyses appear in this context then to fall short of an adequate understanding of the ambiguities of the present moment in which societies that have constituted their own identities by, historically, dispossessing others, now find themselves subject to intensifying fear, anxieties and dilemmas of displacement. Now more than ever we're witnessing the specific tensions and fractures between the modern, nationalist state, and the claims of disenfranchised minorities, whose continuing presence in the cities of Europe disturbs the apparent coherence of the nation's claim to a universalist identity. In the Europe without borders, the loosening of internal borders has been accompanied by a tightening of external borders, and restrictive immigration controls, many of which are exempt from EU race equality directives and thus not yet subject to democratic regulation. What is at stake here then is the modes of inclusion and exclusion in the European sphere, as a political and economic sphere, but also as a sphere of communication, cooperation, responsibility and reciprocity between peoples. The difficulty many Europeans experience in coming to terms with the presence of non-whites and non-Western others in cities, towns and villages, and the hatred and violence that we've seen over the last few years, means that the capacity to live *with difference,* is one of most pressing questions for European culture at the beginning of the 21st century.

From Territory to Border

One of nationalism's specific traits is that it is necessarily territorial. Nationality is predicated on territoriality, and a national existence depends on the boundaries and borders of this territorial realm providing both the metaphorical and physical manifestation of sovereignty. Yet as Hardt and Negri argue, Empire does not establish itself through the imposition and regulation of fixed borders and boundaries, nor anchor itself in a territorial centre of power. Rather it takes the form of new supranational and deterritorialising form of sovereignty, which reconfigures the relationship between territories and states, governments and markets and, in the manner of perhaps its penultimate form and expression—the transnational corporation—redistributes power beyond the control of national boundaries.

Supranational entities of economic governance such as the EU, the World Trade Organisation, the IMP and the World Bank certainly appear then to confirm Hardt and Negri's thesis of the passage of the system of *international* nation-states to a new *global*order, the order of Empire. If the passage to Empire emerges, as they suggest, from 'the twilight of modern sovereignty', then it also emerges from the twilight of a particular conception of citizenship, and the ontological foundations of the national subject and national consciousness. If the bounded territorial authority of the nation-state provided ontological basis that enabled the exercise of a particular form of sovereignty, it also, to a great extent, provided ontological security for the state's national subjects. The demise of the nation-state as a secure ontological container for the organisation of social life and human activity, and as a site of emotional investment and belonging has profound consequences.

As the relationships between territory and border, space and capital become realigned, unprecedented levels of anxiety, insecurity and fear emerge precisely in that space of tension and fracture *between* nationalism and globalisation. For Etienne Balibar, these new relationships between states and global processes inevitably lead to a kind of ontological national insecurity: as the nation state moves from being a stable site of political agency and authority and a container of experience and belonging, 'masses of the population feel unsafe in the very state that is meant to protect them'. Within the transformed relations between the state and market, the government and private sector that globalisation necessarily entails, compounded with the nation-states abdication of its authority and withdrawal from society and social policy, 'all the conditions are present for a collective sense of identity panic to be produced and maintained'. As Balibar argues, although the most deprived and disenfranchised and most remote from power 'fear the state [but] they fear still more its disappearance or decomposition'. This situation, Balibar suggests, leads to a crisis of sovereignty and a crisis of political culture. But it also presents a challenge to rethink the very bases of the monolithic, egoistic and inward-looking nation-state, and to develop an open, responsible and ecumenical citizenship that can respond to the increasing interdependence of cultures in the current transational moment. It leads, above all, to the question of 'what the state is tending to become, how it is behaving, and what functions it is fulfilling in the European space... a space which, in particular cannot simply be reduced to the figure of a "territory"'. Balibar's work is significant here for suggesting that what is needed is a thorough reconceptualisation of the transfomed role, function and meaning of 'borders'. Although some of have proudly declared this a borderless world, less than ever does the contemporary global situation present a world without borders. As his important work shows, borders may be vacillating and may be becoming more capricious, but they are not disappearing. They are intensifying and being both 'multiplied and reduced in their localisation and their function, thinned and doubled, even becoming zones, regions and countries where people are forced to reside and live'. One of Balibar's most pertinent points in the context of this discussion, however, is his observation that it is the very relationship between the border and territory that is being inverted. Borders are no longer merely markers of the limits of sovereignty, borders around the space of the political or even demarcations of the 'edges' or outer limits of national territories. They are then 'no longer the shores of politics, but have indeed become—perhaps by way of the police, given that every border patrol is today an organ of "internal security"—*things within the space of the political itself*''. In this sense, border zones, where cultural differences must be confronted and negotiated, where inequities in rights and privileges are most visible, are not peripheral or marginal in any way; rather they are central to what it means to constitute a public sphere.

The system of Western modernity, along with the borders of the nation-states which conferred the political, military and administrative functions of sovereignty onto territory, is becoming irreversibly undone. But as Balibar's work on the fate of nation-state in Europe demonstrates, this situation precedes the Maastricht Treaty or the Schengen Accords or other political measures to create a European super-state. It comes primarily, he argues, from the transformation of networks of communication and transportation and the unprecedented levels of movement and mobility of populations along these networks. These changes have created: within each territory zones of transit and transition, populations "awaiting" entry or exit (sometimes for several years, sometimes in a periodically repeated fashion), individually or collectively engaged in a process of negotiation of their presence (that is, their political, economic, cultural, religious, and other rights) with one or more states.

As Brian Massumi has put it in another context, it is the very nature of the border that is profoundly changing in meaning: The individual is defined more by the boundaries it crosses than the limits it observes... Every boundary is present everywhere, potentially. Boundaries are set and specified in the act of passage. The crossing actualises the boundary - rather than the boundary defining something inside by its inability to cross. There is no inside, and no outside... Only a field of exteriority, a network of more or less regulated passages across thresholds.

It is this situation we are witnessing today with the movements of immigrants, asylum seekers and refugees. In the increasingly repressive and intolerant responses to asylum seekers all over the world, most notably in Australia and Europe, the state's increasing abdication of responsibility for social justice, as well as the social dislocations arising in the wake of rampant neo-liberal restructuring, are clearly evident. The arrival of groups from the peripheries of Empire (groups deemed redundant to capital expansion) into metropolitan centres of power, exposes the limits of Empire as a supposedly borderless, deterritorialised terrain, just as much as it exposes the theoretical limits of liberal political philosophy. Global migration challenges the practices of exclusion through which the nation-state constituted itself and its 'others', in exactly the same manner as it lays bare the highly uneven and contradictory nature of global interconnectedness, where flows of goods, services and capital and technologies are encouraged while at the very same time new borders and boundaries appear to discipline, restrict and contain the movements of certain groups. The words of Margaret Thatcher sum up the pernicious nature of this uneven mobility and development quite starkly: 'we joined Europe to have free movement of goods... I did not join Europe to have free movement of terrorists, criminals, drugs, plant and animal diseases and rabies and illegal immigrants'.

The EU is a case in point. At exactly the same time as it has relaxed its internal borders to encourage economic integration it has tightened its peripheral borders. This has also gone hand in hand with a racialisation, criminalisation and dehumanisation of the outsiders beyond these boundaries, who, as Thatcher's words indicate, constitute the collective waste and extreme 'otherness' of European civilisation. In her words, we can see these dynamics clearly, as those who are deemed excess and redundant are spatially restricted and condemned to the zones of systematic underdevelopment, poverty and inequality actually produced *within* and *by* the networks of globalised world economic system. Similarly, the decline of the nation-state as the homogenising container of experience has in no way altered the divide between 'majorities' and 'minorities', 'locals' and 'foreigners' which was at its core. Indeed these divisions and exclusions, and the hierarchies between cultures they represent, appear to be reproduced and multiplied at the level of the post-national or supranational community that the European Union is aspiring to become.

The ontology of the nation-state, its particular logic of identity that depended upon the elimination of difference and complexity and the maintenance of firm boundaries against foreigners, strangers and aliens, indeed anyone seen to contradict the image of an homogenous national identity and primordial unity, is inadequate to the times of transnational communities and the responsibilities to those outside our borders. It is this logic of identity, with its fearful and anxious, self-enclosed and egoistic way of being and belonging that went hand in hand with the nation-state and which is now being reinvigorated as a response to the decline of its power and authority. As Andreas Huyssen has argued, the modern, with its dialectical dynamic of inclusion/exclusion, of identity constructed through negation, has been very much an 'adversarial space', always manifest with and defined by, an 'anxiety of contamination by its other'. At a time when boundaries are virtual and continually fluctuating, identity posed along the lines of a limitation or exclusion as constitutive makes, Massumi states, 'a dwelling of the derivative'. The empty container of national identity as bounded, situated and defined by its negation of others, has then no alternative other than to become fortress-like, offering a temporary oasis of relative stasis, 'a local reterritorialisation, guarded frontiers in an uncertain landscape'

Conclusion

In considering the possibilities and the limits of European integration, questions of identity, of collective and cultural identity are paramount. Perhaps the most pressing questions are how do these officially sanctioned versions of Euroculture and EuroIdentity accommodate the large numbers of migrant and diasporic populations and communities now living in the continent? How do these political and economic institutions reflect and relate to the new ethnicities and identity formations that emerge when cultures interact and become entangled? How can the European right to citizenship be in any way compatible with the social and economic realities of globalisation, and yet exist without the closure of national identity or of other fictive ethnicities? Can any of this actually be possible?

There is a quasi-mythical remark by Jean Monnet, one of the 'founding fathers' of the project of European unification: 'If we were beginning the European Community all over again, we should begin with culture'. Monnet's remark has achieved the status of a cliché in European academic and political circles. It acknowledges the fanciful and dangerous idea that something called European identity or European culture could be willed into being overnight, produced spontaneously by the single market or the requirements of a banking system or by a common currency. In essence, European integration has been motivated primarily by the economic and political necessities of global capitalism, guided and shaped by the interests and aspirations of political elites and economic imperatives, but at the same time it cannot successfully rest upon a conception of culture and an understanding of social identitification, identity and belonging so shallow, abstract and bureaucratically determined.

Monnet's remark, despite its nature as an empty rhetorical gesture now constantly cited in an almost meaningless fashion, still serves to highlight the problems that emerge when societies are based solely upon economic principles and considerations, where market forces reorder social life, stripping of it social meaning and turning it into flows of profit and loss in circulation. Free-market capitalism can't provide a meaningful sense of identity, except for the identity of the consumer. Nor can it offer solutions to the social and economic insecurity that globalisation creates. Governments embracing global capitalism must recognise the insecurities, and then the spiralling sets of fears and anxieties they give rise to, which are created when stable social structures are systematically dismantled and when states, in effect, withdraw from societies. Global capitalism may still need the state to some extent, but it no longer really needs the nation. But the old contradiction between the idea of the nation as an economy, and the nation as an ethno-cultural formation, still lingers. It is a contradiction we see appearing in France today, with Le Pen's attacks on North Africans and other migrant groups, millions of whom were accepted in the 1950s and 1960s precisely for economic reasons (labour shortages) but who are even today still being defined as existing outside of an exclusively defined ethno-cultural conception of the nation.

Since cultural diversity is, without question, the destiny, indeed the fate, of the modern world, as Stuart Hall, the black-British theorist puts it, complex questions of cultural identity and issues of social and political rights are therefore crucial. The incommensurabilities of cultural difference and the rights of citizenship must be reconciled if Europe can be anything other than just an enlarged national community. As Hall has argued, the 'more one believes in Europe, or the more the question of Europe appears to be a contested concept worth struggling over and around, the more important are the questions of which Europe, and of what is European culture, and whose European identity, and which version of European modernity? Indeed it is also the question of how and whether it might ever be possible to be both black and European'. Or indeed Muslim and European.

In this important sense then, the issue is about how Europe might move beyond the nation-state model of sovereign power.

The somewhat unfortunate naming of Europe as 'the space of freedom, security and justice' perhaps doesn't bode well. This model, which depended on a coherent and homogeneous social and political order, the grounding of the national culture in a specific, delineated territory, and the attempted elimination of differences, cannot respond to the complexities of the current transnational moment. In the increasingly borderless world of globalisation what is now needed are new images of sovereignty, identity and belonging which are adequate to the plurality, heterogeneity and mobilities of the new global context. What is now called for is the need to come to terms with other cultures and cultural differences, communities and nations. In the context of the changing world order, there is a need to recognise that a community's obligations extend beyond itself. Europe has always been a cosmopolitan project, tied to the destinies of others, variously defined, all over the world. And it has always been connected to cosmopolitan projects, to Imperialism, to dividing up the world and expanding 'civilisation', and now to building the world's biggest single economic and political bloc in the 21st century. The challenge now though is for a cosmopolitan project*within* Europe, for an embrace of multicultural difference and diversity, for a recognising of the discrepant cosmopolitans, the nonaligned transnational identities, cultures and communities struggling for an existence within and against nation-states and new economic divisions and markets. The challenge is to acknowledge the increasing interdependence of cultures, the complicated entanglement and interconnectedness of an increasingly globalised world. It is also to recognise the responsibilities and obligations that this interconnectedness entails.

As Balibar has argued, 'what is currently at stake does not consist in a struggle for or against European identity in itself... the stakes actually revolve around the invention of a transnational citizenship that allows us to democratise the borders of Europe, to overcome its interior divisions, and to completely reconsider the role of European nations in the world'. Well, yes, that is quite a tall order. Perhaps more modestly, we could say that if the European project is to mean anything, if the system of nation-states and the symbolic and physical violence it depends upon, is ever to be replaced by a more open and ecumenical social and political culture, then these responsibilities and obligations must find expression in and through the creation of political and cultural institutions which themselves represent difference, heterogeneity and inclusiveness rather than borders and exclusion.

The challenge then is for a recognition of ways of belonging which are not closed, insular and unitary and which do not automatically presuppose a 'fixed address' or locate 'origins' as the only condition of possibility for attachment and identity, or depend upon the exclusion of 'others' beyond the boundaries of a secure and sovereign enclosure. It is also the challenge to be able to conceptualise a citizenship without myths of identity and without the fictive ethnicities and repressions characteristic of national identity and the national state. It is the possibility of inventing a new kind of identity and a new image of the relations of connection and reciprocity between transnational communities, a new way of conceptualising identity, and also a new kind of openness to the identities and differences of others.

6

Rethinking the Boundaries of the Nation and Identities

Throughout history the land that is now Zimbabwe has had its phases of migration. People have come and gone. But it wasn't until the last decade that the word 'Diaspora' was popularly assigned to migrants who left their country. 'Diaspora' doesn't just represent a people – the place itself it known as *kuDiaspora*. So people say, '*akaenda ku Diaspora*' (he went to the Diaspora). This word is now an integral part of the national vocabulary, complete with its own meanings and usages unique to Zimbabwe.

Becoming Zimbabwe opens in a way that underlines the newness of this idea. It cites Joshua Nkomo thanking the colonial state for defining 'once and for all, our national borders', and hence removing any obstacles in the movement towards 'an unquestioned national identity' (cited in Raftopoulos and Mlambo 2009, xvii). One of the book's main aims is to deconstruct the idea of any such obvious affiliation, and to track the contingency, alliances and contexts through which national belonging and citizenship were constructed. But the idea that national identity and citizenship might be plural rather than singular, or that significant populations of Zimbabweans might want a role in shaping Zimbabwean politics and development while seeking security elsewhere, and embedding themselves over the long term beyond territorial state boundaries, as implied by the notion of a diaspora, did not figure in older nationalist imaginaries. The significance of the adoption of this term is not debated in the book. Moreover the histories of state borders themselves, of borderland regions and border identities are not explicitly scrutinized, though addressing these might also add to the book's central goals, because the 'arbitrary' nature of colonial divides in other African contexts has long been a textbook explanation for the failures, rather than the achievements, of nationalism.

To contribute to this issue of *Critical African Studies*, which debates the themes, emphases and exclusions of *Becoming Zimbabwe*, my focus here is on the way the book treats national borders, histories of international migration and cross border movement. International migrations in and out of Zimbabwe have occurred on a grand scale at various junctures and, aside from their socio-economic consequences,

this mobility played an important role in the development of national consciousness, its meanings and content, and in the practicalities of achieving national liberation. But the legacies of these movements have also been important in shaping the connections and claims of the new diasporic communities formed during the recent crisis. By revisiting this aspect of the book's narrative, and adding a new strand that stretches beyond state borders, I hope to raise the following questions. If modern territorial nationalist ideas have developed partly through transnational flows of people, ideas and connections, is it possible to write a history of nationalism in a way that is sensitive to context, plurality and contestation through a narrative that is restricted by state borders? By confining the narrative in this way, does one inadvertently reinforce the idea of a natural and singular national unity and belonging? If the story were to be stretched to give weight to other contexts, what kind of narrative or narratives would or could emerge?

To rethink possible treatments of cross border flows in relation to histories of nationalism, I shall examine the book's approach to labour migrancy before turning to explore the politics of exile and solidarity during the liberation war. The essay draws on my own work to explore how the development of an international 'diaspora' during the recent crisis might be incorporated into the writing of Zimbabwean history. Before that, however, I begin with a brief explanation for why it might be useful to pay more attention to the borders themselves.

STATE BORDERS AND INTERNATIONAL LABOUR MIGRANCY

The idea that state borders were 'made' at the time they were drawn by the colonial state is true only at one level. Yes, they were the basis of the legal colonial state, conferred the boundaries of the law and limits of state powers, and hence also civic rights and responsibilities. But these limits were not demarcated on the ground immediately, and people initially continued to cross at liberty, using the new divisions to evade the law as much as to submit to it, and it took colonial states significant time to register populations as attached to one particular territorial space. Thus one can see the making of African state borders as a process that stretched over time rather than happening 'once and for all' when the colonial powers agreed on a dividing line. As a new body of scholarship on African borderlands has emphasized, African borders and the state powers they materialized came to have meaning only insofar as border people, other border-crossers and the population more generally came to invest them with such. The manner in which state authority has been made and remade in border regions is a topic for historical investigation rather than a fixed and unchanging set of practices, as I hope to have shown in *Crossing the Zambezi,* which is the story of the making of Zimbabwe's northern border. Though the imperial powers thought of this demarcation as a 'natural border' because it followed the course of the river, for the Tonga, Nambya and other people who lived in its vicinity, the Zambezi was a link rather than a dividing line, and social life stretched across the waters, uniting opposite banks. The process of imagining a national identity within state borders, and the idea of a fixed territorial division that also marked the boundaries of national space and citizenship, developed through the agency and practice not only of the colonial state and the country's leading African nationalist politicians, but required a shift in the ideas and practices of those who inhabited border regions and crossed the borders themselves.

The nature of authority along Zimbabwe's borders, and the utility of crossing or controlling trans-border flows of people and goods have changed dramatically over time, particularly in the context of the liberation war and the recent crisis. Migrations over Zimbabwe's borders have occurred on a major scale, not only because the borders function as political and economic resources for those who cross, but because the settler state and its postcolonial successor have a history of using state boundaries to foster, filter and gain economic advantage from international labour migrancy rather than to halt it completely.

There is a voluminous historical literature on internal and international labour migration because it was so important in the development of southern African political economies, and their associational and cultural forms. In the 1960s, there were heated debates over the causes and significance of the efflorescence of burial societies, ethnic and dance societies that had emerged following the First World War. Much emphasis was placed on the repressive context shaping these societies, and their connections to broader political mobilizations and the growth of Africanist ideas and associations, labour movements and Christianization across the Southern African region. Administrators treated these migrant organizations as threats, but social historians celebrated them as resistance, and analysed the diverse array of associations within one of two competing overarching narrative frames, treating them either as stages in the development of working class consciousness in the case of Van Onselen's *Chibaro* or as evidence of the rise of modern territorial nationalism. *Becoming Zimbabwe* draws on the rich detail of these earlier studies, but is careful not to replicate their teleology. Rather it gives much greater autonomy to cultural forms developed in urban spaces, emphasising the ongoing importance of urban/rural interactions and the compatibility between worker or national identities and local ethnic attachments, as well as stressing the discontinuity over time of political mobilization. Conveniently for a national history, *Becoming Zimbabwe* focuses predominantly on workers *within* Southern Rhodesian space (drawn from the countryside not only of Rhodesia, but also Zambia, Malawi and Mozambique). However, it also tries to make clear the importance of labour flows and experiences outside the country through the potted biographies of key unionists, religious and political leaders whose ideas were shaped intimately by their sojourns in South Africa, and their links to developing Southern African social, political and religious movements.

The book also discusses the legacies of these early migrations and their influence on the post 2000 exodus to South Africa. The generations of migrants that crossed the Limpopo over the course of the twentieth century shaped recent movements through the networks of personal connections they left behind, as well as through ideas and cultural forms that persisted over time. Even those former labour migrants regarded as 'lost' to relatives at home (and therefore to histories of nationalism) because they ceased to maintain ties, could now play a role, if they could be found, or even if they could not, as in their quest to merge in and gain rights, newcomers emphasised the old ties and sacrifices of past generations of workers who had helped to develop modern South Africa. There have been notable continuities in associational means of connecting with home across generations, particularly through burial societies, perhaps the most important and enduring of migrant organisations.

Aside from their self evident role in allowing for the repatriation of bodies, burial societies function to create new bonds, support networks and sociability among members trying to adapt to foreign environments. They have also played important political roles as 'front' organisations facilitating the smuggling of materials and political ideas to rural communities in repressive and wartime contexts. Of course, recent migrants seeking to make claims in South Africa have not only drawn on the connections created through labour migrancy, but have used other historical arguments too. They have tried to unravel older nineteenth century histories of mobility that preceded state borders, capturing memories of common ancestry through family genealogies or shared clan and ethnic names. These efforts to make claims are in some ways about the unmaking of Zimbabwean national identities – in so far as people have sought to become South African – though such claims are also about survival. But they are also about trying to secure civic and political rights in more than one state, and about rights to plural identities in which connections to home can be maintained through diasporic communities.

The echoes of past labour migrations also feature, albeit to a lesser extent, in the narratives of Zimbabwean communities in western destinations such as Britain (though this is not covered in the book). Dominic Pasura notes that men doing manual work who frequent Zimbabwean pubs and *gochi gochi* [barbeques] in the cosmopolitan, industrial cities of Birmingham and Coventry, used metaphors of regional migrant labour to make sense of their loss of status, and spoke of coming to Britain as '*Wenela*' – the acronym of the labour recruitment organization that served the South African mines. But the different class basis of the migrants involved means that collective memories of past labour migrancy within the region (and academic literatures on it) provide an inadequate lens through which to understand recent flows to western destinations, and the related cultural politics.

Unlike their compatriots who crossed the Limpopo, the middle class migrants who made their way to Britain have not generally formed burial societies. The organisations that have filled the role of assistance during bereavement or funds for burial at home, and which have provided sociability in often hostile British city spaces, are Zimbabwean church fellowships, which are centrally important to diasporic social life. As Beacon Mbiba has argued, where burial societies in Britain *do* exist, they bear little resemblance to the beerhall-based male drinking clubs of the older migrant labour literature: rather they function as investment clubs, where professionals with good jobs and mortgages in Britain have grouped together to try to profit from global and Zimbabwean financial markets, choosing the investment analysts and bankers among them to generate wealth for projects at home, politics of Zimbabwean diasporic communities in western locations one would not look to studies of regional labour migration, but to other literature, such as Michael West's work on the emergence of the black urban middle classes, or studies of faith and the Christianization of urban and elite cultures, such as Marja Hinfelaar's study of Methodist and Roman Catholic women's organizations and David Maxwell's work on Pentecostalism. These need to be extended to explore the beginnings of a shift in middle class horizons beyond national borders during the decade of structural adjustment, and the role that international mobility has played in developing ideas about class, status, respectability and accumulation.

In both regional and Western diasporic contexts, however, what is perhaps most notable is the strength of Zimbabwean diasporic patriotism – how flag-waving and national anthem singing have taken on a new social importance for those outside the country's borders. (It is perhaps notable that the anthem sung in diasporic gatherings is not the current Zimbabwean national anthem, but the old liberation anthem, *Ishe Komborera Afrika*, which was replaced in Zimbabwe following South Africa's democratic transition in 1994). To explain this attachment to national symbols amongst those living abroad, one needs to look both to contemporary exclusions and xenophobia in places of settlement, and to explanations for the longevity and strength of Zimbabwean nationalism, and hence to the legacies of Zimbabwe's liberation war.

THE POLITICS OF EXILE AND SOLIDARITY

In relation to this discussion of borders and cross border flows, suffice to say that the tension between exiles and the internal nationalist leadership is an important and recurring theme in histories of the liberation war, amongst the other cleavages that were shaped by cold war politics and military/civilian divides, by ideology, class, education, gender, generation and ethnicity. *Becoming Zimbabwe* offers a nuanced account of the war, which deconstructs ZANU(PF)'s 'heroic' versions and is sensitive to these multiple divisions, and to factionalism and violence. It also appreciates the powerful emotional legacies of the struggle, and the recurring rhetorics of revolution and anti-imperialism. The book does not, however, dwell specifically on the politics of exile or solidarity as themes, although the importance of the liberation movement's personal memoirs on which it draws. I am currently revisiting this topic, in a new research project undertaken collaboratively with the History Department at the University of Zimbabwe.1 Part of the study focuses on the exiles and students who moved to the West in the 1960s and 1970s, re-examining the politics of the solidarity networks in which they were enmeshed, relations with the political leadership within southern Africa, and the alliances and tensions between the Zanu, Zapu, ANC and other committees in London, Europe, USA, Soviet Union, German Democratic Republic and elsewhere. There is more to be said about the role and views of intellectuals who were key in forging these external linkages, about their experiences in the West and in Eastern block countries, about the social life and politics of the camps and exile communities in Zambia and Mozambique. These topics have not been explored in comparable detail to the extensive literature on guerrilla operational areas or protected villages within Zimbabwe. Yet the internationalism of the struggle has had important legacies in terms of post-independence foreign policy and diplomacy and the formation of current diasporic communities. Understanding this history will, of course, depend partly on people's willingness to talk, and trying to conduct interviews with prominent exile figures of the nationalist generation has provided repeated reminders of self-censorship and politicization, and of how key aspects of liberation war experiences remain un-spoken and perhaps unspeakable in the current political context.

Becoming Zimbabwe alludes to the legacies of the internationalism of the struggle, in its treatment of post-2000 diasporic claims-making. The language of exile and solidarity, and the idea of brotherhood in the struggle against illegitimate racist regimes, have been invoked by Zimbabweans in South Africa to make claims to belonging, support and protection. In the UK context too, such legacies are apparent: the Vigil outside Zimbabwe House in The Strand in London, initiated by Zimbabwean activists in 2002, was inspired by Anti- Apartheid Movement precedents, and there are many direct continuities in terms of the people involved, and the strategies and nature of diasporic political activity. In Britain, however, it is not only the legacy of the old solidarity movement that has been important for diasporic claims-making. Historical connections with white Rhodesia have also been important in creating political space. These ties can help explain sympathy for Zimbabweans among the UK's conservative as well as its liberal establishment, such that the otherwise xenophobic, popular tabloid *The Daily Mail* has sometimes been sympathetic to Zimbabweans in Britain, as it cannot decide which it hates most – Mugabe or asylum seekers.

THE CRISIS OF THE LAST DECADE: CREATING A 'DIASPORA'

Becoming Zimbabwe provides a nuanced discussion of Zimbabwe's crisis of the last decade. Appropriately, it provides a narrative that analyses the dramatic changes within Zimbabwe itself, which is an important context for the formation of new diasporic communities. I want to extend the discussion by thinking further about the significance or otherwise of the adoption of the term 'diaspora', which is not analysed in *Becoming Zimbabwe,* and by emphasising the dual contexts that shape diasporic identities, which are also a response to the contexts within the countries where Zimbabweans have settled. The book analyses movements beyond national borders simply in terms of migration and displacement and the pressures generated by the Zimbabwean context. Moreover, when the term diaspora is used in the book, it is deployed in a manner that replicates Zimbabwean popular discourse.

As I argued in *Zimbabwe's New Diaspora,* Zimbabweans are not alone in indigenizing the term, they are part of a broader trend of migrant groups defining themselves as diasporas to claim recognition. The notion of 'diaspora', like that of the 'nation', needs to be understood as the outcome of historical, political and cultural processes rather than as a reified, natural essence – the meaning and composition of a diaspora is fluid, the interests represented and people included are neither natural nor stable over time. Yet Zimbabwean discourse about 'the diaspora', which is repeated uncritically in the book, uses the term in an essentialized manner. Zimbabweans have appropriated the term as a noun rather than an adjective, often in capitalized form, as in Magaisa's article cited at the outset, which talks of 'the Diaspora', or people being 'in the Diaspora', as if it were an ethno-national group or a country itself. (Some leading scholars in diaspora studies do likewise, such as Sheffer, who claims diasporas are 'neither invented not imagined'.) As a result, the term can retain the overtones of a racialised epithet, and an exclusive and naturalised understanding of diaspora as a straightforward extension or scattering of the nation beyond national borders (in some instances, without an actual homeland as a point of reference). The danger of this understanding of diaspora is not only that it masks instability over time, in terms of membership, internal differentiation or complex relations with the homeland, but that it can reproduce fixed, unquestioned and sectional readings of national and diasporic community.

As *Becoming Zimbabwe* recognizes, the country's new diaspora has been highly politicized, and the book explores diasporic engagement with homeland politics (though it has nothing to say about the dual fronts typical of diasporic political effort, important elements of which have been directed at attaining rights in countries of settlement). As Brian Raftopoulos has argued, 'Diaspora activism opened up new fronts in the fight for democratization in Zimbabwe', and networks of opposition party (Movement for Democratic Change [MDC]) branch committees were quickly established that worked with Zimbabwean civic and community organizations overseas to raise the profile of ZANU(PF) human rights abuses and to pursue the goal of political transition at home. At the same time, Mugabe and ZANU(PF) consistently cast 'the diaspora' as disloyal 'puppets' of British and Western imperial interests. In contrast to past generations of exiles, the economic dimensions of the crisis in Zimbabwe meant that this new diaspora developed a centrally important economic role, and as the Zimbabwean economy imploded, remittances became essential to the survival of those left behind. Yet hostile relations between diasporic communities and the Zimbabwean government turned governmental efforts to lever diasporic finance (such as Gideon Gono's Homelink scheme)2 into dismal failures.

At its most straightforward, the term 'diaspora' simply means Zimbabweans abroad. Diaspora political campaigns have often used the term in this way to include the widest possible constituency of Zimbabweans outside Zimbabwe. While many diasporic activists are political exiles who have sought asylum, Zimbabweans abroad include people in a broad range of circumstances, whose reasons for leaving were varied, and who left at different times. Diaspora politics has also (controversially for many recent exiles) incorporated Zimbabwean migrants from the 1960s and 1970s and their children, some of whom have never lived in Zimbabwe. The term diaspora has the advantage of downplaying internal differences and rendering irrelevant the state binaries that divide 'economic migrants' from 'political refugees' in host countries.

Although 'diaspora' is often used interchangeably with the term exile, the two are not the same. Both pre-date the modern bureaucracies that produced the categories of refugee and asylum-seeker, and both are aestheticizable and prone to romanticization. But 'exile' can be individualistic and forefronts the act of banishment, while the notion of diaspora is intrinsically collective and can imply a degree of choice. While being in exile suggests little about relations with the hostland, the term diaspora implies a degree of embeddedness in the country of residence (even if it clearly can also suggest estrangement), helping to explain why diasporic demands for recognition and rights are typically made on a dual front. As the formation of a diaspora implies a protracted separation from home, it can also convey ambivalence about the reality of return. Indeed, some Zimbabweans have explicitly rejected the label 'diasporan' in favour of 'exile' on these grounds.

The term diaspora has also gained elite connotations in the Zimbabwean context. This is evident in the tensions between those 'in the Diaspora' (particularly but not only those who are in the West) and those who stayed behind – a relationship that Magaisa characterises as 'love/hate'. Raftopoulos emphasises the political dimensions to this tension and describes how those still at home 'have criticised Diaspora activists for being out of touch with the political reality on the ground ... or for being cowards who have run away from the frontline of the struggle against authoritarianism'. But Stephen Maimbodei, writing in *The Herald,* emphasises wealth and status, arguing that '"The Diaspora syndrome" has replaced the "been to" syndrome of a previous generation who had studied or trained in the west'. But both new and old labels are selective, he complains: '"my father, who worked as a migrant labourer in Malawi and South Africa, was never called a "been to". *Today's "been-to", or Diasporan, is bringing immense economic benefits to their families ... diasporans are now the new buyers and owners of property'*. The status attached to the term diasporan also emerges clearly through contrast to the meanings of 'migrant', 'refugee' and 'asylum seeker' in countries of settlement, which are related to a range of dehumanizing and criminalizing labels reflecting hostile and xenophobic receptions. As a self ascription, 'Diasporan' is attractive – it implies a certain level of consumption and education, a familiarity with technologies such as the internet and mobile phones, as well as responsibilities and obligations, both towards family and dependents, but also in the political sphere through civic engagements to extend the boundaries of political community both *in situ* and at home.

This emergence of the idea of 'the Diaspora' as a means of talking about the collectivity of Zimbabweans abroad can mask internal conflicts and tensions. Zimbabweans abroad have not spoken with a singular voice, nor have they found it easy to unite, or to forge shared, liberal imaginations of the nation. Much diasporic activism has explicitly aimed to contest ZANU(PF)'s narrow and commandist version of nationalism, based on ideals of rights, the rule of law, democracy and inclusiveness. Yet diasporic politics has often failed to achieve the cosmopolitan and progressive versions of 'diasporic space' invoked by academic writers such as Avitah Brah. Rather, Zimbabwean diasporic politics might be better characterised as a mixture of progressive civic politics, frustrated exile politics, and fractious identity politics. Essentialized expressions of identity have flourished and political divides at home have been exported. The suspicion and instability of diaspora politics not only replicates the main political division between ZANU(PF) and MDC, but also the internal factionalism of the MDC,3 which intersects with broader ethnic and racial divides. The work of homeland and hostland security agencies has also worked to create suspicion and hostility.

THE TRANSITIONAL GOVERNMENT AND DIASPORIC REPOSITIONING

The signing of the Global Political Agreement and formation of the unity government between ZANU(PF) and the two MDCs in early 2009, altered the relationship of hostility between homeland and diaspora populations, and has ushered in a new rhetoric of engagement. There has been an apparent convergence of interests between 'the diaspora' and the Prime Minister's office of the unity government. The latter has headed up diaspora engagement initiatives and started to woo the diaspora, beginning with Morgan Tsvangirai's tour in June 2009, when he called on the diaspora in the UK to 'come home' and help rebuild Zimbabwe. Although he was memorably heckled and booed off the stage in London's Southwark Cathedral, the tour was an important watershed in relations with the diaspora. Subsequent MDC Ministers have been more careful in what they say – they have repeated the call for involvement but have emphasized that this can be achieved from a distance, without the necessity for people to physically come back, arguing that it is possible to engage in Zimbabwe's reconstruction without actually being in Zimbabwe. As Dominic Pasura and I have argued, the new language of engagement is phrased in technical discourses of development and reconstruction, and is dominated by debates over financial investment and the harnessing of skills. It has also been shaped by Western governmental and donor interest, and related budget lines for diaspora engagement.

This context has revealed both the opportunities and tensions of the idea of a diaspora as an extension of a national community. Diasporic demands for recognition at home are being made in the context of a decade or more of separation, in which diasporic communities have been shaped not only by their relationship to Zimbabwe and the Zimbabwean crisis but also by the contexts in which they have settled. The influence of these hostland contexts has been critical: the hostile reception to Tsvangirai's calls for Zimbabweans to come home in 2009, for example, was produced by a divergence of interest between those with and without security in their countries of settlement. For those professionals with legal status and civic rights outside Zimbabwe, calls to return home posed no threat, but for those who are irregular or trapped within a poorly functioning asylum system, this call created deep insecurity as it raised the spectre of forced repatriation and the humiliation of deportation and failure, undermining their quests for rights outside Zimbabwe.

Those within the diaspora heading up calls for engagement with home are often explicitly non-partisan (they do not want to be seen as belonging to the MDC opposition groups or ZANU(PF)). Their conceptualization of both national and diasporic community is inclusive in party political terms, or perhaps more accurately, tries to be apolitical. The new developmental organizations they have created have an elite social base (with leaderships boasting a wealth of PhDs, LLMs, and firsthand experience of global business and financial markets). They want to be part of the action at home, are competing to be the prime point of contact between governments, and want to link responsibilities to Zimbabwe with recognition of their formal political rights at home, particularly voting rights. Despite the explicitly non-partisan rhetoric of those leading these calls, dual voting rights are clearly in the two MDC parties' political interest (as it is widely assumed that diasporic communities are in large part sympathetic to the opposition). The idea of diasporic unity can also downplay class-based internal conflicts, and there is thus a danger that diaspora engagement projects fostered through contacts between elites and governments over- emphasise the role and interests of wealthy and skilled diasporans, thereby ignoring both the interests of the larger numbers of people outside Zimbabwe's borders who are insecure, and the yet greater numbers of struggling, ordinary people left behind inside Zimbabwe.

Even within the main MDC-T grouping, there has been debate over how much effort to put into diaspora engagement beyond trying to secure voting rights. Professor Elphas Muknoweshuro, who holds the portfolio for MDC-T external affairs, has taken a critical stance towards the diaspora, arguing that there has been little impact felt at home beyond private remittances, and that diasporans have developed interests of their own that do not necessarily coincide with the party at home: So far we haven't felt the impact of it all. I take a very tough line with diasporans, and I have learnt to keep my mouth shut. They should not make too many claims – exaggerated, lofty claims. They are there to look after themselves, they have their own reasons for leaving their country ... We feel we're being abused, our party, by people like that [those asking the MDC to support asylum claims]'.

One member of the smaller MDC grouping made similar criticism, particularly of those based outside the Southern African region, arguing that when he had tried to raise funds in Britain, 'they'd always have money for a round of drinks, but when it comes to donations, they'd tell you first we need to put in an application for a grant...'.

Clearly, these on-going debates over constitutional reform, diaspora voting rights and dual citizenship, are far from resolved. It is unclear how diasporic views (or indeed how the results of the domestic outreach on constitutional reform) will be synthesized and incorporated into the process of drafting a new constitution. While it is unsurprising that ZANU(PF) is against dual citizenship, it is more remarkable that there appears to be popular resistance to the idea of dual citizenship more broadly within Zimbabwe among sections of the population. In Matabeleland South, for example, where most households have relatives in South Africa or Botswana, members of the Constitution Select Committee (COPAC) outreach teams noted how members of the public repeatedly expressed hostility to dual citizenship, articulating their views in terms of patriotism, and emphasizing that those who are outside Zimbabwe's borders have developed interests of their own that differ from those at home. Remittance studies have also deflated some of the exaggerated claims about the universal benefits of private remittance flows, showing their greater contribution to middle class/elite households than to high density urban dwellers, while studies of rural areas argue that remittances are often inadequate to meet the needs of poor households. In rural Matabeleland, the Solidarity Peace Trust showed that families with relatives in South Africa frequently associated diasporic kin not with wealth but criminality or abandonment, and complained at length of the problems created by returning relatives who were unsuccessful, or returned home only in coffins.

Conclusion

The scale of movement beyond Zimbabwe's borders during the recent crisis, the instability of the new power-sharing arrangement and the certainty that economic reconstruction cannot happen over night, all mean that debates over the character and role of new diasporic communities, and how they relate to homeland and nation are likely to persist beyond the short term. The importance of remittances to many households, the slow reconstruction of education and other public services, and the persistent political uncertainties of the unity government, mean that families are likely to continue to try to exploit the opportunities of straddling countries and continents for the foreseeable future. Indeed it may be significant that many of those who have returned to Zimbabwe over the last few years during times of persistent political instability, are those with the security of passports or rights of residence elsewhere. Returnees who have felt it is safe to come back are diverse: they include those who have joined an international NGO workshop economy that can lead on to jobs on an international circuit, those who have accumulated significantly and have the necessary connections in Zimbabwe to run businesses, and those who have failed and been deported (authors interviews August and December 2010). For most people, however, the political uncertainties, the shortage of secure work, and the lack of funds and connections mean that the context is not conducive to return.

In this essay, I hope to have shown that we need to subject this new 'diaspora' and 'long distance' nationalisms to the same degree of scrutiny as their domestic counterparts. We should follow the example *Becoming Zimbabwe* has set for a discussion of nationalism that is 'tolerant and is a continuing process of questioning and re-examination' (Morgan Tsvangirai, cited by Raftopoulos and Mlambo 2009: backcover), in which the idea of an intrinsic national unity is deconstructed and subjected to the lessons of contingency, historical agency and context.

The aim of this discussion was to highlight the influence of contexts and experiences beyond territorial borders, and the ways they have contributed to the history told in *Becoming Zimbabwe*. The importance of transnational dimensions to Zimbabwean history has been clearly underlined by the most recent phases of cross border displacement, which have produced diasporic communities mobilising for recognition both at home and in their countries of settlement, whose remittances have become a vital source of survival for many households. These new diasporic communities have been shaped not only by the context of the immediate Zimbabwean crisis, and by the legacies and cultural memories within Zimbabwe of past cross border movements. They have also been shaped by the receiving contexts, and the ways in which past connections have been remembered by others beyond state borders.

My final point thus returns to the question raised at the outset. Is it possible to incorporate past cross border movements and new diasporic communities adequately within a national history, however open it is to lessons of pluralism, contestation and contingency, and to broader regional and international influences? Writing about diasporic communities raises this issue particularly starkly because the notion of a diaspora implies not only a 'homing desire', but also a protracted separation from the homeland and dual or plural embeddedness: one cannot understand new Zimbabwean diasporic communities in Britain or South Africa as simply a reflection of the Zimbabwean context, but one also has to treat the British and South African contexts seriously, as exerting influences themselves. If one does elaborate dual or multiple contexts in any depth, however, can one retain a coherent narrative? Is the problem solved by giving additional weight to contexts, flows and connections beyond Zimbabwe's borders, and fitting this into a story of the making of Zimbabwean national identity that is mostly concerned with the space and people inside those boundaries? Or is there a more fundamental issue at stake here? Does an historical narrative whose primary focus is on a particular national geographical space, inadvertently and perhaps inevitably imply a 'natural' unity or teleology to national belonging, even when one of its main goals is to deconstruct such a notion? The answer must surely depend on the nature of the narrative. As states and borders continue to matter profoundly in their capacity to confer and delimit legal powers and citizenship rights, and as discourses of nationalism continue to play a key role in legitimating and challenging the way these powers are exercised, so it is important that scholars shed light on the historical contingencies, contestations and interests that shape different versions of nationalism, as *Becoming Zimbabwe* sets out to do. My point here is that such narratives of nation and nationalism can be expanded and enriched through greater attention to the histories of state borders themselves and to the changing flows and connections across them.

BORDERS, HISTORY AND IDENTITIES

The situation of the Terena Indians of Mato Grosso do Sul, a group which is settled in villages along an international border. The Terena's situation and that of the border*** create a situation which is different from other indigenous peoples, especially that of Amazonian Indians, or even that of the Guarany in Mato Grosso do Sul itself. The Terena do not circulate across the border, do not maintain marital exchanges with local indigenous groups in other countries and do not have bi-national identities.

The region in which the Terena live today has been of strategic importance in shaping the formation of the Brazilian nation-state: centuries ago. In fact, it was thestage for one of the principal territorial disputes of the Americas. Understanding the history of the definition of the border in what is now Mato Grosso do Sul and the immobilization of ethnic and social groups in the 19th and 20th centuries are important factors today's interethnic situation in the state, an affirmation which can be easily confirmed by a glance at the processes of indigenous land identification and demarcation in Mato Grosso do Sul. In the lawsuits mobilized against the identification and demarcation of Terena lands, political discourses are constructed which seek to reactivate forms of exclusion and symbolic-discursive inferiority in which the border appears as a centrally operative phenomenon. From these judicial processes we see two discursive tactics emerge which seek to delegitimize indigenous demands for lands by annulling the thesis of traditional occupation: that of questioning the Terena's national origin and that of questioning their cultural authenticity and, consequently, their legal condition as Indians.

This chapter thus intends to present some theoretical reflections regarding these symbolic struggles and also the process of development of the border and its effects on indigenous societies. Here, I intend to conduct two analytical movements:

1) Analyse the symbolic struggles which undelie the judicial processes generated by the territorial conflicts between the Terena Indians and rural producers, showing how the border is an active factor in the construction of political mechanisms of exclusion and (de)legitimization of ethnic groups.
2) Analyse state border policies, territorial dynamics and their confrontation with indigenous symbolic policies in different local situations along the border, which also include symbolic struggles for identities and territories that are recognized as legitimate.

Here, I will analyse how indigenous forms of social organization and symbolic-cultural expression produce counter-discourses based upon the appropriation of symbols and strategies derived from different state policies for the border, creating new forms of interpretation for ethnic identity.

Today as in the past, the political demarcation of both national borders and the borders of Indian lands presupposes the drawing of identary borders. In other words, the power to draw territorial borders implies a concomitant act of classification and representation of social groups and their borders, which is in turned at least practically founded upon the material fact of the border.

Borders, in their territorial, social and ethnic sense, are constructed and deconstructed in the midst of struggles regarding classifications; struggles which themselves are composed of a combination of different historical and cultural factors. One fundamental factor in this process is the history of colonization and state formation in these territories, in which the application of different border policies – including policies regarding the assimilation and nationalization of indigenous peoples. Other important factors include the local diversification of policy effects upon different indigenous societies and the effects of appropriation, reinterpretation and ressignification, which – in turn – ensure that ethnic cultures and identities do not unilaterally undergo processes of change.

By analyzing a handful of topics (*borders and classificatory struggles, the border as a laboratory for policies of control, borders and frontiers of economic expansion and identity*), we seek to contribute to the theoretization of the historical development of the border through the interpretation of the history of indigenous groups localized along it and the analysis of present-day conflicts. These efforts can aid us in thinking about other situations from a historical and procedural perspective, based upon a few theoretical-historical points.

THE MEANINGS OF THE BORDER AND THE STRUGGLE FOR CLASSIFICATION

Analyse a few judicial processes involving Terena Indians and rural land-owners, in particular those involving the indigenous lands of Cachoeirinha in the municipality of Miranda; Limão Verde in the municipality of Aquiduana; and Buriti in the municipality of Dois Irmãos de Buriti. In all three cases, the processes of land identification and demarcation began with the formation of the Identification Work Groups of 1997 and 2000 and the resulting lawsuits (undertaken by large and small landowners) which contested these processes.

In the case of the Indians of Buritis, the Federal judge's decision sustained the lawsuit's arguments, alleging that the lands in question were under the jurisdiction of the criteria stipulated in Decision 650 of the Brazilian Supreme Court. This decision was, in turn, appealed by FUNAI (the Brazilian Indian administrative organ), in which the content and objective of the suit was clarified:

In the present declatory action, the plaintiffs have asked for the partial elimination of tutelage so that the labors undertaken by FUNAI might be declared null and void and thus that the lands now occupied by the plaintiffs might be understood as 'lands not traditionally occupied by Indians".

In the documents of the suit we find an order to produce the land analysis based upon expert opinion. The questions raised by the suitors to the experts who produced this analysis clarify the symbolic content of the suitors' legal strategy:

1 Can the expert inform the court where the Terena Indians resided in historical period before 1797?
2 Can the expert classify these Indians as Brazilian Indians in accordance with their origins, customs, traditions and – in short – their culture?
3 In relation to the information contained in these documents, can it be said that these Indians be said to have occupied the mountains and plateaus of the Maracajú since time immemorial, according to the spirit and law of Article 231 of the Federal Constitution?

This sort of questioning also came up in cases involving Limão Verde and Cachoeirinha, in lawsuits of a different nature. When FUNAI sought legal remedy against an order to revert land possession from the Cachoeirinha Indians, the arguments of the plaintiffs were clearly similar to those used in the Buritis case:

In principle, we'd like to bring up a point of utmost importance with regards to the Guauá-Txané, today's Terena, in that they should not be considered Brazilian Indians as they originate in the Chaco.

The same theme of national origins was also brought up in the case of the Limão Verde Indians by the lawyers who represented the accusing parties:

Knwoing that the Terena Indians are not Brazilian, being originally from the Paraguayan Chaco, and that they came into Brazil in the 18th century, where did they first establish themselves...? Thus, the Terena Indians who seek control of the privately-owned lands of the plaintiffs are not descended from Brazilian Indians but from Paraguayan Indians, a fact which evidently removes them from the condition of primitive residents of Brazilian regions, given that there is absolute certainty that their ancestors are in the neighbouring country, Paraguay, in the region of the Paraguayan Chaco, where they should thus seek lands, instead of in Brazil where they did not originate..

In these legal battles, we encounter certain kinds of political-juridical discourses that affirm that the Terena Indians "originate in Paraguay" on "the other side" of the border and that their occupation of the lands along the left bank of the Paraguay River (today Brazilian territory within the Pantanal Region) cannot thus be understood as "traditional" for precisely this reason. These arguments suppose an entire analytical history and a construction of political and legal categories which underpin judicial actions.

As we can see from the above quotes, the judicial process is established in two different spheres: the struggle for land and the struggle for legitimate representation regarding the relationships between social groups and territories. The struggle for material interests is thus transfixed by a specifically symbolical struggle regarding the history of given groups, their origins, their authenticity as ethnic groups. This second struggle seeks to dissolve the legitimacy of a subject (an indigenous society) which portrays itself as the bearer of particular sort of history and origin. At the same time, indigenous representations in the form of myth and ritual (as is the case with the Terena) can invoke specific symbolic means in the creation of a counter discourse which takes in this clash of classifications.

These are the two dimensions which I propose to now explore.

From a theoretical point of view, we should indicate the symbolic forms that also express relationships of power, both in material and ideological terms. In this sense:

Struggles with regards to ethnic or regional identity, or in other words with regards to properties (stigmas or emblems) linked to origins through places of origin and through durable correlated signs, such as an accent, are a particular case in the struggle of classifications, the struggles for a monopoly over seeing and knowing, over giving to know and making one recognize, imposing legitimate divisions of the social world and, through this, making and unmaking groups.

In this way, the struggle for classifications contains a search for the power to fix legitimate identity and, by extension, the power to draw borders of social identity and the material basis for this, thus creating a territory. As Bourdieu indicates, the etymology of the word "region" (*regio*) leads us to a principle of division based up the act of power of the *regere fines*, the act of drawing borders and dividing within from without. The *regere fines* produces and is the product of an act of power, or if we prefer to be more direct, it adds symbolic force which institutionalizes power relations in the plane of social representations, making these appear as if they did not derive from power relations but from nature itself. This reifies a socially produced situation, presenting it as given *a priori*. The power to classify is the power to draw borders which both found what is real and also a given representation of what is real. In this sense, the process of defining social identities and the political process of defining territories are not simply analogous: they are ultimately derived from the same structures of power, given that:

Regionalism (or nationalism) is just one particular case of symbolic struggles in which agents involve themselves, either in a dispersed state or collectively and in an organized state, and seek to conserve or transform the relations of symbolic forces and their correlated advantages, both economic and symbolic...

In this fashion the "border" – understood as a political reality which is imposed upon the relationships of people and nations with territories, or as a metaphor for the interpretation of the processes of definition of social identities – is the fruit of a similar type of process: one based upon the power to create and legitimize classifications, to define the limits between the interior and the exterior.

We have thus arrived at the crucial element in the legal struggles to demarcate indigenous lands. The "nationalist" discourse which creates an opposition between "national owners" versus "foreign Paraguayan Indians" is a form of this symbolic struggle. The national borders appear as an element used to disqualify the indigenous subject within this struggle. However, this symbolic disqualification through the evocation of the idea of nationality in opposition to the idea of ethnicity is more specifically linked to the problem of property titles and the very foundations of the legitimization of the notion of private property as a right of *occupation and work.* The idea of nationality thus serves to attest to the occupation of given territories as private property, but also raises two further questions:

1) Where were the Indians before they crossed the national borders?
2) How and why did the Indians come to be found in the territories they currently occupy?

The classification struggle involves not only the struggle for legitimate representations of "origins" and "social identity": it also involves the power to conserve or transform local sections of a given agrarian structure. Both classifications and the symbolic-cognitive structure which has given partial and contradictory support to the policies and processes which allowed the agrarian structure to define itself in a particular manner along the border are thus in play here. In other words, the struggle over classifications does not hide an economic conflict or material interests: it is itself a struggle for the power to legitimately impose representations; for the maintenance or destruction of hegemonic or dominant representations which themselves express forces and add symbolic power and, vis this, add to the material existence of the subjects which produce them and are produced by them. Thus the search for an identity defined within the bounds of the nation-state and which can be used as a criterion for legitimization, for in this way the power to classify is taken from the groups themselves and is given over to the State. "Nationalism" is thus best seen here as a strategy or a symbolic mechanism activated in order to conserve a certain correlation of forces and a given distribution of lands within an agrarian structure – a structure which cannot itself be comprehended without first understanding the meaning of the border within national society.

We should thus clearly characterize the situation of the border which we are dealing with here in order to point out all the additional theoretical and political questions that are associated with it. A border may first and foremost be understood as the result of a political act that delimits lines of territorial division. But borders also have another, sociological, meaning that is employed as a descriptive operator of social realities in which territory occupies a central position. The border is not just a line demarcating a territory and showing the limits of a nation-state's sovereignty: it is first and foremost an object of social dynamics and relations which constantly (re)define it.

We should thus point out that the political-juridical concept of the border/frontier expresses only one possible dimension or use, to which we might add others such as "agricultural frontier", "forest extraction frontier" and etc. These different notions of the frontier or border are not exclusive and, in fact, are intertwined. Here, we understand border or frontier as a particular type of social organization of space in which conflict over the power to define said space prevails. Borders may be defined as open or closed. The open frontier/border can be defined as a "non-structured space / space which is being incorporated into a fragmented global space" in which "the appropriation of land é undertaken on an ever-growing scale and rhythm, but which is not, however, total, uniform or irreversible". Aside from this, it is possible to assume that in the region of an open border "diversified forms of organization of production coexist".

The concept of the border is in this sense a theoretical tool that can be used to delimit a concrete region in which thinly populated territories (in relation to surrounding national societies) whose local populations have different cultures and forms of organization are being integrated. In this wider sociological sense, the border is where the policies and processes of internal colonialism set ethnically differentiated groups on collision courses. The border is thus different from a "frontier of expansion", which is an empirical object that involves set types of activity, a concrete combination of productive forces an relations of production which are introduced into a frontier area..

The socio-spatial characteristics discussed above permit us to look at the border/frontier as a region that is characterized by unstable relations between social groups and territories, by multiple forms of appropriation, structuring and the utilization of productive territories and resources, Another important element of the border has to do with labour relations:

The alternative hypothesis is that the border is organized as mobile labour, that is with both salaried laborers – both temporary and permanent – and small producers who sell their labour in rural or urban activities. The formation of this labour market implies a process of migration and mobility which is induced through domination.

The frontier or border is thus a region in which a particular type of social organization of space is in vigor, in which internal colonialism is the central operator and in which different forms of use and appropriation of territory exist which, consequently, lead different representations of territory and social identity. At the same time, varying forms and demands relative to the exploration of labour are put into action along the border. The mobility of the labour force is an important point to which we'll return later. On the other hand, the closing of the frontier/border implies a structuring of spatial and social relations and the establishment of a dominant pattern of relationships among social groups and their related territories and spaces.

The idea of the border or frontier thus has a triple meaning: political border as the boundary between two territorial units, social or identitary border between groups and an economic frontier as a space being incorporated into the market and dominant relations of production. In the case under consideration here, the three meanings are deeply interwoven.

Mato Grosso do Sul can be understood as a closed border region, different from open border regions when we look at it in the economic sense. The Pantanal, the area in which the territorial conflicts detailed above are taking place, is, on the other hand, a border region in the sense that it is divided between two different nation-states.

The conflicts mentioned above employ classificatory discourses that constitute mechanisms which define the identity boundaries between social and ethnic groups. In this sense, "border" cannot be understood in the case at hand to mean, simply, a demarcating line or a legal-political frontier. It must be understood in its full sociological sense as indicating different possibilities of territorial and natural resource integration within a context of social and symbolic struggles.

This means that the territories that are today the object of legal conflicts in Mato Grosso do Sul have been integrated into greater national systems via processes of internal colonialism. In terms of State and indigenous actions, the demarcation of indigenous lands and other forms of territorialization such as land occupations and expulsions seek to question localized aspects of the agrarian structure produced by the evolution of the frontier up until the moment of its closure.

This agrarian structure was also constituted utilizing different representations of the Indian and his place in the world, understood as an originating space and as the Indian's rightful place. The search to redefine the limits of indigenous lands, with the consequent questioning of their historically constituted boundaries, is an effect and a development of the process of the structuring of space and of its integration within the political order. Its ultimate effect is to also question representations about the Indian and his "rightful place".

Defining Mato Gross do Sul as a closed frontier region requires us to thus analyse the history of the processes by which non-structured space in this region was turned into structured space integrated within the Brazilian nation-state and the world system, as well as within other correlated processes such as the development and expansion of capitalism in agriculture. This process involves forms of organization of labour and production, territorialization and cultural change. These processes of integration/structuring are the larger contexts within which the current relationships of social and indigenous groups with territories were formed and the social bases (agrarian structure, power relations) of the current social conflicts and struggles over classification were created.

THE FRONTIER AS A LABORATORY FOR POLICIES OF CONTROL

In the 19th century, the Terena Indians occupied Brazil's most important border region – the south of what is now Mato Grosso do Sul state – populating territories that ran up along the frontier with Paraguay. These territories were the result of a complex process of colonization which involved Spanish and Portuguese colonial agents and numerous indigenous societies. The processes of colonial conquest and the formation of the nation-state took centre stage in the second half of the 19th century when, after the war with Paraguay, the Brazilian State took definitive control of the border region and drew the national boundaries which are evident today. As part of this conquest, Brazil appropriated the territories of several indigenous groups, which were subsequently fragmented and put under State management, eliminating the potential threat posed by the Republic of Paraguay. This specific border situation brought indigenous peoples, their localization and social organization to light as a "problem" to be confronted and managed by the Brazilian state. As we can see in the report below, written by the military officer responsible for Fort Miranda:

These marriages also serve as an obstacle to Indian settlement as many are undertaken with members of different and distant tribes. The [Indians] of Albuquerque and Miranda marry amongst each other constantly and also with the Cadiuéos and even other bands neighbors of the Spanish, from which also come men and women here to join in like alliances, which are ordinarily of short duration; and as the men always move to the women's residences, practicing the same sort of thing with their so-called captives, who follow their lords with a similar motive and also for affection, the result of this vague practice is an inconstant circle of change wherein no one ever establishes a set residence...

As this chapter regarding the stability of these Indians is perhaps the most fundamental for to have some future hope of settling them in villages wherein they can be useful in mining and agriculture and to the Portuguese population [in general], I must relate some constant and recent facts at great extent.

External threats and territorial disputes with other States over the lands of Mato Grosso do Sul, when combined with the social characteristics of the frontier (low demographic density, unstable settlement which could be either cyclical or occasional), made the social organization of Native societies a "problem" for the State.

More specifically, the Guaicuru and Guaná Indians had certain socio-cultural traits which became the object of different State policies. In general, we can speak of three major problems associated with indigenous societies from the point of view of the Brazilian state:

1) Spatial mobility, given that Native social organization involved movements over large swathes of lands and marriages between distant groups, which could even cross international borders;
2) Mixture and segmentation, given that the indigenous political systems were characterized by the presence of numerous political leaders and that the practices of marital exchange and the capture and incorporation of enemies meant that any given indigenous societies could, in fact, contain a great amount of ethnic mixture (this was especially true among the Guaicuru and Guaná);
3) Ethno-cultural alterity and the fact that indigenous societies, in general, refused to be passively incorporated into colonial societies as a manual labour force.

State policies between 1790 and 1850 were thus characterized by attempts to settle the Indians in villages, with an eye to achieving several goals in one fell swoop:

1) the breaking of the alliance between the Guaicuru and the Guaná, thus militarily weakening the first group by ending the intermixture between these Indians;
2) Creating a defensive line for Brazilian territory against the Spanish and, later, the Paraguayans, with official Indian villages serving as the social support network for the region's forts and garrisons;
3) Determining more precisely the boundaries of indigenous groups, separating them from their old social relations and creating the basis for the fusion of the Indians into the greater mass of the Brazilian population.

Thus, long before the State began to encourage mixture and mobility along the border, it sought to eradicate certain forms of mixture and mobility. These policies led to the creation of fixed nuclei of Indian settlement in those regions which were considered to be geopolitically strategic. Albuquerque (today's Corumbá) and Miranda were the main settlement areas. The Terena Indians and other Guaná subgroups were encouraged by the State to occupy these regions towards the end of the 18th century. This border region, called the *Pantanaes* by the Portuguese, overlapped a set of territories known as the *Chaco* by the Spanish. The Terenas called the same region *Exiwa*.

The belief in the Terena Indians' Paraguayan origins thus stems from the presupposition that the emigrated from "Paraguayan lands" into "Brazilian territory" only after the 18th century had begun. However, at that time, the territory under consideration wasn't yet identified as "Brazilian". To the contrary: it was an object of some dispute between the Portuguese and the Spanish. The settling of allied Indians in certain areas which are today among the region's major cities was the fruit of State policy which sought to use precisely this sort of settlement to fix and define the border. Indigenous occupation of the region in fact stretches back to the 16th century. The Terena presence coalesced around commercial relations in the Itatins district, near Santiago de Xerez, where today one finds the city of Aquidanana. The region was conquered by the Guaicuru and Guaná during the same period. The supposed "shifting or migration of the Terena to Brazilian territory" was only one population migration among many others which occurred in the territory occupied by the Guaicuru and Guaná. As documents of the Brazilian Army show, it was a migration within territories occupied by Indians and the Spanish.

The territories of southern Mato Grosso do Sul were only defined as Brazilian following the war with Paraguay. This only occurred in large measure due to the efficient mobilization of the indigenous societies of the region by the nation-state. The lands are today under the Brazilian flag and are represented in legal documents as having been Brazilian from time immemorial. However, they were only taken under definitive Brazilian control 140 years ago. Before 1870, three different groups – the Portuguese, Spanish and Indians – claimed them. Some documents can show us the complexity of this nationalization process and how the border which separated Brazil from Paraguay and which imposed itself upon indigenous lands was successively shifted until it came to occupy its current position. The whole region which is today marked by conflicts resulting from the struggle to demarcate indigenous lands was also occupied by the Spaniards between the 16th and the 17th centuries and was a matter of constant dispute between them and the Indians.

Another policy would materialize in the "Regulamento acerca das Missões de Catechese e Civilização dos Índios — decreto nº 426 de 24/07/1845" (Regulations regarding the missions to catechize and Civilize the Indians). This legal instrument sought to create a form of political intervention and the organization of the "work of civilization" among the Indians – what U.S. Americans of the same time period would perhaps call "the administration of Indian affairs". The backdrop for this project was formed by the specific conditions of the frontier in Mato Grosso, which forced state agencies and even certain colonists and military personnel to enact *a policy of Indian administration based upon concessions to Native interests*.

Article #1 of the Regulations contains 33 paragraphs which define the attributions of the Indian Directorate. The first of these paragraphs established the task of examining the state of the settled villages. The second paragraph defines what resources are to be offered up to Native agriculture and the third paragraph establishes the power to "remove" Indians from their lands, recommending "peaceable" means for this task. Paragraph #10 establishes the power to redistribute the "objects" which are given to the Indians. Paragraph #11 talks of the "demarcation" of the lands set aside for the Natives. Paragraph #12 establishes the lands to be used for "plantation" within the villages and those which could be leased out. Paragraph #16 indicates that the merchants who will have access to the villages may either be "fixed" or "mobile". Paragraph #19 establishes the "legal and peaceable methods shall be employed to attract Indians to the villages and to promote marriages between them and people of other races". The 28th paragraph declares that work contracts are to be strictly overseen so that forced labour does not occur. Paragraph #30 speaks about the need for strict control over the villages' production and leases. Finally, Paragraph #32 institutes the Village Director as a "commissioner" for the Indians in the face of the justice system and all other authorities.

The Village Director would thus distribute "objects" to the Indians and administrate their plantations and other agricultural work. He would also command the military force that was stationed in the village. Paragraph 13 of the Regulation's second chapter called for the military enlistment of the Indians.

The Regulations of 1845 thus contain some elements which would be taken up again by the Brazilian state's tutelary regime for native peoples in the 20th century. The structures of power are quite similar in both cases, but there are some important differences. In the first place, the Regulations encourage the Indians to mix with "other races", a policy of state-directed miscegenation. This differs from the indigenous villages of the 20thcentury, where a policy of racial segregation was the norm. The 1845 Regulations also introduce an emphasis on "demarcating Indian lands", agriculture, the "administration of indigenous labour" and the production of the villages. It also establishes the Village Director as a "Commissioner for Indian affairs". In this sense, the Regulations thus prefigured the tutelary regime of the 20th century.

The first attempts to create state-run Indian villages according to the Regulations occurred between 1851 and 1860. They were to be built in the districts of Albuquerque and Miranda:

We have extracted the following information from a report presented to me by the Director General last April 28th:

The primary reason which must be indicated for why the people do not take advantage of catechism is the insufficiency of the sums set aside for the expenses which this entails… [These] hardly meet the needs of the villages of Bom Conselho and Miranda and we cannot, at the present, establish new villages for the tribes which would like to enter into relations with us, nor even distribute a few prizes among all the Indians who have come into this capital.

Having exhausted the initial allocation of funds, we have been forced to suspend the building of the chapels and brickworks in the two villages mentioned, as well as dismiss the music, brick making and tailoring masters who were employed. Their absence has been keenly felt, especially in the village of Bom Conselho where, it should be noted, some intellectual development of the Kinikináo Indians has taken place...

These Indians, of excellent temperament, have already given many services to society as maids on the farms and ranches and as paddlers on the boats which connect the ports of the Lower Paraguay to the capital. The village has a respectable musical orchestra and the Indian children, aside from being well along in learning their letters, are learning the trades of the tailor, blacksmith and brick maker. Miranda village, which was ordered founded by the provincial government in April 1860 under the direction of the tireless missionary, Father Mariano de Bagnaia, who has given much tireless service to catechism, now finds itself in an embryonic state due to the motives described above. A large number of Indians have been attracted to the village by the same missionary and, around the village there lies dispersed another large population of Indians who will probably come to incorporate themselves in the village. The prosperity of the village is of interest to all who live in the municipality because the Terena and Laiana which inhabit it not only work in the same jobs as those who have settled in Bom Conselho, but also supply the village with the fruits and vegetables which they cultivate.

The villages of Bom Conselho (Quiniquináu) and Miranda (Terena and LAiana) were thus the first villages of the Mato Grosso Province, with "village" understood here as a territorial and administrative unit created by the State to localize and settle Indians. The document quote above clearly sets apart those Indians who are in the villages from those who "lie dispersed" around the villages and who are, in fact, the local Indian communities which have escaped State management. The project of catechizing and civilizing the Indians was thus well developed during the period immediately prior to the Paraguayan War. Miranda, the province's second village, was created in 1860.

It is interesting to note that the bureau of public lands was created in 1858 in obedience to the 1850 Land Law, which began operation the following year. This means that the process of measuring lands and defining properties (of establishing land control, in other words) was being established during this period or, at the very least, projected. In the same year, the Provincial President affirmed that "Much has been done to make of Miranda a regular village and I order the Commander of Arms to see that this was done. He encountered some difficulties, however, the principal of which was the lack of a permanent priest who could attract the Indians to the village in a benevolent and insistent manner". In other words, the spread of the villages was parallel to the expansion of controlling mechanisms over the land. The village of Miranda finally began to be constructed the following year.

In the Paraguay Valley resides almost the entirety of the civilized population of this Province. More than 4/5ths of the occupation around the Capital [is situated in] a space of, at most, 1,600 square leagues along the upper part of the Valley, bordered on the west by the Paraguay River and on the east by the São Lourenço and cut by the Cuyabá; at least 1/10th of the above-mentioned population inhabits the counties of Albuquerque and Miranda, [along] the creeks and the great river, as well as its tributary, the Miranda.

What we'd like to call attention to here is the fact that during this period, the villages were expanding. Indian Directors were established to administrate and control said villages and, at the same time, the provincial population was growing in size, especially in the region of the Pantanal where the Guaná and Terena were then located.

In this manner the frontier, understood as a region of conflict over the appropriation and definition of spaces and territories, also became an area for experimenting with policies of domination. Policies of alliance and collaboration with indigenous societies were tested by the State's several apparatuses and, in particular, by the Army as integral parts of a strategy of national defense. During this period, there was little concern about the internal definitions of territorial limits as the Brazilian State's main problem was conflict with other nation-states. The geopolitical problem of territorial maintenance was more urgent than the question of the economic exploitation of these same territories. The State tolerated certain cultural practices precisely because it needed the Indians as military allies. At the same time, the existence of the border – which had not yet been configured in accordance to the systematic activity of the fronts of expansion – allowed the Indians to occupy a wide swathe of territory at different points in southern Mato Grosso. In this sense, then, there was formed a space of relative tolerance for ethnocultural diversity and a certain level of concession to Native interests.

The defense of this territory by the State obliged the Brazilian government to use the Native populations as an auxiliary force. At the same time, as the region became more populated and the fronts of expansion became better established, the mobility of the Guaicuru and Guaná Indians and the deep "intermixture" which existed between both societies became the object of policies for controlling and disciplining the Native populations. Native mixture and mobility along the border was increasingly only acceptable in the eyes of the State if it were subordinated to the demands of the market and assimilation with the non-indigenous population. The State could no longer accept interethnic mixture between Native groups, nor their autonomous shifting from one place to another. Certain State agents learned that indigenous cultural identities were so strong that it would be very difficult to someday absorb them within the general population. Mixture between the different indigenous groups and the spatial mobility that resulted from their different forms of social organization and relations of production became barriers to colonialism.

In this way, the idea that these indigenous groups originated in one place and time, located within the Chaco and outside of Brazil's national borders – an idea so very present in today's legal disputations – is in frank contrast to the historical dynamics of Native circulation and territorial occupation. These dynamics took in many different territorial points (in what is today both Paraguayan and Brazilian land) at different historical moments and involved the exchange of the territories themselves between different political and territorial units (especially within the region now known as the Pantanal), which resulted in their being possessed by different nations (including indigenous nations) at different points in time.

The territories and frontiers were distinct and what is today Brazilian territory was either in dispute or under the jurisdiction of Paraguay or one or another Indian nation. What is today understood to be the Pantanal was part of the Chaco. The border, even though it was the object of experimental policies of control, did not see this control consolidate itself over native groups until after the Paraguayan War. However, the villages that were created as part of the policies of settlement, separation and centralization set the stage in many ways for the post-war period, as they pointed towards a new way of incorporating spaces and territories into national society. In this new formulation, land (understood as a factor of production) would be turned into a highly disputed commodity. These policies prepared the way for the expansion fronts and the definitive incorporation of land into Brazil's agrarian structure.

ECONOMIC EXPANSION FRONTS, THE CLOSING OF THE FRONTIER AND REGIONS OF EXCEPTION

The border of southern Mato Grosso, understood as a political border between two states, was only finally settled in 1870 at the close of the Paraguayan War. The border's instability and its mobility (given that its demarcating lines were not accepted nor recognized as definitive) created a situation in which the spatial mobility of ethnic groups and their ethno-cultural alterity were seen as problematic by the State. It was only after the territorial limits of the national borders had been fixed that the systematic progress of fronts of economic expansion began to create the conditions for the immobilization of the various ethnic groups along the border and their transformation into a mobile workforce, originally subordinated to the State.

The work of these various expansion fronts – and most particularly and agricultural and ranching front – made possible the structuring of space along the border and the incorporation of the lands of southern Mato Grosso do Sul into the nation. This incorporation simultaneously conditioned the structural form of the region's agriculture and the place of indigenous lands within this. The main question is knowing when the systematic action of the various expansion fronts definitively began and when the frontier finally closed. According to Octavio Velho, one of the principal indicators of the activity of expansion fronts is accelerated demographic growth. Even though this may not be a definitive element of the fronts, it generally tends to indicate their operation.

In the 20 years following the Paraguayan War, the total population of Mato Grosso grew by 130%, in comparison with 1850. These numbers do not take in the province's indigenous population. Within this process of demographic growth, one finds the results of the nation's policy of encouraging European immigration: from 1872 to 1890, 5,896 Europeans came into the province; from 1890 to 1900, 3,445; from 1900 to 1920, 15,864; and from 1920 to 1940, 47,002. These demographic dynamics accompanied increased socio-economic dynamization. It meant the removal of the province's manpower problem, which had been cited as the cause of its relative "backwardness" throughout the 19th century. "In this way, the end of the war with Paraguay marked the beginning of a phase in which the economy of Mato Grosso was opened up to the world via commerce and navigation along the Paraguay River" .

It is also important to remember that a large number of military personnel were stationed in Mato Grosso in this period (especially officers), veterans of the Paraguayan War. These men became farmers and businessmen in the region, as well as part of its nascent rural bourgeoisie. We thus have the consolidation of a clear socio-cultural conflict or shock between colonists –foreign or national immigrants coming in from other areas of Brazil – and the autochthonous indigenous peoples of the region. A new phase of colonization was at hand and we can now properly talk of a specific kind of internal colonialism, where new colonists began to occupy the territories of the province of Mato Grosso during the post-war period stretching from 1870 to 1900. This is the beginning of the formation of a capitalist market which would develop under monopoly capitalist conditions, subsidized by the State. Thus, the "economy" gained a strength and autonomy which it did not have in the immediately preceding period.

In general, we can say that two great expansion fronts consolidated themselves during this period. The first was the forest extraction front and the second was the agricultural and ranching front. The forest extraction front saw a boom during the last decades of the 19th century while ranching and agricultural activities developed at a slower – but constant – pace throughout the period. Between 1898 and 1914, production of "erva mate" tea and rubber were responsible for over 80% of the value of the province's exports, a position which they held even after 1911, when the most dynamic element of the economy became agricultural and ranching activities.

Mate tea production began in 1882, when Tomás Laranjeira gained the rights to exploiting the stretch of land between Júlio and Iguatemi (in the southernmost part of Mato Grosso). This activity would later be consolidated with the formation of the Laranjeira Mate Company, which would come to exercise a monopoly over the sector. Laranjeira Mate became a fundamental component of the power structure within Mato Grosso. Rubber, however, would also be an important export of the province. This was extracted in the regions along the Paraguay, Jurena, Arinos and Paranatinga and Alto Tapajós Rivers. After the crisis of 1910, Brazilian rubber production came screeching to a virtual halt. However, within Mato Grosso, forest extraction activities dominated the economy of the first decades of the 20th century.

The greater part of this activity was concentrated in the extreme southern part of the province. Erva-mate and rubber were planted precisely within this region and the development of the ranching and farming economy became fundamental, within this historical framework, for the construction of a new form of power distribution that would completely alter the lives of the Terena Indians.

Ranching and farming were already being practices as an important economic activity in the region since 1850. During the post-war period, its importance as an economic sector would grow: "...during the 1878-1879 economic year, it began to gain significant importance, mostly when we observe that the exportation of cattle, dried meat, horn and horse manes brought in moneys... which would correspond to over half of the value of the province's exports".

In 1915, Mato Grosso had the 4th largest bovine herd in Brazil, with 2,690,454 head of cattle. The principal municipalities concentrating this industry were:

1. Campo Grande
2. Ponta Porã
3. Bela Vista
4. Corumbá
5. Coxim
6. Aquidauana
7. Três Lagoas
8. Miranda

In other words, the Pantanal was at that point already a region which concentrated agriculture and ranching, a tendency which began shortly after the Paraguayan War. Though ranching and agriculture was the third most important activity in the state during the initial years of the First Republic, became a constant source of economic activity and, after the 1920s, took off as the principal economic activity of Mato Grosso. Large companies began to operate within this area, the most important of which was The Miranda Estância Company, which controlled 219,056 hectares in Miranda.

We can thus clearly see how national society's expansion fronts operate in the post-war period following 1870. The development of a farming and ranching front in the Pantanal region exponentially increased the demand for lands in that area and the process of delimiting and demarcating these lands was delayed. Even towards the end of the 19th century, there were few establishments with clear land title, with the vast majority operating as squatters.

Many of these demarcations were the result of federal, state, or municipal decrees, and they led to questions on both the Indians and landowners parts. The demarcation thus did not effectively occur in many cases and was often not accepted in those cases in which it did. From the moment in which the ranching and agricultural expansion fronts begin to operate, a restructuring of space occurs which eventually results in the closing of the frontier. In this restructuring, the Terena are settled on certain parcels of land and are transformed into a mobile labour force under the direction of the State. The old pattern of indigenous mobility and ethnic intermixture gave way before the establishment of the reservations, with each ethnic group settled on a small plot of ground. According to SPI policy, this was an adequate measure which would lead to the Indians' assimilation and incorporation into national society.

João Pacheco de Oliveira Filho has hypothesized that a direct relationship existed between the effectiveness of the demarcation processes of Indian lands and the activities of the Pioneer fronts. He points out that indigenous lands were first demarcated in precisely those areas where the expansion fronts were active. We can also add to this hypothesis, in the case of southern Mato Grosso. Here, the effectiveness of demarcation moved hand-in-hand with the rhythm of the closing of the frontier and the need to regionally define property relations and structuring of social-spatial organization. In the south of Mato Grosso, the expansion fronts affected the closing of the frontier and the demarcation of Indian lands was part of a greater structuring of space that consolidated and institutionalized a given configuration of spatial occupation produced by the shock of internal colonialism. In other words, these demarcations expressed the correlation of indigenous and colonial forces during the late 19th and early 20th century. The closing of the frontier necessarily implied the demarcation of all lands, not just indigenous territories, but all lands in the state. Reservation demarcation was thus part of a larger, global move towards the consolidation of the agrarian structure of the border region.

Another important point is that before the closure of the frontier, a certain tolerance existed with regards to indigenous lands. Indians were guaranteed the use of the land, but were never given formal title to it (something which occurred with regards to most lands in the border region in general, even those used by non-Indians). Although legislation already existed in the 19th century which supposedly assured Indians possession of the lands they occupied, these guarantees stood in frank contrast to the social configuration of the frontier, which insured that conflicts of interest would be resolved by material and symbolic force, due to the instability of territorial definitions and the characteristic conflicts of internal colonialism. In short, land tenure was resolved by the manipulation of the juridical structure and by the systematic use of violence. The border region was necessarily a place where exceptions were the rule in the sense that internal colonialism and the land conflicts generated by all colonial situations could never co-exist within a strict interpretation of the law, given that the law itself was not an instrument for the mediation of interests but a vehicle which expressed the contradiction of interests, as well as an artifact of hegemonic power.

The view that Indians have spontaneously occupied only those territories in which they are currently found is thus in frank contrast with the data that shows that the process of the closure of the frontier was what defined the settlement of Indians and gave birth to the idea that they "only occupied the villages". In reality, the historical data shows the opposite: aside from the state-run villages, there were several other nuclei of decentralized indigenous occupation throughout the territory, as well as official villages which are today extinct.

In today's on-going struggle over judicial processes, however, a model of indigenous society is projected on the past (on the moment when the frontier was still open in the 19th century), stipulating as eternal a form of social and territorial organization that only came into being after the closure of the frontier in the early 20th century. This model holds that each ethnic group occupied a separate and tiny parcel of land which was clearly delimited and that these are properly each group's "indigenous lands". This image, however, only grasps as "true and eternal" the territorial effects of State indigenous policy, produced at the moment in which the frontier was closed.

The closing of the frontier produced the region's agrarian structure and the Indian's modern place within it. This place was established through the conjuncture of two factors: the actions of the Indian Protection Service (the SPI) and the specific social conditions of the frontier. Action on the part of the SPI aided the consolidation of the agrarian structure and, at the same time, introduced a kind of policy which acted directly upon Indian identity. In this fashion, the judicial conflicts around the demarcation of indigenous lands are nothing more nor less than an indirect consequence of the manners in which lands were incorporated into the agrarian structure and the types of policies the State directed towards indigenous societies in the early 20th century. The Terena Indians demands for land are, in turn, a means of questioning the ways in which these spaces were incorporated and distributed within the regional agrarian structure during the initial period of the activities of the expansion fronts.

In a certain sense, then, at the moment in which the process of land regularization begins, at the beginning of the closing of the frontier, when these lands are put onto the market, indigenous lands are situated at an inferior level within the hierarchy of spaces within the region. Regularization of Indian lands not only took place *after*other landowners were given title to their properties (Terena lands only begin to be demarcated in 1906 and, later, after 1920), the demarcation of these lands was seen as a specific part of a greater policy directed towards the forced assimilation of the Indians into national society and their transformation into salaried workers. The consolidation of the closure of the frontier with the structuring and incorporation of spaces within a global system thus combines questions relating to the administration of both identities and territories.

The Pantanal region, as a border region, was the target of Indian affairs policies that sought to nationalize and assimilate Native societies through plans of directed cultural change which also sought to insure greater vigilance along the border. In this fashion, the localization of Native ethnic groups in a region crossed by an international border modified the situation of the Indians of southern Mato Grosso and, in particular, the Terena, transforming them into targets for policies that were simultaneously directed at territories, identities and populations. The problem of indigenous identities thus emerges alongside the question id how to assimilate these identities within the greater Brazilian national identity. The problem of defining the limits of Indian territory is thus replaced by the problem of defining the limits of Indian identity.

BORDERS AND IDENTITIES

The consolidation of Brazilian national borders and the delimitation of internal frontiers into public lands, Indian lands and private properties within an agrarian structure was a process that was also accompanied by the creation of legitimate representations regarding each of these spaces within Brazilian society and its social imagination. The delimitation of Indian lands also implied the attribution of a symbolic place for Indians. They were to occupy the lands set aside for them by the State because these were supposedly the lands they had occupied from time immemorial. Such spaces were also the place where Indians had their duties, given that they were to occupy them only until they had become appropriately assimilated into national society by the SPI. As Lima and Oliveira Filho have both noted, the reservations, agricultural centers and other like artifacts expressed in administrative terms the transitory condition that was supposedly "Indianess". A cyclical argument was thus set up: *Indians exist in determined spaces because they've always existed in these spaces because that is where they should exist.*

The SPI's policies were, above all else, policies geared towards the nationalization of the Indians. The policies for the Terena villages and reservations in southern Mato Grosso sought to consolidate these spaces as a channel for the assimilation of the Terena and their transfiguration from an ethnically distinct people into an integral part of a homogenous national identity. The border was thus also a zone in which the boundaries of social identities were to be the objects of conflict and the targets of disciplinary policies. These policies were in place throughout the SPI's existence and were in evidence even after that agency became FUNAI (the National Foundation of the Indian). They were based upon and expressed the notion that the Terena were acculturated Indians well along the road to complete assimilation. This view of the Terena, established by the Indian affairs bureaucracy, then went on influence other social actors and institutions:

Nationalization discourse continues to revolve around the notion of indigenous groups situated at various points along the scale of human evolution, given that Decree #5484, of 27/07/1928, which categorizes the relative degree of "contact" [between Indians and non-Indians] and which is still the touchstone of indigenist activity, has continued in place... For example, of the two kinds of SPI posts which were discussed at the time, "Attraction, Vigilance and Pacification Posts" were to deal with those peoples who were "peaceful unarmed and in their social infancy, in order to awaken in them the desire to achieve the level of progress that we ourselves have reached"... The second kind of post, the Assistance, Nationalization and Education Post, was set up by the regulations to serve one or more already pacified and settled tribes, capable of being adapted to ranching or farming activities, as well as other normal occupations.

Nationalization was thus conceived as a pedagogic process involving *education and work* or, better yet,*(technical) education for work.* In the 1940s, the SPI's organizational chart was restructured in order to better deal with these two duties, with the agency being encouraged to once again promote the concept of the *Indian as the guardian of Brazil's borders,* and Indigenous Posts and Inspectorates were organized along these general lines. This structure would only begin to be changed in the 1960s. We can see how Indigenous Posts were distributed around the south of Mato Grosso:

The data presented above allows us to see that the tasks allocated to Indian affairs in southern Mato Grosso were different to those allocated to the indigenous bureaucracy in the north of the State. In IR-6, six of the eleven indigenous posts were "attraction posts" (none of these existed in the south) while the remaining five were nationalization posts, most of these serving the Terena. This means that, in this period, the tutelary and political regime of Brazilian Indian affairs was being used to promote policies of*nationalization: the construction and imposition of a Brazilian national* *identity upon the native peoples.* This resulted in an impulse to preserve and guarantee a "slow process of acculturation" while simultaneously accelerating the process of incorporating the Indian into the nation as rural laborers. As anthropologist Altenfelder Silva pointed out in the case of the SPI's activities among the Terena of the Bananal :

By the initiative of the Indian Protection Service, the "feast of the priests", the Oheokoti, was re-established and is now celebrated on the 19th of June, Indian Day, together with other Brasilio-Indigenous civic ceremonies. These include the raising of the Brazilian Pavilion to the sound of the National Anthem, played by the Indians, and the realization of Terena dances, which have now been revived.

But the policies of assimilation that were applied to the Indians of the border region had very diverse effects at the local level. In the case of Terena society, nationalistic political elements were incorporated into the group's ritual and mythic universe. The experiences of the Indians along the border and the political questions produced by these experiences were transcribed into indigenous narratives in such a way that certain historical events gained mythical contours in the indigenous interpretation of indigenous history and the history of colonization.

The fundamental element is that the Terena today present (in ritual and mythic form) narratives that do not oppose native identity and national identity, but rather juxtapose or superimpose the two. Terena narratives, for example, point to the indigenous character Kaly Syny, who appears in the narratives of the Indians of Cachoeirinha and Limão Verde (even being mentioned in pamphlets produced by the Indians) as a chief and a*koixomuneti* (shaman) who supposedly brought the Terena up the Paraguay River and was a principal native figure during the War. Kaly Syny is said to have actively organized the Terena during the War with Paraguay and to have come to the aid of the Brazilian troops, helping them with his shaman's powers to defeat the Paraguayans in several battles.

One ritual which expresses this narrative is the hiokixoti-kipahe (dance of the ema bird, or – as it's more commonly known

– the "stick beating dance"). This dances is ritually practiced on all important occasions by the Terena, including Indian Day and the Saints Festivals undertaken in almost all indigenous communities. Indian Day is particularly emblematic, given that it operates a certain ritualistic duality, enacting nationalistic rituals such as the raising of the flag and the singing of the national anthem, and also indigenous rituals such as the stick-beating dance. The questions that are raised by the interwoven rituals are extremely complex, given that they demonstrate an appropriation of national symbols (such as the Brazilian flag) within indigenous ritual. The flag is held by the Terena or even physically connected to their clothes of bacuri palm fiber and ema feathers in such a way that it becomes literally impossible to separate Terena and national identity.

There are also other interpretations regarding the meaning and origin of the stick-beating dance. In general, the Terena agree that the dance was revealed to a shaman in his dreams and that this shaman then taught it to the other Indians. However, two distinct versions of this myth are narrated, although both are linked to the War and the group's socio-historical experience. One version of the story indicates that the dance portrays a war between two indigenous nations in the Chaco or *Exiwa,* and that it is undertaken to memorialize the dead. Another version affirms that the dance was revealed to the shaman after the Paraguayan War to remember the Indians that took part in it in order to defend their lands and to remember the Indian blood that was shed in this cause. The dance is a ritual undertaken to remember struggles and the Indians which fought and died in them. The identity of the Terena Indians, expressed in this ritual form, links both ethnicity and nationality. Different from what the SPI and FUNAI's nationalization policies sought to create with regards to cultural homogenization and assimilation, national symbols were reworked according to local Indian interpretations in the dance, inverting the logical opposition between ethnicity and nationality and creating a plural identity. At the same time, the narratives that are linked to the ritual express an indigenous point of view regarding their historical experience along the border, emphasizing the element of conflict and war which characterized this experience and creating a counter-discourse that emphasizes the Terena's importance to national history due to the role the group played in the Paraguayan War. This counter narrative, in turn, legitimizes the Terena's land claims, given that the group can point to their defense of Brazilian territory as proof of their "Brazilianess".

In this way, the hypothesis that ethnic identity is necessarily exclusive of national identity, where "ethnic" is understood to mean a supposedly "external" origin which must be either be assimilated or understood as primordial, stands in frank contrast to an observable sociocultural reality in which the Terena's specific ethnic identity is inextricably linked to Brazilian national identity. This linkage is in part due to the peculiar historical conditions of the border region and in part due to the group's strategies and processes of appropriation. The Indians can thus be understood as having produced their own discourse, through myth and ritual, which speaks of the group's origins and which links historical and magical-religious elements, justifying not only the Terena's presence in the territories which they currently occupy, but also the legitimacy of their demands for land. Ethnic identity and its boundaries are thus not closed to the effects of historical processes and the policies applied to the economic and political frontier regions. In reality, Terena ethnic identity transformed itself throughout its history, linking itself to national identity in such a way that national and ethnic identity have become interposed – even though the Indians never became assimilated in the sense of being folded into the greater population, losing their ethnic identity. This fact makes the struggle for classification in today's judicial processes regarding the Terena that much more complex.

This struggle highlights yet another conflict over the power to create legitimate representations regarding social identities and the maintenance or transformation of certain aspects of the agrarian structure. In the case of the Pantanal region in Mato Grosso do Sul and the Terena Indians which occupy this region, we can clearly see that the border affected the group's process of territorialization and the definition of its current identity. The experience of occupying territories along the border determined the Terena's spatial location and the form and content of their ethnic identity. It's not just the territorial limits of the border that are mobile, but also the boundaries of the social identities of the groups which are located along it, given that this location implies their subjection to different types of policies, both symbolic and economic, which condition the development of social groups and territories and which give them their specificity.

Ethnic and national identities – like borders, frontiers and boundaries – are re-elaborated according to power relationships. They are essentially mobile, in time as well as in space, and this fact makes the questions brought up by the struggles to demarcate and identify Indian land even more complex. The judicial processes and the political-juridical strategies adopted in the fight against the demarcation of indigenous lands impose certain representations as legitimate. However, when we analyse history and the evolution of the border, we see that a century ago, neither territories nor social groups were encapsulated within the limits in which they are found today and that, furthermore, their identities have not remained static over time but have progressively been shifted, cut, regrouped, and reformulated by political struggles, wars, colonization and the workings of expansion fronts. We then see that the representations contained in the discourses of the actors who are today in conflict with one another should be understood as a part of a greater struggle over classifications and not as a key to understanding reality as it is classified and represented by these actors.

7

Conceptual Issues in the Study of Borders and Surveillance

The Canadian Sociologist Everett Hughes advised that the study of society should begin at home. In fact it should begin (and continue) wherever the observer is. In that regard the conference at which the papers in this volume were delivered can illustrate some border issues.

One that stands out is the common form of a *temporal process of linked border crossings*. Here the initial crossings of various personal borders are a pre-requisite for some kind of permissive or restrictive action on the part of border guards (as broadly defined). This permits the subsequent crossing of *organizational borders* (which can, but need not, be linked with geographical borders) in the form of *exiting* and then *entering*.

Consider those of us who passed through one or more international borders in coming to Canada. We were permitted to cross into the physical and organizational Canadian border, but only under the prior condition of permitting a variety of our *personal borders* to be crossed —first by the country that we were permitted to exit, perhaps were in transit through, and then the country we entered.

These personal border crossings included "non-public" information (both that personally known by the subject but not immediately manifest to strangers, and information not even necessarily known by the subject). Take for example the biographical and bio-metric *identity information* encoded into a passport or visa and offered to (or "taken" by) an agent and the disparate and disaggregated details of prior transactions and behaviour which are accessed, combined, cross-checked and compared against watch and risk profile lists.

This checking in turn can render asunder knowledge inhibitors stemming from the *logistical borders* of fragmentation, incompatible formats and time. Consider the resurrection for decisional consumption of events long past (which in an earlier age could be easily concealed and were often beyond human memory) or in widely dispersed records and those in varied non-combinable formats. Note also how inspectors go beyond direct searches and through x-rays, electronic, chemical, canine and other scans pierce the protective *border coverings* of the unaided senses offered by our bodies, clothes, backpacks and suitcases. For some travelers the transversing of the body is a transgression.

In these border crossings we see several central characteristics of contemporary surveillance – the breaking through previously protected information barriers/borders of the person often in a low visibility or invisible fashion; the use and integration of multiple kinds of data (no border is an island); and the use of acontextual, non-local and abstract categories to construct profiles of, and for decisions about, the individual.

As with video cameras applied equally to guards and prisoners or workers and managers, we see the reproduction or generalizability of these means as they are also applied to those licensed to cross the personal borders of travelers. Consider the use of drug tests, background investigations, biometric identification and video—including a recent proposal for cameras in airline cockpits, as applied to those in the transportation industry.

The articles in this volume emphasize the juridical and geographical national border. This form which can be so vital with respect to issues of citizenship, identity, economics, security and culture can be located within a broader conceptual space which permits comparisons across kinds of borders and an emphasis on the links between borders.

At the broadest level border issues are central to the idea of any system, whether physical, cultural, social or psychological. Thinking about society as a system is of course fundamental to modern social theory. Parsons 1956) Any notion of society involving a system of interdependent parts implies the ideas of internal and external borders and means of defining and regulating them. The parts are differentiated from each other, even as there are points of connection and exchange between them.

Many forms of surveillance can be usefully viewed as techniques of boundary-maintenance. Surveillance serves to sustain borders through defining the grounds for exclusion and inclusion –whether to physical places, opportunities or moral categories. Differential treatment based on surveillance results is central to many forms.

Surveillants (whether at an airport, a welfare office, a credit card company, a highway, a mall or in a family) serve as gate keepers, compliance inspectors, social-essence definers and guardians, assessing aspects of individuals to determine who they are, what categories they fit into and how they are to be treated.

Conversely, while it usually generates less attention as a policy issue (because it can more easily be framed as legally and often ethically wrong) surveillance is also a tool for undermining borders.

At a very general level there are likely some universal border structures or forms regardless of specific content which serve to define and protect organisms as well as groups. Borders which serve one group's interest (and are functional for it) may of course be challenged by those whose interests are not served and for whom the border is dysfunctional. The topic involves a fundamental natural and social process of border differentiation and creation/ re-creation, which has accelerated under modernization. We see a kind of boundary musical chairs, as actors and organizations strategically pursue their ends in ever changing environments.

Changes in life conditions, social organization, cultural values and technology re-arrange borders, generating various combinations of the new and the old. Borders may become ever more inclusive and generalized and simultaneously (in other forms) ever less inclusive and more specialized, as well as becoming more permeable for some elements and less for others. Depending on from whose point of view and the analytic component, surveillance may serve to maintain or undermine borders.

Beyond its' broad usefulness in thinking about social behaviour and organization in any context, the concept of borders offers an organizing perspective for considering contemporary surveillance issues. When these are sociologically and socially significant and newsworthy, it is often because defining, crossing, or failing to cross, a border of some form is at issue.

I hypothesize that when individuals feel their personal borders are wrongly invaded (their privacy is violated) one or more of four conditions are present. A natural sense border protecting information is crossed (e.g., the presence of secret video or audio transmission devices). A social border assumed to be protective of information is breached (e.g., violations of confidentiality). The temporal and spatial borders separating various periods or aspects of one's life are violated (the matching and mining of diverse computer data sets). The assumption that unless notice is given, interaction and communication are ephemeral and transitory like a river and not to be recorded and shared with others for future use.

From the early stirrings of surveillance studies in the 1970s through the end of the century, empirical research and moral concerns focused on the use of new computer technologies to break through personal borders, as well as their potential for bringing greater organizational accountability. Those concerned with privacy and civil liberties argued for tightening the newly vulnerable borders around personal information and they met with some success. At the same time, fallout from the 1960s and Watergate led to increased pressure for greater organizational openness and transparency. The technological and social changes related to economic globalization also meant the weakening of several forms of organizational border, resulting in the freer flow of goods, information and persons.

Yet after 9/11 in some ways the above was reversed. We see less public concern over the invasion of privacy and less support for governmental and organizational openness. Pressures to cross personal borders in order to protect organizational and national borders have greatly increased. Many in government argue that the privacy and openness of recent decades, and the unrestricted use of new technologies such as encryption and the web, undermine national security. Contrary to the trend of recent decades, many social borders are now more difficult to cross – whether leaving or entering a country, a neighborhood or a building, seeking immigrant or asylum status, or accessing information, while some individual borders are easier to cross as a result of new laws such as the Patriot Act. This can confuse the righteously indignant researcher on the side of the angels. Is the social problem the difficulty of crossing the borders of the individual and the ease of crossing organizational borders, or the reverse? Of course there is not one social problem and much depends on the context.

But however viewed, we need to attend to enduring, as well changing aspects. Toward this end I first suggest a framework and questions for analyzing and seeing the connections (whether theoretical or literal) between various border structures and processes.

CLASSIFYING BORDERS

The border demarcation may be metaphorical, symbolic and largely definitional as with the borders between good and evil, loyalty and disloyalty or art and kitsch. Or it may be more literal, material and tangible as with the borders of a printed page, the walls of a prison, or an expressionless face.

I am interested in the norms and physical/technical conditions involved in the discovery or protection/concealment of information, particularly as this involves the borders of the individual in relation to other individuals, as well as to organizations. The area can also be analyzed by considering organizational borders and inter-organizational relations.

The topic may be usefully approached by studying the interplay of the cultural and the physical/material as both border-barriers and border-breakers. Border barriers are intended to serve as blockages in defining edges and border breakers intended to overcome these.

Borders as barriers can be understood as literal containers or excluders of persons, objects and information e.g., as in a prison, a purse or an encrypted communication. Some of this is done using "hard" physical factors (e.g., closed doors, clothes, locked display cases, armor) and some using "soft" normative factors ("don't ask, don't tell" rules, "you can look, but don't touch", "stop on red") and very often both (e.g., doors on restrooms and the expectation that "ladies" and "gentlemen" signage will be appropriately directive).

Border breakers may also involve physical (e.g., explosives, night vision or decryption technology) or cultural factors (e.g., search warrants, self-disclosure and notice rules), as well as combinations (e.g., the voluntary offering of information on customs declarations forms and electronic and chemical searches of persons and luggage at international borders).

A fundamental question is how agents and subjects of surveillance create borders around themselves and/or their opposition and, in game-like fashion, seek to transcend or undermine their opponent's borders. To pursue this we need a comparative and dynamic framework for thinking about types of barrier borders and barrier breakers and the questions they raise.

Knowledge advances through identifying variation in outcomes. Below I suggest some of the main forms of border variation. A next step is to analyse their causes, correlates and consequences. For ease of presentation these variables are discussed in either/or terms, although many are best seen as continua. The dimensions of the presence or absence of physical and cultural factors in the determination of borders. This yields four types helpful in considering the sociology of information. Cells 3 and 4 involving barriers to border crossings are most applicable to technological surveillance issues. The cases in Cell 1 (absence of cultural or physical barriers) are likely characterized by greater trust, equality, resource abundance and cooperative group and individual relations, and lessened hierarchy than borders with barriers. That pattern holds for the single barriers of cells 2 and 3 relative to the cases in cell 4, where we see both cultural and physical barriers.

Key issues here are the extent to which a border is naturally "readable" and "crossable" without special disclosure rules or technological means of access, or in contrast serves as a barrier. The barrier may be natural as with limits of the unaided senses or because a border (whether to movement or perception/comprehension) has been created.

The compulsion of disclosure norms and the frequently involuntary (for the subject) character of surveillance technology represent major social markers for understanding and evaluating the ethical and public policy aspects of personal information collection.

In the same fashion the use of borders to restrict access and information (sometimes as a result of initial personal border crossings to determine eligibility) are relevant to understanding current questions around the privatization of public space and access and new restrictive copyright rules. The latter block access to what, in their absence, would be otherwise available (e.g., the right to physically be in a given place, to access information without restrictions or to reverse engineer and modify software).

Contrast a bank visitor with a Halloween mask bearing a threatening note and a customer without a mask also making a withdrawal; calling from an unlisted (or listed) telephone number to phone numbers with and without Caller-ID; a supervisor seeing or smelling employees smoking dope as against inferring dope smoking from a drug urine test; observing police behaviour on a public sidewalk vs. in the back areas of a police station; or driving within, as against beyond borderless EC countries. My discussion will focus on the border barrier cells.

What is the purpose or immediate *goal* of the barrier from the standpoint of its owner/controller/responsible agent? By definition a border demarcates. But beyond its denotative function, a barrier can be intended to keep in, keep out, or to do both simultaneously and differentially, depending on the category. A fence around an electrical power facility is intended to exclude persons. Physical borders—whether high mountains, islands or limitations of the senses also serve to exclude, as do sealed or confidential records. Countries that deny residents the right to travel freely (whether within or beyond their national territory) use borders to keep the population within. The walls of a prison are intended to keep prisoners within, and a sometimes-wrathful public out.

Whether the purpose is to wall in or to wall out, we can ask *what* is included/held within or excluded/blocked? What is a border intended to be open or closed to? A mobility metaphor is often appropriate with any consideration of the idea of a border. The question being what elements (under what conditions) are kept in or out, or permitted/able to pass through and how often and in what direction? Major forms here are persons, valuables, information, communication, animals, insects, germs, heat and coldness and chemicals.

Given the richness of physical and social reality, all barrier borders are partial and limited with respect to what they can include and exclude. A mapping of even the most basic elements that can be contained within the cachement areas of a border and those that may cross in one or both directions is far from simple. Thus cyclone fences inhibit the movement of persons across them, but not sights and sounds (or movement over or under them). A broadcasting booth protected by a window permits light and the visual to go back and forth, while internal sound is kept within and external sound without. As a Los Angeles teenager, I recall watching films I was unable to hear while parked beyond the fenced Griffith Park Drive-in theater. Conversely, I recall hearing, but not seeing, concerts outside the Berkeley Greek Theater (rather than doing both from inside with an admission ticket). A cattle grate keeps bovines from going from one territory to another, while permitting persons and vehicles to go both ways at will. However, it has no impact on seeing, hearing, or smelling what is happening on opposing sides.

What is the barrier's *operative principle*? What is it based on? How does it keep out and in? What is it that must be crossed/ broken through in order to enter or leave or be within or beyond? The distinction between the cultural and the physical applies. Cultural restrictions involve barrier norms –manners, diplomacy and secrecy, privacy and confidentiality rules. Physical barriers that restrict or block may be inanimate as with cliffs, walls, safes or clothes. Solid doors –with and without locks, windows with "blinds" or curtains, drawers, and secret compartments are related examples.

More permeable borders may be "voluntarily" maintained out of habit or to avoid sanctioning for wrongful crossing (e.g., fear of electric shock, land mines or setting off an alarm and other deterrents). More gentle forms such as a mall store that keeps teenagers away by playing classical music can also be noted. An armed guard, geese trained to quack at intruders and guard dogs and alligators in a moat (who threaten to eat unauthorized entrants) offer examples of sustaining borders through animate means. Skin can be the functional equivalent of a wall in preventing access to body conditions. The *face* can be a potential mask of inner feelings and attitudes. Animals mark territory with their scent and skunks and squid use their resources to deter predators in creating a defensive perimeter.

We can also note borders of an ecological or logistical nature in which there is a separation/compartmentalization/segmentation of activities, or the dispersal and disaggregation of information. Thus the absence of a national id card or universal identifier means that personal information in distinct databases can not be immediately joined. There may be cognitive borders to communication as with incomprehensible languages and incompatible codes.

Time is a distinctive form of information barrier. Here the physical and cultural may be combined, as when rules provide that records kept in a locked vault not be released for a fixed period of time. Time may also protect information as a result of memory loss or record disappearance or degradation. Time shares with the senses the idea of a border between the known and the unknown. To the extent that the past has been experienced or known, it stands in the same relation to an unknown future as does the unseen lying beyond the power of the naked eye.

The Senses

A final operative principle for borders beyond the physical, cultural, logistic, ecological and temporal lies in the zones within and beyond, which the *unaided senses*work, and fail to work. Erving Goffman implies this limitation in his definition of front and back stage regions as applied to group interaction. In suggesting that "a [border] region may be defined as any place that is bounded to some degree by barriers to perception", he identifies a central way that borders can vary and is discussing the senses. I would broaden this definition to "any place bounded to some degree by barriers to the senses". This avoids narrowing the topic to just the sense of vision as implied by "perception". For borders and surveillance a key element is access or inaccess as these involve the various senses.

The senses stand in special relation to other border factors since persons may be the object of a border (whether having things taken from or imposed upon them, or being kept in or out). Persons may be the carriers of a border as with those wearing location monitoring transmitters (e.g., children, paroles), the boy encapsulated in a plastic bubble for medical purposes or high and low caste Hindus. Persons are also of course the vehicles for comprehending borders through their senses. Many forms of surveillance as border crossing tools and border enhancement tools rely on extending or constricting the senses (whether of the agents or subjects of surveillance and in varying combinations).

Border barriers and breakers often aim at limiting or strengthening sense data. The former thus can involve the construction of barriers that block or limit the normal range of the unaided senses (soundproof rooms, encryption, masks, blindfolds, concussion grenades), as well as impeded human physical mobility and access. Border breakers may seek to extend that range by magnifying the sense in question, or by offering new forms of data and means of transcending physical limitations.

The senses, while invariably connected to perception and cognition, can also be seen as a distinct border form. The senses of course are not a border that one can physically cross as when going between countries or places. Sense borders are different from those that block the mobility of persons or objects. Nor are they a conceptual border involving opposites as between the sacred and the profane, or hot and cold. The senses involve cognitive or experiential borders between the known and the unknown, or the experienced and what can only be imagined. The ignorance associated with the "beyond" of a sense border also differs from limits to cognition that stem form being unable to give meaning to data because they are not understood, or are unknown as a result of disaggregation or being hidden.

Borders of the senses occur naturally when their thresholds are reached. Thus the horizon's border offers a barrier to sight, as does darkness. The borders beyond which we can not hear (or smell, or touch and taste) are logically equivalent, if involving much shorter distances than sight. The later two even require immediate proximity to the stimulus. The territory included in our unaided senses is miniscule relative to what there is to be sensed.

Asking what is on the other side of a border or a frame is a related question. How does what is within the border differ from what is beyond it? With the conceptual border, there is a logical opposition (if not always opposite) based on what is included or excluded from the category. Physical borders may separate places with different social definitions (e.g. a river as the marker between countries) or simply different physical attributes.

The elements distinguished by a border may be basically equivalent (other than for their differentiating factor) as with the river banks separated by flowing water, a national or state border defined by latitude, or the two halves of a basketball court.

Such *symmetrical* borders contrast with *asymmetrical* borders which separate fundamentally different elements (whether beyond, below or above). Consider what lies beyond the edge of a cliff, below the wire of a tight rope walker, surrounds a submerged submarine or the in and out of bounds lines of an athletic field,. Or consider buildings with a concierge or gated communities and what lies beyond them or the jagged and shifting lines of police using fire hoses aimed at crowds.

The finite crossing of a physical border, such as opening a sealed envelope or in hiding a video camera in a wall, creates transparency—the act of border crossing reveals what is on the other side. But sense borders stand in a different relation to their other side. Sense borders may be extended through technology (e.g., binoculars, telescopes, microscopes, and sound transmitters).

However those extensions simply push the opaque threshold beyond which one can no longer receive sense stimuli. The ratio of what is known to unknown is altered as the border is extended, but it is not obliterated.

We may also ask about *directionality* and *frequency* of border crossings. Where border crossings are permitted we may ask if they are uni- or bi-directional. Steve Mann's work in trying to take pictures of surveillance agents (in the tradition of Garfinkle's breaching experiments) illustrates the one-way nature of much surveillance and the question of how, and by whom, a social border is created.

A related factor is whether the *transition* across borders is sudden or gradual. The border change may be immediate and discontinuous as with the edge of a cliff or a town wall. Or the border may be slow and continuous (even as a qualitative difference eventually appears) as with day and night and ecological regions that fade into each other.

Gradual transitions may be marked by in-between areas and intermediate buffer zones traditionally known in geo-poliitcal contexts as "no man's land" (which did not make them woman's lands). Contrast the direct division between entities as when leaving the U.S. and entering Canada or Mexico with the DMZ separating North and South Korea and equivalent contested areas.

Such interstitial border areas (while partly designed as conflict minimization means) are particularly likely to be contentious, as those on opposing sides claim the interstitial area as their own, or one they are entitled to control and use to pursue their own ends. As we will note this contention goes far beyond traditional issues of geography to the location and meaning of borders between the person and others under the stimulus of new surveillance technologies.

We may ask if the border is relatively *fixed* involving geo-coordinates and stationary barriers, or *shifting* and *fluid*. Consider for example the relatively fixed borders of an inland home as against a property line determined by tide levels or a bluff constantly eroded by wind, rain and waves. Diplomatic immunity and international planes and ships involve borders that move with the diplomat and vehicle, as do mobile homes. While Foucault noted how scientific measurement led to lines around presumed normalcy, many devices are fluid and their cut off points specific to the situation and issue (e.g., the advisory note attached to credit score reports that there is no passing or failing grade).

When Frost writes "something there is that doesn't love a wall" he implies both natural processes of erosion and the more purposive activity of insects, animals and hunters in undermining borders. Barrier borders are always partial and to varying degrees leaky. Many surveillance technologies rely on border seepage.

The logistical and economic limits on total monitoring (or perfect borders), the interpretive and contextual nature of many human situations, system complexity and interconnectedness, and the vulnerability of those engaged in border work to be compromised frequently provide room for the inappropriate border crossings (whether involving legal or merely social violations).

In addition, new surveillance technologies give a momentous boost to crossing several forms of traditional border. They call attention to contentious interstitial areas whose meaning is defined through political struggle. They also help create new types of border.

BORDER CHANGES

Old borders never die.

They just get re-arranged. —General Douglas McDialectic

In one form of intact border we see re-arrangement in the individuals who pass through them. With role transitions persons continually cross social and cultural borders. The normative borders remain around categories, but role occupants move on. The game is roughly the same, but the players are different. Consider the move in childhood from being a non-swimmer restricted to the shallow end to being able to cross the line into the deep water reserved for swimmers, not to mention the transitions from childhood to adulthood and beyond (and the gradations there 18, 21, 25, 65 etc.) and the border crossings of immigrants, migrants and tourists.

There is also variation in the individuals passing through ticket controlled perimeters on different days (e.g., sporting and musical events). Consider too, the less common transitions in role and identity entrances and exits –whether entering or leaving a school, marriage or religious order, or undergoing a sex change operation.

Another kind of change involves the borders themselves. Closer to contemporary questions we see the link between surveillance and borders and how technology may change borders. Central topics here are how the agents and subjects of surveillance create, apply, sustain, challenge and change borders under conditions of the new surveillance.

George Simmel has written that "the bridge symbolizes the extension of our volitional sphere into space." In the same way new border creating and breaking technologies extend our volitional sphere into areas far beyond space, including the senses, bodies, selves and time.

Recent developments in communications, surveillance and related technologies in some ways undermine and alter traditional physical, geographical, spatial, juridical and temporal borders, making them more vulnerable to crossing and, partly in response, new borders appear.

New forms and borders whose meaning is unclear or contested are appearing at an accelerated rate. New technologies that overflow and change the meaning of traditional borders, may create disputed interstitial areas.

Consider changes involving the borders of the person and personal information. In the past, walls, darkness, distance, time and skin were boundaries that protected personal information and helped define the self. Information about the self resided with the individual and those who knew him or her. The number of records on an individual was limited. But now with so many new ways of collecting personal data and the growth of data banks, we see the rise of a shadow self based on images in distant, often networked computers.

New ways of defining the self have greatly expanded. We become not only the sum of our own biographies, but part of broader social types believed to have the potential to behave in certain ways. Individuals are defined relative to quantitative scales generated from enormous amounts of data.

Traditional borders blocked information about the self from flowing too freely to others without the individual's knowledge or will. This limitation enhanced the value of personal information to the individual, who could use it as a resource, doling it out as was appropriate. The boundaries of the body/self also served to keep out unwanted influences and information.

But with recent technical developments, the self may be less protected from covert intrusions and manipulations.Technologies being developed that seek to infer meaning from personal involuntary emanations such as brain waves and scents suggest the question of who such data belong to. Consider the case of a California man with a rare blood disease whose virus was cloned in an effort to help treat others. His claim that he had a property interest in the cell line that was subsequently developed was rejected by the court. Determining identity from DNA "prints" left on a drinking glass or by how a person walks can also be noted. Where does the person stop once elements associated with the person are expressed? With visual image, especially if it is used for commercial purposes, the individual has a property right. Should that apply to other forms?

Related examples can be seen when previously unavailable information protected by limitations of the senses are accessed and given meaning through technological supports. Night vision technology takes what had been existentially private (regardless of whether it is in a legally protected private or public place) and makes its visible. Urine, hair and sweat analysis are used to infer drug use patterns. The effort to read subtle facial expressions, voice tremors, handwriting, and heat patterns around the eyes as clues to the person, also seek to profit from porous borders.

Various forms of electronic and chemical scan are used to infer the presence of contraband "seeing" through closed objects such as suitcase or clothes worn. Consider also unseen cameras with zoom lens that look beyond location in a private mall to a "public" street, or a "public" street camera that reveals the interior of a "private" shop or home.

A nice example of how heretofore meaningless personal data associated with a legally private place comes to a public place and is suddenly given meaning through a new technology can be seen in thermal imaging. Here heat from inside a house can be picked up by a device 'outside', revealing the outline of interior areas.

In crossing borders the above efforts take from the person and or their possessions. But technological border crossings may also impose upon the person and in so doing often create contentious marginal zones in search of legal and social definition.

Consider a bakery pumping its smells onto the street, a factory pumping scents through its heating system or a department store spraying its' "perfume of the day" or the intrusive cell phone talking in a public place. These examples create and call attention to buffer areas traditionally free of such stimuli. Telemarketing and spam fit here. Auditory and visual subliminal messages may involuntarily and subtly cross personal borders of perception, just as tear gas, light or acoustic micro-wave crowd control means may not so subtly cross personal borders.

A related border blurring involves the line between the human and the non-human and the living and the machine. We are increasingly seeing humans with artificial parts and research is well underway on artificial skin and blood.

Computer chips have reportedly been implanted in chimpanzees, and a variety of implants have been proposed for humans.

Cyborgs are not just science fiction. We see robots designed to behave as humans and efforts to have humans become more efficient by modeling their actions after machines. The ease with which we divided the human from the non-human and the organic from the inorganic is challenged.

CHANGES IN INSTITUTIONAL, ORGANIZATIONAL AND PLACE BORDERS

The personal border changes noted above are a strand of a broader tapestry of blurred borders that also involve organizations. The lesser clarity re the separation of individuals and groups from each other, and from their environments, has counterparts within institutions and organizations. New communications and surveillance technologies (along with new crises, threats and opportunities) are also blurring and re-arranging organizational structure and goals.

In some ways it becomes more difficult to draw clean clear lines separating the centre from the periphery, the rural from the urban, the national from the international and the private from public (whether involving material or intellectual property).

In the case of formal social control organizations, for example, we see if not outright merging, at least fogging up of the traditional lines between national and international authority, foreign and domestic police, military and police, and intelligence gathering and criminal prosecution. With increased internationalization and globalization of crime, terror and social control, the meaning of national borders and foreign and domestic actions is less clear. The links now made between dealing in contraband (drugs, weapons) and terror weakens the traditional distinction between crime and political activities. The previous separation of the military from domestic police, and intelligence from operational units, is also weakened by new legislation and new forms of cooperation. The emphasis on prevention blurs the line between intelligence and crime fighting activities, freedom of speech and association and crime, and weakens the tradition of a predicate before invasive surveillance is undertaken.

Consider also the boundaries of home and work. For an increasing number of people the traditional boundaries between work and home are blurred (in one way they are even restored to aspects of the pre-industrial age). With telecommuting, we see an increase in the number of people working at home. As well, fast-track employees with beepers, cellular phones, computers with modems and fax machines are expected to be constantly available for work no matter where they are. In addition, company rules such as those against smoking or using drugs are applied to off-duty, as well as on-duty behaviour. The workplace becomes everywhere the worker is. At the same time, with child day care, health, lounge, recreational and commissary facilities, workplaces become more like homes.

The use of electronic monitoring to incarcerate people in their home breaks and create borders in another form. Since the development of modern rights, the home has represented a sanctuary and a refuge, relatively inviolate in defining one of the lines between the public and the private. But with electronic monitoring the home can become deprivatized for both offenders and members of their families. The latter may also be seen and overheard on the video and audio means that frequently accompany home confinement programs.

We also see the weakening of selective borders of domesticity with respect to an increase in the hard and remote wiring and sensoring (and potentially censoring as well) of the home. Here the membranes that bring inputs into the home for entertainment, telephone and computer communication, electric power and heat, as well as various security sensors, send back records of internal activity to distant centers.

Developments in communication and surveillance tools over the last several centuries (and markedly accelerated in recent decades) fundamentally alter temporal lines. The ephemeral past is not what it used to be. With modern technologies, elements the past can be preserved and offered up for visual and auditory consumption. Temporally bounded events move from a flowing river to a stagnant pool. This goes beyond filming of a birth, a wedding or a battle to surfacing and preserving elements of the past that were previously unavailable, such as images of a growing embryo or a brain wave pattern in response to a given stimulus.

The growth of computer records offers a different type of preservation and access. In extending our ability to know the future (particularly on a probable basis), we see the weakening or even breaking of yet another border. Traditionally many elements of the future were open-ended. This supported American optimism and a belief that with hard work or good luck things might get better. DNA analysis or expert systems which yield predictive profiles based on the analysis of large numbers of cases claim to offer windows into a determined future.

Another weakened temporal border involves the lag between the occurrence of an event and communication about it. Such time frames have been greatly shortened as the immediate past and the present almost merge and the temporal buffer offered by slower, more restricted means of communication is reduced. There is less time for judgement and greater pressure for instant action in our twenty-four hour globally connected informational world. For people who are 'on call' regardless of the time or where they are, the borders between action and inaction, on-and off-duty and public and private that were available with the 'natural' rhythms of day and night, weekends and holidays and distance are shattered.

Resistance and Efforts to Create New Borders

Of course these efforts to change traditional borders occur in a dynamic environment. In Western liberal democracies the advantages of technological border breaking developments are often short-lived and contain ironic vulnerabilities. Border creation and border crossing involve a dynamic adversarial social dance of strategic moves and counter-moves and should be studied as a conflict interaction process.

Elsewhere I identify 11 behavioral techniques intended to subvert the collection of information based on crossing personal borders can be noted. While my emphasis is on crossing personal borders, many of these tactics are relevant to other forms of border as well. Here I note several forms particularly relevant to the topic at hand.

For *discovery moves* (known as surveillance detection in the intelligence trade), the goal is to find out if surveillance is in operation and where it is. Examples of discovery moves include locating a hidden border breaking device through use of bug, tape and video camera detection devices.

Avoidance moves may follow the discovery that surveillance is present and involve self-regulation. The subject's behaviour varies depending on whether or not surveillance has been found to be in operation. For example drivers slow down when their anti-radar "fuzz buster" warns them that police radar is in use.

With *piggy back moves* the surveillance is directly faced rather than avoided. A border control is evaded, or information protected, by accompanying or being attached to a legitimate subject or object. For example systems requiring an access card can sometimes be thwarted by walking or, in the case of a parking structure, driving quickly, behind a person with legitimate access.

Blocking and *masking* call explicit attention to the communicative aspects of surveillance. Surveillors desire to read the signals given off by their subjects. With blocking, subjects seek to physically block access to the communication or, if unable or unwilling to do that, to render it (or aspects of it such as the identity, appearance or location of the communicator) unusable. The Faraday cage, which encapsulates space in metal or a metallic net, blocks electronic transmissions.

A simpler version is the shoplifter who uses a large shopping bag with a familiar logo within which is a second bag lined with aluminum or duct tape. Wearing a Halloween mask and writing in invisible ink are familiar children's games which have adult counterparts.

A "photo flash deflector" fluid which blocks the photographing of a license plate became available soon after systems for monitoring red light runners appeared. Some "fuzz busters" send white noise back to a police radar gun producing a blank reading. The encryption of communications is another example.

Electronic surveillance may easily intercept a message, but meaningless absent decryption. Masking involves blocking in that the original information is shielded, but it goes beyond it to involve deception with respect to the identity, status and/or location/ locatability of the person or material of surveillance interest. Efforts to disguise identity, whether involving wigs, died hair, elevator shoes, padded clothing, plastic surgery or fake documents. Remote computer entries, whether taking or sending information, by using another's identification and password, are a nice example of masking. The goal of *breaking moves* is to render the surveillance device inoperable, often by stopping a border breaking or defining device. For example RFID chips can be fried in micro-wave and a video monitor immobilized by spray painting the lens or aiming a laser pointer at it. A male guard dog may be neutralized with a tranquilizer dart, mace, poisoned food or a female dog in heat.

Terminus

In conclusion, I have suggested questions and concepts that may, consistent with the opening epigram from Simmel, help connect the separate and separate the connected with respect to border phenomena. The prism of the border offers a way to order and reflect upon questions of surveillance, communication, privacy, accountability and social change.

It is tempting to see a linear pattern with the knowledge of science and technology leading to the breaking of ever more borders that seemed impassable and immutable to previous generations.

Yet we are hardly at the age of the end of borders. The pushing back of borders and frontiers does not mean they disappear given their functionality, social and cultural supports and the richness and complexity of an onion-skinned universe.

It is just as reasonable to note the discovery and invention of new borders and the pushing further back (or ahead) of older ones in a continuing process. We see continuity in the progressive erosion of borders, but also in the creation of new borders. What changes is content, not form.

Developments in communications and surveillance create new forms and destroy, re-arrange and alter some of the physical, geographical, spatial, juridical and temporal borders that have traditionally defined and protected the integrity of individuals and groups.

When surveillance topics are controversial it is often because defining, creating, crossing, or failing to cross a border of some form is at issue. Policy issues in a wide array of contexts often revolve around the appropriateness of crossing or failing to cross, personal and organizational borders and the wise and unwise use of border barriers.

Concepts such as those offered above can identify questions and variation. A next step is to study correlates, consequences and causes of this. Studies of the structures and dynamics through which agents and subjects of surveillance strategically create border barriers and border breakers around themselves and/or their opposition ought to be a central topic for social inquiry.

8

Global Concept of Borders, Borderlands, and Frontiers

At first glance the concept of borders, borderlands, or frontiers would seem to be straightforward. A border or boundary is a line on a map delineating a territorial boundary or the limit of a political jurisdiction. Borders are primarily, but far from exclusively, seen as properties of and under the control of states. Nevertheless, this has generally not always been the case. Even in the contemporary world where such an interpretation often does apply, the concept of borders frequently becomes much more complicated.

COMPLICATIONS OF A SEEMINGLY SIMPLE CONCEPT

The first complication is semantic. In many European languages, including British English, the term *frontier* is a synonym for border. In the Americas, and especially in the United States, *border* means boundary, between countries, between the states of the United States, or between provinces in Mexico or Canada. *Frontier,* typically but not exclusively, refers to a historical boundary between expanding European settlements and indigenous settlements. Thus in English usage in the United States, frontiers and borders are very different concepts and refer to quite distinct social markers. This usage has often been generalized to any sort of border zone or borderland between different sets of peoples coming into contact. It is frequently extended metaphorically to refer to any boundary between known and unknown, an extension discussed further at the end of this entry. The second complication is historical. Since the founding of the first states in human history in Mesopotamia some five thousand years ago, boundaries or borders have generally been vague, imprecise zones in which political—and to a lesser extent economic, social, and cultural—control fades away. That is, borders, boundaries, borderlands, and frontiers are zones or regions with some dimension, where there is a shift, more or less gradual, from control by one state to another or to an absence of state control. An important corollary of this complication is that the lack of precision is not necessarily a problem in semantics or conceptualization. Rather, it is often an accurate reflection of an actual fuzziness of boundary zones.

A third complication is that at different times and in different places these concepts have had different meanings, and they have been implemented in different ways. Often a word translated as *border* from one language to another had behind it a different meaning, a different concept of markers, and even different ethical and political implications of what that "border" entailed.

A fourth complication is that the meanings of these terms and how they have been implemented have changed over many millennia. Throughout these changes there have often been disconnects or divergences between their social reality and what various actors (individuals or states) thought they should be.

Finally, there is a problem of scale. Almost any border or boundary zone, when viewed from a sufficient distance, appears as a sharp line. When viewed up close, however, it becomes a zone having some width and often having blurry edges. So from a central capital, a border or frontier may seem precise. Yet from the perspectives of those living on or near the boundary or frontier, or even from the perspectives of those charged with administering or controlling it, it can be quite vague and often contentious.

Defining Borders, Borderlands, and Frontiers

In order to discuss these issues it is useful to present somewhat general definitions of these terms. The following definitions carry two caveats or cautions. First, as with any generalized concepts, they will not be precise for all uses. Second, these terms shift meaning over time and through space. Still, the following are useful for further discussion:

boundary —a demarcation indicating some division in spatial terms

border —an international boundary line; when a border is seen as a zone it is often called a borderland or the borderlands

frontier —a zone of contact with or without a specified boundary line

The term *borderlands* straddles the distinction between frontier and border and is often used as a synonym for frontier as a zone.

The contemporary concept of a border as a sharp, precise line stems from two sources. First is the Peace of Westphalia, which established the modern nation-state system under which a state had full sovereign control of the lands and peoples within its borders. The second source is the development of private property as a concept, in which one individual, or state, had exclusive rights to land or territory. While in the early twenty-first century these conditions are taken as "normal" or "natural," they are neither. Rather, the idea of a border as a precise line grew out of the needs of states to define boundaries. The idea of exclusive control of land developed from the transformation of control of land from a matter of use rights to a concept of land as an economic commodity, that is, something that can be bought and sold. In other words, these contemporary conceptualizations, which are often seen as a part of the process of modernization, were themselves socially constructed under very specific historical, political, and economic conditions.

In premodern times, that is, approximately before the sixteenth century c.e., land was most often thought of as a resource to which individuals, or more typically groups, had rights to use. In many nonstate societies, if the individual or group did not use the land—usually for a considerable time—then they lost their use rights. This is almost always distinctly different, however, from the European concept of *terra nullius,* which means "empty or unused land." For those groups who foraged for a livelihood or who practiced shifting agriculture, "use" of land often included long fallow periods. To groups that practiced intensive agriculture—from classic civilizations to modern states—such fallow land appeared empty, hence unclaimed and available for settlement. These differences in how rights to land are conceptualized have been the source of much conflict over many millennia between agricultural states and nonstate peoples. For example, such conflicting viewpoints are at the root of the myth that the island of Manhattan was "purchased." Dutch occupiers presumed that they were buying a commodity with exclusive rights. Indigenous peoples thought that in consideration for a gift marking friendship they were granting rights to joint use of common lands.

At least two caveats are in order in regard to such conflicts. First, nonstate peoples could and did come into conflict over use of land. Indeed, one of the major mechanisms of the spread of humans derives from such conflicts.

Although they were sometimes resolved through fighting, such conflicts were more often resolved by one group moving deeper into unoccupied land, which over time led to the spread of humans over most of the earth. Second, many claims by civilizations or states that land was unused, or was *terra nullius,* were in fact veiled rationalizations for seizing land from peoples who had less complex social or political organization and who did not use the land as intensively.

From the development of the first states some five thousand years ago until the early twenty-first century, though abating somewhat since the Peace of Westphalia, land could be, and often was, seized by conquest.

To be ethical, such seizures often needed some sort of justification, such as a "just war," reparation for previous harm done, or evidence of illegitimate use by those from whom the land was seized. Obviously, such claims could, and often were, readily invented and rationalized. Still, states did develop a territorial sense and became concerned with boundaries, borders, borderlands, and frontiers. A primary concern, however, was control, mainly political and economic but sometimes also social and cultural. Even constructed barriers, such as the Great Wall of China or Hadrian's Wall in northern Scotland that marked the edge of the Roman Empire, barriers that did constitute explicit boundaries, were primarily used to control movements of peoples and goods. They were seldom intended as absolute barriers.

Such walls and other barriers were often constructed with military and control functions in mind. They served to regulate interactions between the state or empire and the surrounding groups, whether those were other empires, states, or nonstate peoples. They were constructed to keep members within the state or empire, to keep others out, and to regulate which individuals, groups, or objects could cross the barrier as well as why, when, and under what circumstances such crossings could take place. Such barriers often marked a shift from direct control to indirect control, wherein local leaders controlled the area, but via assorted agreements with the state or empire. In essence, such barriers were not sharp or precise lines but rather the visible centerlines of zones of transition. Some people tried to avoid these controls. Such avoidance is typically defined as "criminal." Thus borders give rise to smuggling and smugglers.

Frontier as Membrane

These sorts of considerations led the historian Richard W. Slatta to describe frontiers as membranes. This is a singularly appropriate metaphor for frontiers and to somewhat lesser extent for borders, borderlands, and boundaries. Membranes are differentially permeable with respect to what may pass through them and what is blocked. Their permeability often is different for opposite directions. That is, some goods are allowed to pass, say horses entering China from the central Asian steppes and silk leaving. Other things, such as armies, are not allowed to pass. Horses came into China but seldom left, unless mounted by soldiers seeking retribution for raids; silk left China but seldom came in. Membranes have thickness. When viewed from a distance they seem thin, almost like lines. When viewed up close they are zones through which objects, people, and ideas may pass.

BORDERLANDS AND FRONTIERS AS ZONES OF ETHNIC CHANGE

Because borderlands and frontiers are zones between different human organizations, they are also zones of intense interactions of objects, peoples, and ideas. These interactions can range from very peaceful, mutually beneficial relationships to incessant warfare. Oftentimes, several types of interactions along the range from peaceful to warlike can occur simultaneously. For instance, along the northern frontier of New Spain (what is now the southwestern United States) various indigenous groups would have peaceful trading relationships with some Spanish villages while they were raiding others. This also occurred among various indigenous groups. Indeed, at times these opposite relations were not between different indigenous groups and villages but varied from family group to family group on both sides. In short, frontiers are zones of intense interactions, often of several types at the same time. These interactions can change rapidly with local circumstances. This locally variable volatility is a special characteristic of frontiers and borderlands.

These were and are zones where different products and processes mixed and intermingled, often leading to the development of new products and processes. On frontiers one process of this sort, called ethnogenesis, is especially salient. Ethnogenesis is the formation of a new ethnic group via the amalgamation of two or more previously distinct groups.

With the interactions of different peoples, interbreeding and intermarriage were not rare, even in cases in which one or both sides tried to prevent such mixing. When the mixing became sufficiently regular and frequent, it could give rise to an entirely new group. The Metís in Canada and Genízaros in northern New Spain are examples. The Metís grew from unions between French fur traders—typically males—and indigenous women. These long-term relations were mutually beneficial. French fur traders gained access to furs collected and processed through their wives' groups (such unions were frequently polygynous, with the trader having more than one wife, often from different groups). The indigenous groups gained access to European trade goods acquired through traders who were relatives and hence under considerable kinship obligation to trade fairly. In the early twenty-first century the Metís are still negotiating with the Canadian government for recognition as a people distinct from both indigenous or first nations and from European immigrants.

In northern New Spain there was an active trade in captives, both indigenous peoples captured by Spaniards during fighting and Spaniards captured by indigenous peoples; in both cases, the captives were typically women or children. Indigenous children raised in Spanish communities developed a separate identity that was neither fully Spanish nor fully of their natal indigenous group. If an individual Genízaro or his family rose to prominence, typically as a frontier soldier or sometimes through economic success, he or they could be assimilated into Hispanic society. When the United States annexed the region, the trade in captives rapidly ceased, and the Genízaro population gradually assimilated into either Hispanic or indigenous societies.

The anthropologist Frederick Barth describes another role for boundaries with respect to ethnic identity. Barth argues that ethnicity is not defined by its content but rather by the boundary or boundaries that separate one group from another. This seemingly counterintuitive view developed from studies showing that when individuals or families crossed ethnic boundaries (which may or may not coincide with political boundaries), they often changed identity. Such events are not all that rare in the ethnographic record. Furthermore, some individuals and families made such changes more than once in a single lifetime. Typically, such changes are associated with changes in ecological adaptation. Chinese farmers who moved onto the steppe and became pastoralists typically joined a nomad group and took up that group's culture. If or when they moved back and again took up farming, they again became Chinese. In such cases, not only is the border or frontier a membrane, but it also is a catalyst for identity change. As noted, such ethnic boundaries seem most common where local ecology forces changes in productive strategies. Changes in climate and especially the development of new technologies allow such borders to shift over time.

Recent research by the biologist Mark Pagei and the anthropologist Ruth Mace supports Barth's interpretation. Pagei and Mace argue that boundaries help maintain a sense of group and enhance social solidarity and cooperation, but often at the cost of promoting conflict with other groups. Thus boundaries and borders play an important role in group formation, even while generating conflict between groups.

The Puzzle of Borderlands and Frontiers

These complications give rise to yet another, enduring aspect of borders, borderlands, and frontiers. On first glance they all seem the same or certainly similar. But with closer examination, each border region seems unique. This puzzling aspect of frontiers has fascinated and frustrated scholars who study frontiers comparatively.

The sociologist Thomas D. Hall argues that this puzzling quality derives from the complex way in which frontiers are formed. In a nutshell, frontiers are constructed by the interaction of two or more different groups. The location, extent, duration, and changes in any specific frontier zone entail a complex mixture of factors external to the frontier zone and local factors, all mediated by the actions of the peoples who live in the frontier zone.

The broad similarity among frontiers derives from the small number of factors, in the following example numbering five, that shape most frontiers:

- the types of groups that come into interaction (three types: nonstate, tributary [or ancient] states or empires, or capitalist [or modern] states);
- the type of boundary involved (four types: local economic, political or military, long-distance economic, and cultural);
- the types of nonstate groups (three types, such as those conventionally labeled bands, tribes, or chiefdoms);
- the type of frontier (four types: buffer, barrier, internal, or external); and
- the type of ecological environment (four types: steppe, sown, hill, or valley).

These few factors, when divided into only a few basic categories, will generate 576 different types of frontiers. This immense variety—which could easily be expanded with finer categorization—explains why each specific frontier seems unique. The point of this example is *not* the specific list of factors *nor* the number of specific categories into which they are divided. Rather, it is that with only a few factors divided into a small number of categories an immense variety of frontiers or borderlands can be described. This then "solves" the puzzle of how and why all frontiers seem similar at first glance but on closer examination seem unique. The similarity derives from the small number of factors involved; the uniqueness from the large number of ways they can be combined.

BORDERS, BORDERLANDS, AND FRONTIERS AS SITES OF SOCIAL CHANGE

Because of the various complex interactions that occur along borders, in borderlands, and on frontiers, such places are very fertile areas for studying how social, political, economic, and cultural changes occur and how individuals and groups both shape and are shaped by those changes. They are zones where the local and the global interact very intensely and hence exhibit processes that are rarely, if ever, seen in more central areas. This is another reason why the study of borderlands and frontiers is often so fascinating to scholars.

Frontiers are often seen as sources of change, as in the famous frontier thesis of the American historian Frederick Jackson Turner (1861–1932): that the frontier zones of the United States shaped the country's national character. Turner has often been criticized for having the causality backwards: It was the central areas that shaped the frontier. The literature of these debates is enormous, even leading some U.S. historians to question the utility of the concept of "the frontier." A major problem here is in the definite chapter: "the frontier" was in reality many, highly fluid, and changeable frontiers.

One very positive result of these debates has been the development of a growing body of writings on comparative frontiers. By comparing different frontiers, scholars have begun to uncover both common, underlying factors and their various unique constellations. Such studies have done much to further blur the distinctions between history and sociology, anthropology, and geography. A conventional, if caricatured, view of these disciplines is that history is idiographic, concerned with painting detailed pictures, whereas sociology, anthropology, and geography are nomothetic or seeking lawlike regular patterns. This conventional view is flawed in at least two ways. First, it sees the two approaches as opposites or as in conflict rather than complementary. Second, it fails to recognize that there is a vast array of possibilities of combining both types of explanations and descriptions. Studies of frontiers or borderlands, especially comparative studies, must combine both approaches in ways that often render disciplinary distinctions unrecognizable. Phrased alternatively, comparative studies of frontiers are inherently multi- and interdisciplinary. Thus the comparative study of frontiers itself forms a kind of intellectual borderland.

Borderlands and Frontiers as Metaphors

No discussion of borders, borderlands, and frontiers would be complete without some attention to the metaphorical use of these terms. Most readers of English are familiar with such phrases as "the frontiers of medicine," "the frontiers of science," and "space, the final frontier." Behind these metaphors is a state-centered view of borders, borderlands, and frontiers in which such areas mark a zone of transition from well-known territory under control of the state to little-known territory not under control of the state. This metaphor breaks down, however, if pushed too far. Spatial frontiers most often had residents on the other side who were obviously not unknown to themselves. Indeed, at first contact, from each side (and there often are or were borders or frontiers with more than two sides) the other side(s) seemed unknown and were seen as strange or mysterious by the other side(s).

The unknown quality of the "other side of the border or frontier" simultaneously generates curiosity, promise, threat, and fear. It is this combination of reactions brought on by approaching unknown and often uncontrolled territory, peoples, or ideas that is the key difference between frontiers and borderlands on the one hand and a border or boundary in the conventional sense on the other. Presumably with a conventional border, what is on the other side is known but is held separate and distinct by the border. The combination of mystery and danger accompanied by promise and curiosity seems to be at the root of the popularity of the use of frontier (and less frequently borderlands) as a metaphor. In that sense, of course, it is singularly apt for describing or labeling a transition from the known to the unknown.

Thus concepts of borders, borderlands, and frontiers seem at first glance straightforward, simple, and clear. Yet when examined more closely, they are mysterious, complex, and murky. This is why they are often regions of such fascination to scholars and thinkers in many disciplines. Also because of their transitional qualities, they are often excellent sites to study a wide variety of social, cultural, political, and economic change.

THE ARAB SPRING AND THE BORDER PEOPLE OF TETOUAN

The border of Ceuta is famous. The discourse behind the scene described is about nation-states and the establishment of borders. It is linked to narratives about structural power-relations among and within nation-states, as well as the images and boundaries which people have in mind. It is about defining identities. In daily social realities this comes down to a rather arbitrary division of people: people with a "good" passport, people with a "wrong" one. Freedom of movement along one of the most protected borders in the world, the border of Ceuta, is thus a question of citizenship and has become an issue to ongoing, current local, national and supranational debate. The above example shows how powerful discourses institutionalized in macro-level structures manifest temporarily as very practical processes in everyday-life at the border: State-officials controlling passports, people can pass depending on to which territorial unit, national or regional they belong to.

As every border the border in Ceuta, between Spain and Morocco, is thus meant to separate legal systems, cultures, politics, mentalities, religions and people from each other in order to guarantee sovereignty about territories and people to the two states. Those people are expected to subject themselves to the discourses of national identities and nation-states with all their sovereignty. In the case of Ceuta the border is even more contested: It is also the separation of the European Union and Morocco, Europe and Africa. Therefore identification with collective identities congruent with the territories of those units is expected to be proved by the people living on the land considered to belong to the respective territorial units.

Identification and subjection to discourses linked to the territorial units can vary spatially in extent and quality. This is crucial here and based on the assumption that discourse is always renegotiated by people in their everyday routines and practices in certain places –people make their own meanings of discourses and that way reproduce the discourse, adding their own discursive pieces. As everyday lives are often bounded to a certain region and networks of activities, which are somehow spatially concentrated, the national discourses will be regarded here as being place-specifically reproduced.

To make things more concrete: We are dealing with the network of institutions, activities and people of the border region of Ceuta and the way people renegotiate collective identities and discourses in their very special spatial context. An important assumption about the border-region and its people has to do with the vital function, the border has for interaction between Ceuta and the areas and people on the Moroccan side, including illegal activities such as smuggling. The border is much more permeable than its physical appearance might suggest. The people who have an objective in passing are diverse: There are European tourists wanting to visit Morocco or wanting to visit Ceuta, there are salesmen with Moroccan passports with a special permission to enter the Spanish enclave daily and there are those who only watch the fence from distance – thousands of potential immigrants to Europe, the desired continent of their hope for a better living.

Many of the latter desperately run into the fence, experience violence or even death. Inspite of this, there is cultural exchange, interrelation and normality embedded in the everyday routine at the border.

Especially the group having a permission to cross the border from the Moroccan side to Ceuta every day is interesting: This group "benefits from a 24-hour visa-exemption granted by Spain". This is applied by "special provisions for bilateral trade" with the neighbouring province of Tetouan: citizens of this city "require only a passport for a maximum 24-hour stay" and can do business in Ceuta. This group of border-people, daily crossing the border, represents more than everyone else the permeability and interaction inherent in the border.

A paradox appears at borders when discourses related to the territorial units of nation-states and the people inhabiting those "national" territories are renegotiated in the lives of border-people who to diverse extent and for the realization of spatially separated activities spend their days on both sides of the border. People such as the citizens of Tetouan described above, are involved in practices on both sides, have built up trans-boundary-social networks and may have a sort of own collective identity (an own discourse) which is spatially spread to both sides of the border among border-people.

Many intelligent, studied people have thought about the issue of borders and the life of people in the region around them. In this chapter focus lies on the possibilities inherent in borders, the interaction and permeability. It is about the assumption that the everyday meaning making at the border can create a fluid and hybrid culture, a discourse and collective identity. My assumption is that this culture might be possibly even seen as more "connected" and powerful than and thus resistant to cultural unities called ´Morocco`, ´Spain`, ´Europe` or Ắfrica`– in the sense that geographical proximity in the border-region and shared experience in everyday life are embraced. Everyday routine is local and powerful. People profit from the border and the imposed structures by a commonly experienced culture of everyday, different from other far away parts of nation-states. Emotions, rational decisions of people living in the Moroccan part of the border-region might be much closer to emotions and decisions of people living in the part of the border-region of Ceuta, than to those of people living in Casablanca, the Sahara or Agadir. The ´Other` does not necessarily have to be *felt* at the other side of the border and is always sustaining the self –so that the distinction can never be clear-cut. This is based on assumptions about discourse and meaning-making which are presented later on in this chapter: If the powerful national discourses are not fully resisted, the everyday life practices of border people and their meaning-making will at least provoke renegotiation and reproduction of the national discourse in a very unique way, due to very unique circumstances in the border-region.

A powerful, territorially bound, national discourse has been recently produced in Morocco. Ideally, thus recently things should have been changing on the Moroccan side of the border. Morocco is facing one of the greatest social movements going on in the Arab world,–the "Arab Spring" starting from the 20th February movement, which made so many Moroccans go out into the streets, calling for a change of the system they live in. A strong sense of collective identity brought diverse groups of different goals and interests together, reinforcing national identity by claiming the same thing and fighting for a common goal. Even though some people do not subject to the discourse and collective identity, it has become an issue, and the national identity has become subject to renegotiation. For some it can reinforce a patriotic sense of belonging. It might also stimulate the hope of a better future in Morocco and have broken with the taboo of speaking about borders –following ideas of Moroccan students borders might play a role even in demands to the king.

The relevance of the research is contributing to knowledge about borders with a more distant aim of furthering transnational cooperation and decenter the discourses of nation states and the Arab Spring in Morocco. The aim of this particular research is therefore to develop an understanding of, if possible, how border-people with a presumably strong own discourse and identity resist or renegotiate a powerful national discourse in their everyday life. If as supposed the national discourse is too powerful to be totally resisted, it is thus worth researching how the border-people combine the influence of the powerful national discourse of the Arab Spring (20 February Movement) with their own discourse and meaning-making. This finally leads to the main research question:

How have Moroccans in the border-region possessing an exceptional 24 hours visa to work in Ceuta renegotiated the discourses of the Arab-Spring movement in Morocco in their every-day practices with regard to their relationship to the physical border in the region and borders in mind?

This research question may be answered by focusing on the following sub-questions about

The physical border

A) What was the every-day practice of the Moroccan border-people in relation to the like *before* the Arab spring? How did they relate the practices to the border?

B) What is the every-day practice of the Moroccan border-people in relation to the like *after* the Arab spring movement has begun? How do they relate the practices to the border?

The borders in mind

A) How did the 'border-people' at the Moroccan side define the Other, the Self and the commonalities of the border-region and the border *before* the beginning of the Arab spring? What did they think about (people on) the other side of the border?

B) How do the 'border-people'at the Moroccan side constitute the Other, the Self and the commonalities of the border-region and the border after the beginning of the Arab spring? What do they think about (people on) the other side of the border?

The goal of this research is thus to understand the role of the physical border on the one hand and " borders" in minds of border-people on the other hand before and after the beginning of the influence of the Arab Spring discourse. This is purchased by finding out about changes of relations with the physical border and the imaginary boundaries in people´s minds as indicating change or combination of practices and discourses. It is a question of how the individual renegotiates and how much he subjects to the discourse, border-people might do less. My first assumption is that the nation-wide discourse of the Arab Spring has been subjected to the more purely by a person participating actively in the movement, identifying with the collective. This means that I assume that the supposed interaction, the permeability and the relationships of people with/across the border can have changed for the individual because the process of crossing itself (e.g. sharpened controls as reaction by Moroccan authorities to calm down the population, and avoid contact with a democratized outside) and the feeling at crossing are experienced differently. If subjecting to the discourse (collective identity) of the Arab Spring more purely, people can change their image of the other side of the border, feeling a higher self-esteem as belonging to the Moroccan collective, more equal and united with Europeans and carry it on into their daily lives crossing the border. This implies changing the mental boundaries of the other and the self, of the common and shared between the ´border-people` on both sides. Yet, I assume that the sort of collective identity of border-people makes them resistant to the nation-wide discourses of the Arab Spring much more than other people: Individual renegotiation takes place in the context of the border region and it´s "resisting" networks. The notion of "European paradise" is different from the daily life of the ´border-people`, who have a more diversified, realistic idea of Europe. Instead of feeling different from the "other" located at the other side their daily contact has an economic, practical value so that border-people feel belonging to Morocco and simultaneously silently resist the wider discourse of national identity and Arab Spring.

The research methods chosen here is an explorative, qualitative one, based on triangulation of qualitative research techniques. In order to achieve these goals in a structured manner, the following themes will be dealt with: First some regional background information will be given in paragraph number two, to make the reader more familiar with Morocco as a country and the special role of the border-region. The next paragraph gives a theoretical framework on borders, discourse, meaning-making and social movements in order to focus on the most important related aspects of the border-region´s daily culture. Then a paragraph is dedicated to the chosen methodology, giving more insights into the choice of places and research group as well.

REGIONAL BACKGROUND – PLACING THE REGION OF CEUTA AND TETOUAN

Variety is something that can be found in many aspects of life in Morocco: Variety of landscapes and land-use, a history of diverse periods of domination and a plurality of a former tribal society. Various dominant political systems throughout history, diverse ethnic and other population groups, linguistic pluralism, economic class differences and disparities are important intermingling issues. On the other hand there are some features of similarity in Morocco such as common beliefs and a common religion, as well as the shared love for the king Mohammed VI, national identity and a certain range of traditions and cultural rituals. This chapter is to describe and give some background information about what Morocco and its diverse interrelated features might be like, giving the very Northern part, the border-region of Tetouan and Ceuta, a place.

Basic data and social economic situation in brief

The constitutional monarchy Morocco is situated in the outer North-West of Africa, belonging to the region of the Maghreb. The king, and religious leader at the same time, rules over 16 regions and a population of 33 million people. The population is young with an average age of 24,3 years and to 98,7% Muslim. Suiting this situation the official language is Arabic, however there is a great variety of spoken languages due to historical developments.

Morocco has a very much rainfall dependent economy due to the crucial role of the agricultural sector to economy. Yet the growth of the non-agricultural sector makes the GDP slightly less vulnerable. What is interesting is that Morocco still allows for the informal sector to take 45% of non-agricultural workforce and in the North for smuggling goods and people. Having a look at the socio-economic dimension the HDI is still low, indicative especially for the low adult literacy levels and great inequalities between urban and rural, men and women, considering physical and social infrastructure. The above information contributes to understand the current social movement and situation of Morocco as a nation-state in a global system, helping also to understand the current discourses on the border issues.

Most significant historical developments with crucial impacts on present-day Morocco

However, society in Morocco has changed throughout time and is changing, having important impacts on the border debate. Various forces have been dominant in provoking changes in the past: Morocco has once been an important "powerful Muslim Empire". Hereby a religious leadership has been established.

At the beginning of the 20th century the colonial era of the French and Spanish – the latter in the North along the Mediterranean Sea - started.The legacy of the colonizers was "ambiguous". Economic reforms made especially benefit the French, using Moroccans as tools and employees, so that export quotas did not help the Moroccans but the French - Moroccans instead. The dependence on Europe even did not finish after independence in 1956, which is described by the term of "neocolonialism", referring to the appreciation of French culture but also to economic dependence both especially fostered by the pro-French elite. This short historical background, nicely illustrates the struggle about territory, power, dependency and legitimacy which has played for centuries and has by no means stopped.

The functioning of the political system and the Arab spring

Having a look at the political system of Morocco one can notice that there has thus been "stagnation" in monarchy after independence, building on "pluralism in name but not in practice" until the 90s of last century. The practice was rather to "sideline challengers" in order to keep on "centralized power" and guarantee a "weak fragmented political party system". This strategy has even been maintained in slightly different way each by the second king, Hassan II and the third, the current king Mohammed VI hiding it behind an "aura modernity" and an "'executive constitutional monarchy". This means that reforms are organized "top-down" and despite "significant changes" the process is very long-lasting and not digging deep enough. Reasons might be the power of traditional institutions, the 'makhzen`, which make the "king rule [...] but [...] not govern". Some even doubt if the measures actually ought to be called reform and hint at `corruption' in the system (Y. Saghrouni, personal communication, September 8th, 2011) stressing again especially the power of the "makhzen monarchical institutions network". However, "Moroccans love their king" (Y. Mahtat, personal communication, September13th, 2011) and trust him in his role as religious leader, which even increases his power, so that many efforts made by the grass roots movements would be taken over by the king later on and his people is merciful to him (Y. Saghrouni, personal communication, September 8th, 2011). On the other side it is certainly fortunate for Morocco, that the new king shows himself sensitive to people – at least if he has no choice for not further endangering his status (Y. Saghrouni, personal communication, September 8th, 2011). Yet the parliamentary elections of 2007 can be considered somehow a setback for the monarchy, because of a negligible participation of only 25%, which shows that the practical functioning of the institution is doubted. To sum up, the "implementation lags behind", and still the reforms have stimulated movement and more openness, less taboo, women rights and more freedom of press has been attained. Prospects for reforms depend on how much pressure the movement can exercise, on how and to which extent the traditional institutions support it, especially referring to parties inside the country (such as the growing Islamic forces) and the support of grassroots by the external world. In the light of the Arab spring movement with its peak on February, 20th in 2011 recent reforms are meant to introduce more rights for women, decentralization, a new constitution and Amazigh as language for the Imaghzen minority with written language (Y. Saghrouni, personal communication, 8th of September, 2011).They also go along with a reinforcement of a collective, national identity as talks to some Moroccans students have revealed.

Wider changes influencing every-day life cultures in Morocco

Since the independence in 1956 and recently since the beginning of Arab spring movement societal and cultural changes have taken place. This can be seen in the role of women, the status of minorities in society, the role of religion and the influence of globalization.

Women have become more self-conscious and although their fight has been long, nowadays their rights have been much strengthened and they are present in the public (Y. El Kirat, personal communication, 15th of September, 2011). However men remain in a somewhat superior position because of religion, social norms and practice have another impact, e.g. the underrepresentation of women on the streets at night. To "minorities" and ethnic groups such as the Imaghzen applies a similar, but ambigious story (Y. El Kirat, personal communication, 15th of September, 2011). Globalization might be with its transmission of especially Western can be seen as a challenge to Moroccan society especially to the role of religion. Islam, however, is still of great importance, if not even greater than before. Globalization and other modern life-style features generally have brought along challenging features such as the schedule of work in relation to the praying practice, women calling for equality and independence, individualism versus family ties and social obligation and secularism. As a response surprisingly many different copying strategies have appeared in different states (ranging from real secularist adaptation to theocratic, strictly religious regimes), with Morocco being a constitutional monarchy with a religious leader at the same time. People seem to find ways to combine both religion and new influences some returning to stricter beliefs, whereas others chose to interpret the Qur´an less strict allowing them for a "westernized" life-style (Y. Mahtat, personal communication, 13th of September, 2011).

The role of diverse languages has changed, but the issue is still being regarded as a severe obstacle to many people- since there is a close link to identity formation and status in Moroccan society. The most spoken languages are still the least recognized, whereas French-Arabic -bilinguism dominates the public sphere: One still stands for prestige as facilitating communication in the business sector and the world of intellectuals and the other respectively being the language of belief, religion and state.

What has to be said, however, at this point is, that all the issues discussed cannot be seen independent of each other, because of very strong interrelated features and affects among each other.

The border-region in the very North

Historically, during colonial Morocco the North has belonged to the Spanish protectorate zone. Unlike the French, the Spanish colonizers did not establish different legal systems for different ethnic groups – although the group of Amazigh people, the Rifis, was much bigger in the North than the Arab ethnic group. Rule was instead established through existing structures of tribes and notables.

But there were fights for many years about territorial dominance between groups of Moroccans, different tribes and the Spanish army – wherein the Spanish would often succeed by using leaders for their own purposes when they were without chances by mere fight. However, the Moroccan groups caused them plenty of struggles, especially in the 1920s during the Rifwar. The colonial rule was even less approved, when, during the Depression of the 1930s, the Spanish zone was the poorest among all regions in Morocco, due to the least economic stability. This period in combination with the Civil War in Spain gave opportunity to the rise of a national movement, which was supported by Spanish agitation and social activism mostly out of anxiety (of officials before unrest and the pressure of Franco)– and after the Second World War out of lack of forces. Moreover hunger and disease had increased throughout the war as well as discontent. Also in the French zone tolerance of colonial authority was "fading fast". The protectorate came to an end by internal pressure- except for the enclaves along the Mediterranean coast and the delicate issue of Spanish Sahara.

The era of independence had begun but still the economic situation was not good in the North so that there was a strong trend of outmigration in the 1960s, but also rural –urban migration to smaller and major towns. At the same time Morocco as a state was engaged in winning the competition about Sahara to be attained from the Spanish in order to realize the idea of "'Greater Morocco'" and finally succeeded. Anyway the annexation is widely criticized and is subject to conflict even nowadays.

The Spanish – Moroccan diplomatic relations thus have always been overloaded with tension and rivalry (much more than the French- Moroccan relations) about territories and are still not friendly, which is to be seen in acts of aggression such as the occupation of an island close to the Spanish enclave Ceuta being interpreted by the Spanish as some sort of provocation. Another struggle is about fishing grounds in the Atlantic, leading to tension between Morocco, Spain and the EU.

The border between the enclave Ceuta and Morocco thus marks the separation of two states with very diverse political systems with a tensed relationship but at the same time forms the line of division between Europeans and non- Europeans. In that sense the border is even more contested since a lot of possible irregular migrants seek to enter the "European paradise" but are mostly left without any chance : "*Considered for decades as a land of opportunity and asylum, Europe has adopted more and more severe measures with respect to immigration [...] notion of 'illegals' attempting to profit from a more favourable situation* ". A highly sophisticated security system has been established and "*over the past decade, Morocco has in its turn experienced increasing pressure from Europe to respond to migration flows and institute a legal framework with respect to those who pass through its territory*". After the confrontation between Spanish and migrants in 2005 leading to death of many migrants and the deportation of even more, the Sub-Saharan migration has climbed even higher on the political agenda. This shows how the impact of a small piece of border (certainly after Spain had joined the Schengenstaaten in 1991 has impacted on global migration reaching far into Africa, creating suffering among so many people who are not allowed to cross the border legally.

However, in the daily routine, the economy of the Spanish enclave, Ceuta, and the province of Tetouan are highly interwoven and therefore the border between the states plays a significant role.

The social, cultural changes mentioned in earlier paragraphs about Morocco in general certainly have impacts also on the very North of the country – where many Amazigh people will hopefully experience the benefit of reforms. Still, the question of language might be regarded as even more contested because of the heritage of Spanish as language of the colonizers, which can lead to more serious consequences in relation with the fact that French is the formally most acknowledged and prestigious language in the state of Morocco. Globalization – e.g. the conflict between being an open trading region with international harbours and the influence of media etc - and the strong Islamist forces in Tanger is a good example here, especially in times of the Arab Spring impacting the region.

The cities of Ceuta and Tetouan

The situation of the zone of Tetouan and Ceuta at the Mediterrraenean Sea has had important impacts for the region. Ceuta itself is a Spanish city and province of 77.389 inhabitants which is economically dependent on the relation with the Moroccan areas in its direct neihbourhood. There is a regular flow of workers from those areas, since Moroccans from Tetouan profit from a 24-hour visa-exemption granted by Spain. Hernandez et al. describe the interrelation as "thriving from commercial relations with Morocco including narcotics and humanTrafficking", including smuggling to a huge extent. For the Moroccans the profit is even higher since the introduction of the Euro to Spain and Ceuta, reinforcing the attractiveness of the Spanish city as a site for work. The economy is moreover rather dependent on the harbor, some industrial areas, commerce and benefits from special, generous fiscal conditions. Small and medium enterprises are numerous in commerce and services, the internal consumption is augmented essentially by the tourism sector and Moroccan citizens consuming in the city as well. This leads to the important issue of how the 4 religious groups have come to settle in the city : Before the Arab conquered the city, it was mostly Christian and became Christian again after the conquest of the Portuguese in 1415. From 1668 the city was in Spanish-hand and is since then claimed to have preserved its "Spanish-ness", even during the period of the protectorate and after the independence of Morocco and it has been even ratified as part of the Spanish Constitution. Since 1986 when Spain joined the EU, there has been financial support by the latter. In 1995 Ceuta obtained the status of an autonomous city in Spain. Due to the special geographical location many diverse groups have come to the cities with diverse religious backgrounds – except for the Spanish-Christian-occidental majority, Arab Islamic forces entered during periods of Arab domination and remained. The Arab community is even growing and diversifying nowadays, mostly by Moroccan immigrants. throughout periods dominated by arab Islamic forces. They are the second largest group, followed by a small number of Jewish who have been trading in Ceuta ever since and a Hindu-community, which has established due to trade relations in the 20th century and has integrated into the population and is still nowadays growing in number. All of the different cultural, religious groups then have their very sites of religious practice and ceremonies in the pluralist city of Ceuta.

The city of border people on the Moroccan side is Tetouan, a city surrounded by mountains: Tetouan has been a Roman City, Tamuda oppidum on a high plain, belonging to the mountain of Djebel Dersa, but was given up then again. Only in the 11th century the Arab conquerors built a city at the same place which was then mostly dominated by Amazigh until the Arab conquerors arrived again in 1307 to protect the city against conquerors from Ceuta. Tetouan had been a pirate place for a long time until it finally conquered by Spanish and burned out. However, when Jews and Muslims were fleeing from persecution in Spain the pirate city was reestablished again and went on expanding as a trade centre, together with Ceuta under the authority of Sultan Moulay Ismail (1672-1727) – The structure of the city of then can still been recognized nowadays. In the 19th and 20th century Tetouan was governed one more time by the Spanish and only after independence it became part of a Moroccan state.

Nowadays Tetouan keeps on expanding, there is growing tourism along the coast, which is eypecially benefitting from proximity to Europe. It is a main trading centre for Western Rif-area: Beside tourism, fishing, textile-, cigarette and electronic industries are dominant as well as the agricultural sector of especially olive production. By nowadays the city has 500.000 inhabitants.

THEORETICAL FRAMEWORK

In this theoretical framework the most important concepts related to border-theory and Arab-Spring are presented and further the way they will be used and applied is explained. This includes a clarification of the chosen theoretical perspectives and approaches – also giving a grounded argumentation in order to make clear the use for answering the research question of this research design. The theories and ways of approaching issues presented here are generally very much interlinked: Border theory is based on ideas of discourses, but discourse and meaning-making have to be seen here in the context of border theories and social movement. As making a choice for beginning with one of the issues here border theory is first elaborated, focusing also more specifically on borders in mind and physical borders. As a second step discourse and meaning-making are presented, also focusing on the formation of collective identity more specifically. The last part is a short outline of social movement theory based on meaning-making and discourses of collective identities.

Border theory

Borders have been an "active problem for thought and action" (Anderson et al in Kramsch, 2010, p. 1006) for a long time and scholarship has increased substantively especially during and from the 90s of last century. Issues which have become central are borders, border regions and border identities in interrelation with diverse factors beyond physical determination such as the "changing role of territoriality, nationalism, everyday life and state power". Following Brambilla we can first reformulate the idea of defining borders: Instead of thinking about answering the question of "What is border?" one can better think about an answer to the question "What does it mean to be a border?". Gibson – Graham gives a very useful thought about boundaries and borders, which can be used as a first understanding of terms: Borders are "binary structures" which can be "boundaries between [...] terms, highlighting similarities on both sides of the divide, undermining the solidity and fixity of identity/presence, showing how the excluded ´other` is so embedded within the primary identity that its distinctiveness is ultimately unsustainable". This quotation elegantly illustrates the contradictory, contested nature of borders which is to be stressed in this research.

A list of related terms and definitions is given by Cassarino :

- Boundary (territorial demarcation; symbolic dimension)
- Frontier (area of interaction across the border; synonym of border and frontier)
- Borderland (transition zone; a 'system of closure and openness')
- Border Region (region shaped by the dynamics of boundary; the notion of 'hybridity')
- Border Landscapes
- Barrier (may be assimilated to a fence).

The most relevant aspect here is the concept of "border region". In this research we understand a border region to be constituted by all the movement and interaction, which contribute to the establishment of a fluid, dynamic, non-static network of institutions. Using the concept, it is important to define also the concept of the "region". Here this is not about a strictly defined territorial unit, but it is about regarding a region as a *sort of network* of activities, institutions and agency, in this case around the border. For reasons of restrictions of mobility even in the 21st century these networks, however, might be based on proximity, in this case to the border and thus concentrate in the direct territorial surroundings of the border – in the North East of Morocco and Ceuta.

Moreover there is an important term which Cassarino does not mention in his list, but which is crucial for this research: It is the term *"border-people"*, the people who are part of the networks surrounding the border. Those can be the citizens of the network region, some of which are the research group of this chapter, but for Driessen also and especially the people trying to reach Europe – which he calls clandestine cross-Mediterranean migrants. Kramsch instead uses the term ′borderlanders‵ for border people, meaning the same group of people.

What goes in hand with defining concepts is the approach to borders and methods. Recently, a call for methods of border studies with temporal specificity have become popular, taking into account history and everyday mentalities of inhabitants of "lived borders". The "problem of the Other" is considered to be a central issue here and will be elaborated in the following paragraph on borders in mind. The call is about elaborating a geo-historical approach and taking serious the possibilities inherent in borders as opposed to some geographical determinism of e.g. natural frontiers. The approach therefore has to do with the reassessment of narratives, myths, and demystifying nationalizing discourses which Kramsch argues is especially relevant for European border spaces today, by reopening possibilities. It is meant as an "escape from binary oppositions" such as distinguishing hard or soft borders, because this would mean "ignoring lived spatiality borderlands and borderlanders". This incorporates the idea of "resistance to territorially institutionalized power, [a] repoliticized understanding [and] recognition [of] worlding capacities" of border-people. It is about the *"notion that the arena of local everyday life experience is the scale where "the meanings of (state) boundaries are ultimately reproduced and contested"*.

Thus focusing on border-people here is taken as a meaningful way of understanding the borders in times of changing discourse in order to be sure to be attentive to contestations and power-relations in the renegotiation of those narratives. As Kramsch puts it : "the bearers of border differentiation" and their agency and power are part of the process of othering and constructing borders.

What applies to the border of Ceuta Kramsch even argues that internal state borders and external frontiers of the European Union have been "coproduced in dialectical tension". This is an interesting thought, because it means that an external European frontier as the one discussed here, the border at Ceuta has been constructed discursively, in relation: Renegotiation of interwoven Other and the Self within political spheres and everyday life has thus played a crucial role especially at "moments of institutional rupture and change". For the fortified physical appearance of the border in Ceuta this idea gives an explanation: The imperial and postcolonial recent (maybe ´current`) past had decisive impacts, since it constitutes the "impermeable hard edges external Eu borderland – as European transboundary imagery" and has produced an "acute inner –outer contradiction". For the life of people this implicates that bordered identities are involved to (re)inscribe "national narratives of territorialized home and belonging". The fortification of the border in Ceuta has increased since Spain joined the Schengen agreement in 1991, in order to increase transcendence of borders *within* Europe. For the external border of the EU in Ceuta this meant an increase in surveillance even on the sea and the construction of double fences. Before this change Spain was rather easily accessible for Moroccans and other Africans. However, the possibilities embedded in borders at different scales, including the one in Ceuta, make them "privileged sites of contestatory politization of space. The focus can be given to "local cross-border arenas" but even better to the "transnational actors" themselves, to the people. As Driessen puts it, the border is nontheless permeable and migration to the "European paradise" will not stop, even if Europe seeks to reinforce the demarcation of political, economic and cultural boundaries by legislation.

These ideas will be elaborated by making a concrete differentiation between the physical border as indicator and borders in mind, in order to understand how the current national discourse of the Arab Spring has entered the discourse and is reproduced by the border-people. The two indicators as discussed in literature are described in the following two paragraphs.

Borders in mind

"There is a border when, having crossed this line, one finds oneself in the presence of a different world (monde), a complex of ideas of

sentiments, enthusiasms, which surprise and disturb the stranger. A border, in other words that which marks it firmly on the ground, is neither gendarmes, nor customs officials, nor cannons behind some ramparts. Sentiments, yes; exalted passions and hatreds''

The above quotation illustrates the role of 'feeling different' as being the most relevant to the notion of borders. This idea undermines the institutionalized character of so many borders in the world, showing that a 'real' border is linked to experience and the feeling of otherness, which is always to a vast extent subjective and in process. Following the argumentation of Kramsch, "the Other" is the central criterion and problem, it is a key to "to understand the spatiality of borders".

The Other here has to do with "narratives", discourse, and refers to widely spread ideas in literature about social construction of boundaries and the role of language, as a "dialectic of regional transformation and the Other". The question whether this process can be uncoupled from space is highly debated. As Kramsch shows, there are researchers who stress the role of globalization in erasing and undermining physical borders and there are those, who try to bind up the construction of boundaries to territorial units, such as the nation-state. However, for this chapter the perspective is taken over, that boundaries – and this actually means a discourse of boundaries - can be uncoupled from territorial units. Yet, it comes down to space in the every-day life of people: "Symbolic, cultural, historical and religious meanings are carried by boundaries" and are part of cultural practice in every-day life, where they are re-negotiated. In this sense, there might be a kind of "national", "institutionalized" discourse about boundaries – "us" and "them"- but this discourse takes spatiality in particular places and everyday-meaning making, where other discourses meet, merge with or resist it, taking the form of the interwoven Other and Self.

Identities of nation-states are shaped and shape the borders and frontiers in the world, connecting the nations within them and are meant to reinforce cohesion, "yet, they are also the sits of division, fragmentation and political conflict".The role of the nation-state and other territorial units would be too "binary" to capture the contested-ness and powers shaping boundaries and borders beyond the spatial units of nation states. However, construction of identities by searching for "the Other", as being a central element to constructing boundaries and simultaneous process of the construction of a Self, is always linked to finding aspects in common and contest the notion of clear boundaries - which thus remain powerful discursive narratives.

Kramsch points to the notion of possibility inherent in borders and describes borders as spaces of re-worlding, where boundaries in mind result into "complex and contradictory sentiments and mentalities of borderland people". The institutionalized discourse of "Us" and "Them" e.g. used by nation-states in that sense must be reconsidered and focus on the Other, which is not confined to territorial units defined by physical borders. There is no clear division at the borders, there are symbolic boundaries linked to culture and politics beyond them, shared notions of belonging, internal heterogeneity within nations, social cohesiveness among people in border regions, memories and exclusivist identities and there is territorial attachment - even to the border. You can even question if the territorial division is far close to reality, in the sense that there can be a lot of tension between actually framed borders and virtual boundaries of human communities. The idea here is then that although border-people can be influenced by the national discourses of "us" and "them" and are subordinate to the system of the state they live in, to some extent, they might still have different boundaries in mind, due to their every-day life experience in which they produce their own discourse and narratives of boundaries. This also means, that they might share a sense of a Self (as opposed to inherent Other) with people living at the other side of the border and belonging to the nation-state at the other side.But since they share an everyday routine and make meaning within this scenario they might identify with each other and their border-people discourse much more (as question of proximity to their everyday experience) than with overarching national discourses, although these are mostly institutionalized and powerful. Yet this does not deny the influence of and subjection to the national discourses in meaning-making in everyday life at both sides of the borders. The flows across the border bring people closer to each other, simultaneously the physical border is meant to harden for the sake of institutions. This assumption is crucial for this chapter and understanding the borders in mind of border-people living in the area of Ceuta as well. The next paragraph is to elaborate the physical dimension of the border.

Physical borders

"Border areas [...] contain local and regional social forces that can in turn shape the nature of cross-border relations and by extension ´modify the interstate and geo-political influences on border regions`".

Some more radical authors even go to call the act of drawing borders "arbitrations" and "simplifications" of geopolitical and political and social struggles, which to them means to oversimplify social realities. They regard them as a real paradox being "undemocratically imposed by states claiming democracy". What is emphasized here is that power-relations determine how borders are constructed and negotiated. However, the weakness of the argumentation above is that the permeability and interaction at borders are neglected, which parallels neglecting the power of agents at the border, the ´border-people` and their own discourses.

Kramsch instead argues in favour of the exploration of limitations of the state and the power which powerless can develop resisting the dominant discourse, e.g. the discourse of nation-states within clearly marked territorial boundaries. The border between Germany and France during the 20ties and 30ties of last century is used by Kramsch to explain his idea: A so called "natural" border between states, the Rhine, was recognized as "a vast integrating force" by some advanced thinker of the period, resisting the dominant, existing discourse in sciences. The river was described as a "espace vitale (lebensraum)" for the close-by areas through its relational character being a "connector of cargo, people, ideas, and religious fervor". Although borders have been always object to discussion of nation states, thus becoming a battle ground for "myths", they have been "frontier[s] of intense and long-standing interaction and exchange among the populations in habiting the territories composing it. The role taken by the Rhine has therefore been more that of an integrating force than of nationalist separation.

The integrative power of the border and interaction across it are also essential for the border region of Ceuta: According to Driessen the economic survival of the city is dependent on daily cross-border flows of goods and people and thus the interaction with the province of Tetouan. Driessen even goes further and states that tens of thousands of people profit from the open border exchange and a disappearance of the border, giving the territory to Morocco, would have disastrous economic consequences for the region and especially its people on the Moroccan side. Therefore the inhabitants of Ceuta and the bordering area e.g. Tetouan have special permits for moving across the border. Yet, all this implies a high selectivity of people who can cross the border freely. The existence of borders and trans-national regional processes does not contradict each other in the sense that both are mutually preserving: Friendly relationships between countries go along with profiting from rent-seeking opportunities so that governments may have an interest even in enhancing and stimulating illegal activities. A clear separation between formal and informal is not possible. Formally, however, new regionalism as an approach is ever more subject to debate in wide regions of the world, also concerning regional initiatives aiming to progress towards sustainable development regional initiatives. Overcoming the division of informal and formal categories of activities regionalist strategies might be even more successful – which shows the possibilities characteristic of borders in general. In this approach also "the people of the borderlands are recognized as playing an active role". The idea is thus, that one cannot define the nature of borders only by political-diplomatic terms, as independent of social, economic relations and can better regard a border as "space of possibilities". The construction of political, social and cultural difference and the activities of social, cultural and economic networks represent the "paradoxical nature of borderlands.

Here the underlying epistemological assumptions have to be clarified: Kramsch argues very much in a tradition of awareness of ′myth- making′ (narratives) and power relations. This is to some extent related to a perspective on borders, which puts social practice, language and discourse to the centre of social construction of space, instead of considering boundaries as "expression of territoriality" and the state as a "spatial system with more or less exclusive boundaries". This incorporates the idea that territorial units are historical, discursive products of cultural meaning-making.

These understandings and assumptions implicate that borders are considered to latently carry a "dimension of political possibility", giving a space to challenge socio-political self-understandings of nations "in particular national territories and places". There is also an inherent, dialogic dimension of interaction to be taken into account "between borders, regional territories, and people". This is based on tension between the power of state discourses "and the `everyday life' practices of those inhabiting, negotiating, crossing, and navigating borders via interactions that may simultaneously cathect more worldly ´overlapping territories, intertwined histories`". The power of the discourse of the ´border-people`, which to some extent could be even regarded as a collective identity and is produced in their everyday life and interaction at the physical border, renegotiates the wider powerful discourses of institutions. For this chapter it means, that the renegotiation can be observed physically. Processes and events taking place at the physical borders as well as the frequency and kind of interaction of people at the different sides of the border can reveal very useful information about how people combine the discourses of everyday-life and institutionalized national discourses, drawing on national collective identities, in their own meaning-making. The latter is what the following paragraph will deal with.

Discourse and meaning-making

"The production of new knowledge is a world-changing activity, repositioning other knowledges and validating new subjects, practices, policies and institutions"

Following Hall´s description of the post-structural philosopher Michel Foucault´s famous concept of ´discourse‘, one has to understand it as group of statements giving a language to talk about, a representation of knowledge on, a topic. Those diverse meanings and statements are subject to negotiation and renegotiation through social practices, which, again, entail meanings which shape what we do - our practices. In that sense all practices have discursive aspects and shape each other mutually to varying extents. Thus topics are actually constructed by discourse - as indicated by Hall the "concept of discourse" is about *where* meaning comes from.

Taking over more ideas of Michel Foucault we can think further here and consider the statement that the "material takes on meaning and is endowed with [...] value only *within* discourse". What is meant by this is that not only topics are constructed in discourse, but also "meaning is constructed in discourse" and serves to construct it. For Foucault the ´production of knowledge` (which is considered as more than meaning-making) by discourse has to do with understanding oneself in culture. Thus shared meaning-making "takes place" in time and space and contributes to the construction of relations of power as well as it is limited by those. One can also say that people operate within limits of discursive formations which they submit to: they stick to their rules and conventions and by this become bearers of the discourse. However, "vulnerability to destabilization and reconstruction" as mentioned above is a very characteristic of discourse.

In the case of this research the people under research become "border people" as bearers of the border discourse. They make meaning within the framework of a wider discourse and thus renegotiate it, as they do with the discourse of the 20th February movement as well.

An interesting aspect which is linked to the power of discourses and meaning-making is performativity. Gibson Graham indicates that "performativity for Butler is ´the reiterative and citational practice through which discourse produces the effects that it names`". Thus a discourse is recognized to have effects and to be powerful – even a research itself is thus regarded as creating more or less powerful narratives. In a post-structuralist tradition knowledge is consequently seen as "multiple, contradictory and powerful".

In this research those features of knowledge and discourse will be traced, however, on a collective as well as individual basis: Here the border discourse is examined and the way it is changed by the wider discourse of Arab Spring, given the arbitrarity of permeable practices at the physical border, which could be also influenced by the Arab Spring discourse.

The individual aspect is based on the earlier mentioned idea of ´meaning-making‘:

"Meaning is understood to be produced under specific social and intellectual conditions, and knowledge is not a ´true reflection` but a productive and constitutive force. Although knowledges cannot be differentiated according to their greater or lesser accuracy (their success or failure in reflecting the world), they can be distinguished by their effects – the different subjects they empower, the institutions and practices they enable, and those they exclude or express"

What is described here is that there are always conditions and a context to meaning-making and meaning can be considered as a "result of a system of social conventions specific to each society and to specific historical moments". Space and time thus play a crucial role here. For this research then the characteristics of the moment (after the beginning of the Arab Spring) and the place (the border-region) have to be taken into consideration for every discursive piece of analysis.

This leads us to a crucial point related to what people´s discourses might be like: "´taking the meaning` must involve an active process of interpretation" and [is] never exactly congruent with the speaker´s meanings". The ´reader` of meaning, in space and time, is consequently as important as the writer, for, as Hall argues, only then meanings become meaningful. Gibson-Graham adds that there is a "possibility of disruption and invention in cultural process" for the individual (consciously and unconsciously) which "opens a space for ´agency` and unpredictability".

In that sense some degree of individuality of shared meaning will always be present in narratives which individuals tell - although they act within a certain discourse, they add their own meaning, their own, nuances to it and reproduce the discourse. Thus for the research this means that among the group of people under investigation discourse will be not only renegotiated by telling to the researcher but also vary slightly among individuals.

This opens up the way for the main ideas and assumptions of this research: Finding out how the discourse of Arab Spring has entered every-day meaning-making and life, in the sense that the relation to the border to Ceuta might be different and mental boundaries are under continuing reconstruction. At the same time there is an assumption that the meaning-making of the individual contributes to the reconstruction of the shared meaning and discourse as well. The research is thus to show resistance to and renegotiation of "narratives of regional change", focusing on a certain group of border-people in a certain border-region, influencing discourses of the "local, regional, global". The formation of shared meaning and identification with it is also known as collective identity formation, which is what the following paragraph is dedicated to.

Collective identity

Collective identities are described to be "multi-faceted and dynamic cultural productions" which are created and recreated in time and space - in a socio –historic context. In these features collective identity seems to be very similar to discourse in general, but having a look at a definition of collective identity differences become obvious:

Holland et al define two distinctive dimensions of collective identity - belonging and action. The first one has is based on the idea that collective identity is usually created in relation to difference and thus based on a differentiating characteristic of people belonging to the collective, which is thus a condition for a potential solidarity and individual belonging. Then the terms of inclusion and exclusion become very defining. The authors also stress, that belonging implicates a sense of "connection: cognitive, moral and emotional", which is part of the process of identification with the community, practice or institutions which the collective identity is about. However, they emphasize that the perception of a "shared status" is often more "imagined" than "experienced". Thus if one is searching for difference between discourse and collective identity, one could refer to the process of identification taking place at the formation of collective identities, since people can become bearers of a discourse or subject themselves to it without identifying with it in a cognitive, moral or emotional way. To put it into another way: Maybe collective identity is a sort of discourse with a process of identification as basis to its construction.

What is striking is the notion of process. A collective identity as a discourse is dialogic in nature, "emerging, forming and reforming between people and groups in multiple sites and places of contentious practice", a construction "across differences ". The latter indicates that it is likely that there is not one singular collective identity: There are versions of collective identity e.g. of a social movement, created in "multiple sites" which reveals that decentered-ness can be crucial in approaching the "formulation of collective identity" as a "place-based process".

The second dimension is built on the belonging and identification: Belonging is a basis to "collective action, choices strategies, tactics, targets" and can be regarded as rather pragmatic, as a sort of "organizational form".

This is decisive to formation of "collective identity of social movements" as Holland et al.. Participants of social movements have "a shared sense of the movement as acollective actor – as a dynamic force for change" which is object to a common imagination. Thus identification leads to "support of their own actions" for an image, evoked through interpretation of "shared activities", "power opponents" and "possibilities for change". In this sense a shared definition or common interests creates solidarity which is first seen in "claims of belonging" and can then be transformed into an "action system".

Because of dialogic construction of the identity across differences as basis for belonging "alter versions" of a social movement are important contributions to the movement´s identity. But they also constitute "challenges to collective identity after movement success" : The identifications with differentiating characteristics brings along identification outside the collective, being confronted with a 'world'. The movement's "self-understanding and alter versions are engaged with one another often contentiously". Holland et al describe this engagement as a "process of negotiation".

For this chapter the dimension of belonging is most significant: The 20th February movement is known to consist of a variety of different groups, identifying with a variety of distinct discourses, which means that there is a variety of collective identities within the movement. Yet at the same time they come to identify with a wider common "umbrella"-identity, the wish for change, for taking action ultimately for their own good. However the identity is eager to embrace the whole nation of Morocco. If this notion of identity also plays in the border region as assumed in this chapter, then there might be an impact on borders in mind of the border-people, which is linked to identities, and the relationship with the physical border – where the other side of the border cannot feel involved into the collective, as they lack the differentiating characteristic of being Moroccan and longing for change. The research deals very much with the idea of what the boundaries of these differentiating characteristics are like in the mind of "border-people".

The action-dimension instead can be seen as somewhat less significant here, since emphasis is given to the infiltration of the Arab Spring discourse into meaning-making and formation of discourses around and with the border. The way collective identity and meaning-making take a role in social movements is presented in the following paragraph.

Social movement theory

"Perhaps it is possible to examine how people's understandings of the world shape the way that they respond to the conditions and processes that academics may call variables and mechanisms. If people come to view their community's institutions as resources for social movement activism, for example, and they attempt to act on this understanding, then the understanding constitutes the resources as resources".

Social movements can be defined as a mobilization of people against the established, dominant discourse at a time. Meaning –

making is the essence of it because as Kurzman puts it: "social movements may be a particularly conducive site to privilege meaning-making, because their activities foreground resistance to the dominant norms and institutions of society". In that sense meaning-making is how people express their wish for change, how they construct a social movement. Meaning-making in social movements also implies that people have an own understanding of the world and on that basis give meaning to it. In this context Kurzman stresses the concepts of "'framing'" (meaning the way of putting the movements discourse) and "'political opportunities'" (pointing at a moment in time which creates more stimulating circumstances for "'mobilizing structures'". These ideas show that a common discourse has first to be created, since maybe there are already small groups of people being no longer satisfied with the existing, overarching, institutionalized discourse, but because of diverse reasons. Thus they first have to find each other and negotiate a shared discourse for mobilizing people and a "collective identity", which gives power to the movement. Mobilization and presentation of the discourse can be realized by making use of the "culturally available" set of activities, the social movement's repertoire. Kurzman moreover emphasizes that the establishment of a collective identity as a condition for mobilization and the development of social movements has to be seen as a process, which is not static, but which instead can develop further, can be undermined and be revived. This implies that time is an important aspect for social movements: preparation and construction, mobilization, articulation, and maybe even opposition or criticism of the movements - creating conflicts and dividing groups - are part of the continuous re-negotiation of the collective identity and of the social movement itself.

What applies to the Arab Spring or 20th February movement in Morocco many aspects of the theories can be used to explain the processes which have led to the establish the movement and which are still going on at the moment. For the purposes of this chapter the above mentioned aspects of

- meaning-making
- discursive (re-) construction of the movement

- discursive (re-) negotiation of a collective identity constitute the basic idea of this chapter: Observing how the Arab Spring and 20th February movement discourse is renegotiated among the group of border-people under research, how they make meaning of it and thus reconstitute the discourse in their very special situation of "living at the border" and how it makes them renegotiate their own mental boundaries concerning the border and the Other.

The approach chosen here follows the idea of Holland et al treating social movements as in a decentered, dialogic manner "that is particularly congenial to anthropological emphases on cultural processes" and is thus fits the dialogic process of collective identity : The Arab Spring movement is not regarded to be a "unified actor", but instead to have " multiple sources of cultural discourses competing to inform the everyday actions of movement participants". The latter is related to the stress given to daily experiences of people at a micro-level scale at the border "paying more attention to the diversity of place-based participants who are incorporating movement relations, concepts and practices into their every-day lives". The Arab Spring, as assumed in this research, is based on a certain kind of collective, even national, identity, which does not necessarily have to be the same all around the country, and thus does produce a very particular way of treating it in every-day life experiences of people living in the border-region of Ceuta.

Methodology

This part is dedicated to the methodological choices made for this research. First the selection of the research strategy is outlined. Then a more detailed description of the methods of triangulation is given each about interviews, observation, focus group discussions, informal talks and the analysis of contents.

Choice of research - strategy

Choosing for a suiting strategy for a research is about being aware of what kind of knowledge is to be obtained – or to put it the other way round: choosing a certain strategy one determines the kind of knowledge obtained. As this research is about giving deeper insights and developing an understanding of the meaning-making of border-people in social reality, focusing also on a limited territorial unit and as mentioned a specific group of people one can summarize that it is about one special case.

The case-study is thus the preferable strategy, compared to more generalizing quantitative surveys or experiments where an artificial environment would be created. The research will be descriptive in nature answering a "how"-research question, explaining the case, the methods chosen are ethnographic because The focus is primarily on "culture and people" as well as "daily experience", which ethnographic methodology fits best. The role of the researcher is to be mostly a participant-observer in the field, staying among people under study and at the same time investigating their life.

However, integrating fully into the everyday-routine of border-people will not be possible, due to different visa-conditions for crossing the border of researcher and research group, the occupation of border-people, the lack of homogeneity of the group (e.g. characteristics, different workplaces) and the limited time available for fieldwork. Instead a more "hands-off role" will be taken here, but the main advantage of participating remains : Gaining insights into an "insider", also called "emic", deeper understanding of the research group. The latter is a decisive aspect, since the central goal here is to try to understand the "´native point of view`", the views and meaning-making of border-people in this study. This indicates the task for the researcher here, namely to interpret the data and materials gathered. He or she must always be aware of his own role interpreting, concentrating on studying one single culture, the one of the border-people in the border-region, crossing the border to Ceuta regularly for work. The underlying assumption is for this is that the culture can be understood best "as an interconnected whole or system" fitting the idea of investigating the *network of border-people and the border-region*. Isolation of components of culture is opposed, resembling a more etic approach to research. Methods thus rely on wide-ranging observation and "more structured programs of interviews".

The surrounding and context of the research is still to some extent unknown to me, the researcher, which means that the research is also rather explorative. Underlying assumptions are based on literature and theory, so that the fieldwork will be sometimes issue to improvisation. Deepening of knowledge will take place throughout the entire period of fieldwork : The assumptions of the researcher are not yet confirmed and are object to be revised, which can lead to the formulation of new hypothesis maybe even after finishing the analysis of data gathered in the field. In that sense the research might later on contribute to the formulation of relevant pieces of theory – as far as possible - by an explorative, ethnographic approach with a given time limit to fieldwork.

As mentioned before awareness of the role as researcher and of the researched is necessary during all the investigations: Assumptions have to be noticed and documented; a structured interpretation of data has to be applied during the phase of analysis. The access to the research group and experts has to be properly organized and meetings and treatment of data has to follow ethical rules. Besides, choices have to be made consciously and have to be reflected as well – especially in the phase of analysis they should be made in a responsible and reflective manner.

A useful tool for not gathering one-sided data is to make *use of triangulation* – which generally augments the reliability and validity of the research process and results. This means that the basis of the research and work in the field is to operationalize main- and sub-questions into interviews, observation, informal talks, qualitative analysis of literature and focus group discussions -the common tools of qualitative research methods. Those diverse tools and methods will be described in more detail in the following paragraphs, referring also to the way they will be used and implemented in this research.

Interviews

The research is about finding out about the change of discourse and meaning-making in the life and minds of one specific group with common characteristics but possibly differences in meaning-making of a wider discourse among them. To become aware of differences and similarities in answers it is most practical to prepare the interviews to be held according to a certain standard of questions – which does not mean that there cannot be any spontaneous interaction if interesting topics are raised by the interviewee.

Also considering the fact that interviews will have to be conducted or with an interpreter, either in another language than the researcher's native language already prepared entirely formulated questions might support the flow of the interview and facilitate the researcher to concentrate on the content of answers, the behaviour of the interviewee and ways of how to stimulate the interviewee to reveal the most information possible. Comparing answers of different interviews in the analysis of data will be much easier as well and more reliable. However, to give space to every possible ideas, answers may not be fixed. For all these reasons here it is chosen to work with standardized, but open-ended types of interviews.

During the process of interaction of interviewing there are some factors to be aware of, which can impact the resulting data. "Possible mistakes in the process of communication" have to be prevented, e.g. by formulating carefully, a neutral but stimulating way of asking questions, clear and receiving body-language by the researcher (suggesting that he is an attentive listener). What is said has to be interpreted carefully. Taping and taking notes at the same time might be useful to prevent mistakes as well. Stimulating to elaborate answers spontaneously and the avoidance of suggestive questions are basic skills to be applied. Holding interviews always carries the burden of an artificially created situation: The interviewee can feel uncomfortable if he does not know very well the researcher, having own assumptions about what the researcher might want to hear and therefore being selective in what telling. Certain information is not considered to be made to be overheard and known by the researcher. In that sense the researcher's task is also to be careful in interpreting, concerning the influence of the interview-situation and the relationship between interviewee and researcher.

Observations

Observation is a way of obtaining information and knowledge without intervention, aiming to be as true to social reality as possible. For this explorative, ethnographic approach meaning that participating observation from inside, focusing on the emic, is preferable to other kinds of observation. Observation can add a lot to the research because it makes the researcher understand the circumstances of life of people, practices and interaction, reasons and occasions.

It gives background information to interpret other data from interviews. It helps to find out about the emic point of view. Being with people and listening to them and observing them and their interaction at the same time, makes the observation a participative one. Opportunities for useful observation can occur throughout the entire period of fieldwork, spontaneously or planned. However, even now certain interesting sites of observation can be even named: One will be to observe the physical border and the process of crossing it.

The behaviour and interaction of the research group, the border-people, among themselves, with outsiders and with the officials controlling are crucial. This might reveal characteristics about the border itself, institutionalized power-relations, emotions of people related to passing the border etc. Another interesting site for observation will be the place and activities of people working in Ceuta itself –observing and participating for one day in their routine would fundamentally enrich the whole picture. Yet, this is based on trust by the research-group, which has to be built up through time. Moreover one would have to check first, whether passing the border with different passports (a Moroccan 24-hour Visa and a EU-passport) at the same time and place will be possible. Observation can be always interesting where borders in mind or the relation with the physical border is revealed. This can happen at any time. What is sure, is, that taking more notes is always better than taking less – one gains a broader view and increases the reliability of data. Yet, perception and observation always depend on the researcher, his or her abilities to interpret – also here reflectiveness on the researcher´s role is necessary. Researching in an unknown, foreign context, such as being German in Morocco, but also being a student with a certain academic background, being a woman etc. can have impacts on the information and processes observed and analyzed. Making distinctions between pure ethnographic observation and own ideas, thoughts etc. will be also part of analysis and writing in a later phase.

Informal conversations

During the period of fieldwork the researcher can meet people and talk to them by coincidence or unexpected occasion. Throughout conversations some important statements or pieces of information might be revealed, even though these talks are informal and casual. The researcher then should take notes of relevant information, without creating the more artificial setting of a formal, taped interview. Information out of a spontaneous context can be worthful, in the sense that it is really born within a real-world situational context and serves to elaborate other tools of research –such as interviews, observations etc. Moreover the frequency of informal talks can be higher than formal interviews, so that a diversity of views on different topics can be gathered - especially unexpected aspects can show up and should be integrated in the conception of the research – this is likely to happen in an unknown context as it is the case for this research. Informal talks are very useful and relevant; they can even serve to test assumptions and do add relevant details to the research.

Focus group discussions

Focus group discussions are meant to bring together people of different opinions and make them discuss topics linked to the research question. Unlike interviews with a single interviewee, they are meant to confront a group with a topic of debate and observe interaction. Thus, the aim of a focus group is confront and provoke people to take a position towards a certain topic listening also to other people and their opinions (L.A. Brouwer, personal communication, 20th of November, 2011). The task of the researcher is very complex in this method: He or she has to structure a debate, involving all participants, organize the flow of the discussion and to reformulate and specify questions, whenever the debate seems to shift away from the actual topic of debate. He or she should try to ideally be a neutral pole among the discussing, although he or she might have an own personal opinion about the themes. He or she has to keep the overview and determine the time of debate per topic and try to comfort the participants, to keep their concentration by moderating the discussion (L. A. Brouwer, personal communication, 20th of November, 2011).

A proper preparation and time-planning are the keys to reach a smooth discussion (L. Brouwer, personal communication, 20th of November, 2011). It is also worth considering the relationships among the participants and the degree of familiarity, impacting the debate (L.A. Brouwer, personal communication, 20th of November, 2011). Gestures and non-verbal behaviour of the participants should be noted already during the debate, to be sure to record nuances of what is said (L.A. Brouwer, personal communication, 20th of November, 2011). Again the role of the researcher leading the conversation has to be reflected as well as the personal background of the participants, the setting of the discussion etc.

In this research a focus group could be possibly organized – if participants of different backgrounds with some controversial standpoints were willing to join a discussion, of which the topic has to be figured out during fieldwork. Yet, those possibilities will be revealed as well during fieldwork, so that a discussion might anyway take place only in a later stage.

Qualitative analysis of contents

The whole process of research is of course iterative, which can serve to deepen insights and make the research more reliable, especially the (final) interpretation. Interpretation as the capacity of placing oneself into the emic point of view to understand people is a key-factor. Further on the researcher should avoid "over"- interpretation – by being aware of the difference between own ideas and assumption and the ethnographically observable.

Coding is a very useful device for handling the various "truths". Based on the theoretical framework facts can be interpreted and key-terms can be identified, revealing decisive information. Vennix e.g. makes a distinction between descriptive and issue-specific codes according to the theories chosen for a research. Which way of coding is the most suiting for this research will be revealed during the research process depending very much on the data obtained. Thus during or after fieldwork schemes for analysis will be developed for the structured analysis of results with the aim of answering the main- and sub-question of the research schematically. Overviews of information per respondent and sub-question can be very useful in order to compare data. This way to data is reduced and filtered.

Ongoing reflection on theory and data (iteration) is the only way to guarantee good results and are a challenge to researcher. This leads us to the next important paragraph: The possible difficulties and obstacles to be encountered and overcome.

POSSIBLE DIFFICULTIES DURING FIELDWORK AND ANALYSIS

Besides the possible difficulties inherent in the methods of triangulation ethnographic, qualitative research brings along some inherent general difficulties as well. One is the direct involvement of the researcher in setting up assumptions, realizing fieldwork and interpreting at the same time as well as analyzing later on. This involvement means that there is always some subjective input by the researcher, making selections and decisions on the basis of his own worldviews – the researcher is his own research instrument. Thus again awareness of the own role is a condition for reliable research. The kind of data, personal testimonies and observations, cannot lead to generalizing, universalizing conclusions. There is never an absolute truth to be looked for. Further on the process of the research takes a long time – the longer it takes the more reliable and deeper insights can be gained, but this specific research has a very much restricted period of fieldwork, meaning that results have to be considered carefully within the specific place-based, temporal context. Conclusions are thus unique and limited to the same criteria.

Another general problem is language as most important tool of research– as the researcher´s mother tongue is not the same as the one of the research group communication is always somewhat less precise especially if using a third common language instead of one of the mother tongues. Even more difficulties can arise from making use of an interpreter (which can be, however, the only way of communicating at all)– communication is then interrupted by a third stage of interpretation and will be probably even less precise.

Accessibility of the research group is another issue here: The topic of borders used to be a sensitive one especially in Morocco – asking questions about the topic might lead people to reject to give answers out of fear for authorities. The latter have to be treated respectful and modest behaviour is appropriate whenever the research and researcher get in touch with the public during fieldwork.

All in all, circumstances and occasions might be unique then and the study cannot be replicated – the study is unique and the researcher has to show awareness for this fact. Thus specificity and uniqueness imply that no generalizing conclusions will be possible about a wider group of people, places or periods in time.

Bibliography

Anderson, J.: *Transnational Democracy: Political Spaces and Border Crossings*, Routledge: London and New York, 2002.

Anderson, M. and Bort, E.: *Boundaries and Identities: The Eastern Frontier of the European Union*, Edinburgh: International Social Sciences Institute, University of Edinburgh, 1996.

Bachelard, G.: *The Poetics of Space*. Boston: Beacon Press, 1969.

Balibar, E.: *We, the People of Europe? Reflections on transnational citizenship*. Princeton, N.J.: Princeton University Press, 2004.

Barth, F.: *Ethnic Groups and Boundaries*. London: Little Brown & Co., 1969.

Bartlett, C.A. and Ghoshal, S.: *Transnational Management: Text, Cases and Readings in Cross-Border Management*, Boston: Irwin/McGraw-Hill, 2000.

Campbell, D.: *Writing Security: United States Foreign Policy and the Politics of Identity*. Manchester: Manchester University Press, 1992.

Cheek, Timothy: *Mao Zedong and China's Revolutions: A Brief History with Documents*. Boston: Bedford/St. Martin's, 2002.

Coakley, J.: *The Territorial Management of Ethnic Conflict*, 2nd edn London: Frank Cass, 2003.

Dalby, S.: *Creating the Second Cold War: the Discourse of Politics*. London: Pinter Publishers, 1990.

Deepak, B R : *India and China : 1904-2004 : A Century of Peace and Conflict*, Manak, Delhi, 2005.

Diener, Alexander C., and Joshua Hagen. *Borders: A Very Short Introduction*. New York: Oxford University Press, 2012.

Donnan, H. and Wilson, T. M.: *Borders: Frontiers of Identity, Nation and State*, Oxford: Berg, 1999.

Galluser, W.A., Burgin and W. Leimgruber: *Political Boundaries and Coexistence*. Bern: Peter Lang, 1994.

Gupta, S.: *Disrupted Borders: An Intervention in Definitions of Boundaries*, London: River Oram Press, 1993.

Huntington, S.P.: *The China Modernisation Military and the State*, N.Y., Vintage Books, 1964.

Johnston, R.J.: *Geography and Geographers*. London: Edward Arnold, 1991.

Kapur, C.K. : *Chinese Military Modernisation*, Manas, Delhi, 2003.

Mary, W.: *Military Space Force: the Cultural Dimensions of Authority*, Cambridge, Belknap Press, 1985.

Nayyar, K K : *National Security : Military Aspects*, Rupa, Delhi, 2003.

Ohmae, K.: *The Borderless World: Power and Strategy in the Interlinked Economy*, New York: Harper, 1990.

Prabir De: *India and China in an Era of Globalisation : Essays on Economic Cooperation*, Bookwell, Delhi, 2005.

Prescott, J.R.V.: *The Geography of Frontiers and Boundaries*. Chicago: Aldine, 1965.

Radhakrishna: *Military Ethics: Guidelines for Peace and War*, Sumit Enterprises, Delhi, 2009.

Schneider, S. and Barsoux, J.L. : *Transnational Management: Text, Cases and Readings in Cross-Border Management*, Boston: Irwin/McGraw-Hill, 2000.

Shapiro, M. J. and Alker, H.R. : *Challenging Boundaries: Global Flows, Territorial Identities*. Minneapolis: University of Minnesota Press, 1996.

Stuart R. Schram: *The Political Thought of Mao Tse-Tung*. New York: Praeger, 1969.

Velez-Ibanez, Carlos: *Border Visions and Management*. University of Arizona Press, 1996.

Wilson, T. M.: *New Borders for a Changing Europe: Cross-border Cooperation and Governance*, London: Frank Cass, 2003.

Wilson, Thomas M., and Hastings Donnan: *A Companion to Border Studies*. Hoboken, NJ: Wiley-Blackwell, 2012.

Index

S

❑❑❑